THE AMERICAN NARCISSUS

INDIVIDUALISM AND WOMEN IN NINETEENTH-CENTURY AMERICAN FICTION

JOYCE W. WARREN

Rutgers University Press

New Brunswick and London

Library of Congress Cataloging in Publication Data

Warren, Joyce W.
    The American narcissus.

        Bibliography: p. 309
        Includes index.
        1. American fiction—19th century—History and criticism.
    2. American fiction—Men authors—History and criticism.
    3. Women in literature.   4. Individualism in literature.
    5. Feminism and literature.   I. Title.
    PS374.W6W28   1984   813'.009'353 0 9 83–23018
    ISBN 0–8135–1040–6 (cloth)   War
    ISBN 0–8135–1495–9 (pbk.)

British Cataloging-in-Publication information available

To Frank—
who sees beyond the self

CONTENTS

ACKNOWLEDGMENTS

There are many people whose lives have touched mine in ways that have been significant for the writing of this book. Some influences have been personal, others primarily academic. In considering the latter, I want to thank first of all Hyatt Waggoner, who, when I was a first-year graduate student at Brown University, instilled in me the techniques of scholarship that I have found so valuable in writing this book. Quentin Anderson and Joseph Ridgely, who were my advisors at Columbia University during the writing of the dissertation from which this book derives, initially gave me the encouragement I needed to pursue my ideas and continually asked the provocative questions that enabled me to develop them effectively. I want to thank particularly Ann Douglas, who read the original manuscript and took time from her own busy schedule to give me many useful suggestions. I am also grateful to Elaine Showalter, who read the manuscript for Rutgers University Press and whose careful reading and suggestions for revision were immeasurably helpful.

The research for this book was done at a variety of libraries. Most significant were Butler Library at Columbia University, the Paul Klapper Library at Queens College, the Cambridge University Library, Hofstra University Library, the Berg Collection at the New York Public Library, and the Pierpont Morgan Library in New York. Invariably, the librarians were helpful, courteous, and thorough, but I owe special thanks to the reference librarians at the Bryant Library in Roslyn, New York. Their cheerful competence and willingness to pursue obscure questions have made difficult tasks a pleasure.

Finally, the typing and retyping of this manuscript were done with great efficiency and good humor by Mimi Eisenberg and Jane Churchman. I cannot thank them enough.

The personal influences that led to the writing of this book began long before the book itself was conceived of. My mother, Violet Hill Williams, was the first major force in my life that made this book possible. It was she who read to me as a young child the books that she herself had loved—books that help to give a little girl a positive image of herself. It was she also who insisted that I should have the opportunity to go to college like my brother, despite financial difficulties. But most important, unlike so many mothers, she was not concerned about her daughter's clothes and popularity; she never worried me about whether or when I would marry. Instead, she seemed always to care most of all about what I thought and felt, what I had accomplished, and what kind of person I was.

The other important person during my young years was my father, Robert Williams, the friend whose company I always enjoyed, a man who never talked down to the smallest child and always made one feel like a significant person. I also want to thank my brother, Alfred Williams, who, before I was in my teens, introduced me to the books of Raphael Sabatini and Edgar Rice Burroughs, thus ensuring that the spirit of adventure that is missing from so many conventional "girls' books" was an important part of my development.

After childhood, the person who has been most valuable in the writing of this book is my husband, Frank Warren. Not only has he been personally supportive and critically helpful, but his warm concern for persons has provided an essential touchstone for one engaged in writing a book about the self-orientation of the American male. My children, whose companionship is one of my greatest pleasures, have played an unconscious role in the writing of this book. I think first of my three daughters, Victoria, Catherine, and Charlotte, whose individuality and intelligence, creative spirit and lust for life, have made me see most graphically the tragedy of a literature that is so lacking in female characters who can speak to such as they. My son, Frank, was born during the writing of this book, and the down-to-earth concerns of this new little person have been an important factor in preventing me from succumbing to the pitfall of abstraction that I have criticized so severely in the American Narcissus.

THE AMERICAN NARCISSUS

CHAPTER 1

CHAPTER 1

THE AMERICAN NARCISSUS: BACKGROUNDS OF CULTURE

*A woman was nothing to David Hersland.
Something to content him . . . a thing useful to
him or not existing for him. . . . He needed a
woman who would be inside him.*
Gertrude Stein, *The Making of Americans*

If I were a serious actress looking for a good, strong role to play, I would be hard pressed to find such a part in nineteenth-century American fiction. There would be plenty of subordinate roles—ingenues, character parts (usually old ladies), or colorless romantic leads—but there would be no female Captain Ahabs, Huck Finns, or Natty Bumppos. In fact, there would be almost no female character that I could really get my teeth into, no part that I could play to the hilt, because most American female fictional characters are not people. They have no individuality, no entity that says, "I am myself, this person and no other." Like Catherine Barkley in *A Farewell to Arms*, they say instead, "There is no me anymore." Or, like Marilyn Monroe in the film *Don't Bother to Knock*, they submit: "I'm anything you want me to be." No male character, however enamored,

1

would say these things, even by implication. He might say, "I'll *do* anything for you," but he would not offer to erase his individuality.

Until very recently, women writers who seemed to question this portrayal of women were either overtly censored or simply unpopular and unread; or if they were popular in their own day, their popularity did not survive into the twentieth century.[1] There were, of course, nineteenth-century American writers who created complex female characters and did not lose their popularity by it, William Dean Howells, Harriet Beecher Stowe, and Sara Orne Jewett, for example. Most major American writers, however—those whose works are regarded as classics in nineteenth-century literature—did not grant the individuality to women that they were willing to accord to men.

The lack of fully drawn women characters in major American fiction has not gone unnoticed. Richard Chase observes in *The American Novel and Its Tradition* (1957) that no American novelist was able to portray a fully developed female character until the time of Edith Wharton and Henry James.[2] Critics after Chase have commented on the limited or stereotypical role of women in American fiction. Whether elevated to abstract symbols of idealized traits or reduced to images of sin, female characters in American novels have, for the most part, been uninteresting nonpersons. Except for Hester Prynne, who is usually recognized as the great exception, few female characters can compete or even share the spotlight with the male heroes of American fiction.[3]

As feminist critics have recognized, this lack of strong female characters has meant that women readers cannot see a place for themselves in the literature of their own culture. The woman reader must identify with the male protagonist in order to find a role model that encourages the development of her individuality. However, most American literature is written from a masculine perspective in which man acts out his destiny apart from society and from women. Women are associated with the pressures of society and seen as entrappers, unattractive adversaries of the "American" experience. For the woman reader to identify with the men in the novel is to identify against herself.[4]

The failure of American writers to create fully drawn women characters has been increasingly recognized, and the problem it creates for the woman reader has been noted. However, the *reason* for the lack of autonomous women in American fiction has not been explored.[5] Why have American writers not been able to create strong women characters? One cannot say simply that American literature reflects a sexist society. European society has been no less sexist in its restrictions on women, yet European literature has no shortage of strong women characters—Antigone, Madame Bovary, Anna Karenina, Eustacia Vye, Hedda Gabler. But they have few counterparts in American literature.

In *Love and Death in the American Novel* (1960) Leslie Fiedler attempted to deal with the difference between American and European fiction. Citing the failure of American novelists to portray adult heterosexual love and the consequent typecasting of women as either innocent fair maidens or evil dark ladies, he concluded that American male novelists suffer from unresolved oedipal complexes. They are afraid of passion and marriage. Such involvements would mean the end of childhood, and the male is afraid to grow up, afraid to accept the responsibilities of society. Hence, Fiedler notes, American classics are "boys' books."[6] My principal objection to Fiedler's thesis is that it does not really help us. If we accept his assertion, we still do not know *why* American literature developed the way it has. Why are American writers afraid to grow up? Why is the same not true of British writers? Or French? Or Spanish?

It is my contention that something peculiarly American in our culture has produced this literature of female nonpersons. If women were not granted personhood in nineteenth-century literature (the focus of this study), it is because they were not regarded as persons in American society. It may seem strange to claim that women have been denied their individuality in America—the nation of all nations that has emphasized the importance of the individual—and particularly

3

in the nineteenth century, the heyday of American individualism. Yet herein is the cause: it is *because* of this emphasis on the individual that American women have not been recognized as individuals.

In a nation that stresses the development of the individual, there has been little room for the "other" person. Nineteenth-century individualism, particularly as reflected in the writings of Emerson and the prescriptions of the American myth, encouraged an insular self-assertion that prevented the individual from recognizing the selfhood of others. Persons regarded as outside the American experience—persons who by their society's definition did not themselves qualify as individualists—were not seen as individuals. Women, blacks, Indians, and other "others" had no place in the drama of American individualism. Like the legendary Narcissus, the American individualist focused on his own image to such an extent that he could grant little reality to others.

INDIVIDUALISM IN AMERICA

Before we can understand the effects of individualism on women and other groups, it is necessary first to examine the character of the individualistic strain in American culture, what it was, and how and why it was unique. Americans took the concept of individualism—in Europe, a negative concept connoting selfishness and social anarchy—and transformed it so that it not only came to represent the positive qualities of freedom and self-determination but actually became synonymous with Americanism and the proudly proclaimed "American way of life." In this respect, American republicanism differed from democratic tendencies in other countries, where the emphasis was on collectivism and social unity rather than on individual rights. In European democracies, sovereignty remained in the state; in America, sovereignty rested instead in the individual. Individualism became a peculiar characteristic of American life. All of America's institutions are an expression of individualism; all of its major political parties have made individualism part of their platforms; the philosophies and religions developed in America were based in individualism; and even most reform movements in America have been individualistic in their aims.[7] Eighteenth-century America represented a dream of individual fulfillment. Hector St. Jean de Crèvecoeur wrote in 1782 in his *Letters from an American Farmer* that in America the poor of Europe were regenerated: "Here they become men." There is something for everyone; "each person works for himself."[8] Benjamin Franklin, who formulated the maxims by which generations of Americans have guided themselves, wrote in his *Autobiography* in the late eighteenth century that what most aided him in getting ahead was his *own* industry. He insisted that all questions, even moral questions, could be decided by considering whether or not they were beneficial to the individual. The value of religion, poetry, virtue, friends, public office, marriage—everything, in fact—was to be measured only by its usefulness in helping the individual to advance himself.[9] That Franklin's advice was being followed by his countrymen in 1815 is suggested by an editorial in the *Niles Weekly Register*, which observed that America was marked by the "almost universal ambition to get forward."[10] This emphasis on and faith in the individual was an underlying assumption in the way America conducted its affairs. As John Taylor noted in his analysis of the American government in 1814, "Individualism is the substratum of our policy."[11]

It was in the nineteenth century that individualism took hold and flourished in America. Andrew Jackson's election in 1829 marked a turning point, after which it was impossible openly to support any other ideology.[12] The *Democratic Review* wrote in 1839 that American society recognized the "individual man in himself as an independent end." American democracy, it continued, is the final stage of civilization, and its goal is to liberate the individual man for the full development of his capacities.[13]

The predominance of individualism in nineteenth-century America is particularly apparent in the observations of foreign visitors. Alexis de Tocqueville wrote in 1835 that, because of the emphasis on individualism in America, the individual was apt to imagine that his whole destiny was in his own hands. According to Tocqueville, the new democracy led Americans to "a presumptuous confidence in their own strength."[14] Writing around the same time, Michel Chevalier believed that individualism had reached its height in America.[15] And when British historian James Bryce visited America toward the end of the century, he observed: "Individualism, the love of enterprise, and the pride in personal freedom, have been deemed by Americans not only their choicest, but their peculiar and exclusive possessions."[16]

Twentieth-century analyses of the American character indicate that this belief in individualism is still strong. In *People of Plenty* (1954) David M. Potter examines the work of representatives of cultural anthropology, social psychology, and psychoanalysis and finds that all three disciplines agree on the basic definition of the American character: all stress the competitive spirit and individual achievement.[17] Other studies confirm that, despite individual failures and worldwide depression, Americans have continued to believe in the self-help myth: the concept that the individual is responsible for his own destiny.[18] The American cultural ideal, writes John William Ward in *Red, White, and Blue* (1969), is "the individual, unconstrained in body or mind, free from all adventitious circumstance, steering his way unaided through the world."[19]

WOMEN AND INDIVIDUALISM

All of the observations cited above about the development of the individual in America focus exclusively on the male.[20] Little is said about the female. All of the studies of the American character are analyzing men in America, for it is the man who has been encouraged to achieve, who has sought the expansion and development of the self. The role of the woman was not to *be* the achiever but to be available to be *used* by the achiever for his advancement. In the American Dream, woman figures not as the dreamer but as an object in the dream.

It was for their usefulness to men that women were valued in nineteenth-century America. Crèvecoeur's American Farmer tells his wife that he would not have married her if she had not been useful to him. And he concludes that the German immigrants achieved more than other nationalities because their wives worked harder.[21] As the West was settled, wives were a useful commodity. Writing in 1846 of her trip west, Eliza Farnham reports an interview with an Illinois bridegroom, who tells her that he acquired a wife because "my neighbors went ahead of me with 'em." Marriage for him is a business proposition: "I reckon Women are like horses and oxen, the biggest can do the most work, and that's what I want one for."[22] The diaries and recollections of women who traveled by covered wagon to Oregon and California from the 1840s to the 1860s reveal that not one of them initiated the trip, and less than a quarter even agreed that it was a good idea. The majority went against their will, and for women the trip was a lonely, unhappy experience. They did all of the "women's work" during stopovers when the men could rest, and they also helped with the "men's work," driving the team and stock, while on the move. Once arrived, women provided the major source of labor on the new land without sharing the autonomy of the men. A study by Dr. W. W. Hall in the 1862 report of the Department of Agriculture notes the "enormousness of women's work-load" on farms and concludes that men were using their wives' labor for their own profit.[23]

The Industrial Revolution affected this view of women only by adding a new means by which women could be used. Both George Washington and Alexander Hamilton supported employment of women in factories, not because the women would benefit, but because the men saw how women's labor could enrich the community and the individual man. According to Hamilton: "Women and children are rendered more useful, and the latter more early useful, by manufacturing establishments than they would otherwise be. . . . The Husbandman himself experiences a new source of profit and support, from the increased industry of his wife and daughters."[24]

This attitude, of course, applied only to women of the

lower and yeoman classes. The upper- or middle-class woman was not expected to work in the factories; in fact, she was not expected to work at all. Rather, as Thorstein Veblen pointed out in his *Theory of the Leisure Class* (1899), her domesticity was required as a gauge of male success. When a class had attained enough security to be free of the necessity of physical labor, said Veblen, leisure became a badge of prestige, and a man's success was measured by the number of nonproductive servants he could afford to keep. A man's wife and daughters were regarded as the chief servants, whose enforced leisure reflected honor on the husband and father.[25]

Despite the emphasis on individualism in nineteenth-century America, women in all walks of life were seen not as individuals but as secondary characters in the drama of the American individualist. What this meant for women in nineteenth-century society has been the subject of a number of studies by feminist historians. Of primary significance is the recognition that women constituted a distinct culture, a culture separate from the national (male) culture. Women's experience was not the same as men's experience. They were a part of, but apart from, the competitive world of business and industry and the adventure of Jacksonian individualism. The creation of this separate "women's sphere" has been linked to the rise of industrial capitalism. Women and the home represented stability in a rapidly changing society, and women were forced into a more circumscribed position to facilitate the transition to an industrial society.[26]

The nineteenth century marked a significant diminishment in women's freedom. By the 1830s women enjoyed considerably less social and economic freedom than had seventeenth- and eighteenth-century American women, and their role was further restricted by the developing "cult of the lady."[27] As feminist historians have noted, one cannot equate prescriptive behavior with real behavior. The focus of this study, however, is the cultural attitude toward women, not the behavior of women themselves. The literature of the period praised as the qualities of a lady the virtues of submissiveness, piety, purity, and domesticity, and a woman was judged according to how well she lived up to this ideal.[28] Yet even when American women seemed to have more freedom, as in the colonial period, they were never allowed to exercise that freedom as *individuals*; they could use it only to enhance the position of the male members of their family or to contribute to society in general.[29] Moreover, although colonial women may have had a greater latitude in professional options, one cannot assume that they exercised political or economic power.[30]

Perhaps the most significant aspect of women's status in nineteenth-century America was their powerlessness. Women had little social or economic power; they were gradually excluded from the professions; and their legal rights were restricted (where they had had the vote, it was withdrawn). Lacking any real power, women sought compensatory power in various ways—but usually only within the accepted bounds of women's place.[31]

In the nineteenth century, although seeds of change were growing, and although individual women challenged the traditional restrictions on women's place, opportunity for most American women remained limited. Women of all classes and in all regions of the country shared in this lack of power and personal autonomy. The urban middle- and upper-class woman on the eastern seaboard was restricted by the conventional image of the lady; the pioneer and farm woman was held in thralldom by her heavy workload. In addition, the working-class woman in the cities not only received the lowest wages in her class and suffered the lowest status of any white woman; she too was in some respects influenced by the cult of the lady. Although forced to forgo the virtue of domesticity by the necessity to work outside the home (as well as in the home), belief in the importance of proper feminine behavior was so prevalent that, as Gerda Lerner notes, working-class women were sometimes prevented from organizing and unionizing to better their situation because of their allegiance to the ideal of the lady.[32] The other significant group of white women in nineteenth-century America comprises the Southern lady.[33] Little is known about the poor white woman of the South at the time, though her situation would in many respects have been similar to that of the pioneer and farm woman. But in the antebellum South, the lady was even more restricted than in the North.[34]

How did the position of American women differ from that of European women? Nowhere, of course, did women have the power and autonomy of the male members of their society, but European visitors to America consistently commented on the greater circumscription of American women. In 1835 Tocqueville observed that American women were more repressed and more submissive than European women. Although the young American girl is more independent, he said, she gives up that independence totally when she marries. In capitalistic America the circumscription and dependence of the wife were necessary, Tocqueville concluded, as "security for the order and prosperity of the household."[35] Another French visitor to the United States, Gustave de Beaumont, although he differed from Tocqueville in his appraisal of the nation's problems, agreed wholeheartedly with his countryman on the question of women. In his novel *Marie* (1835), Beaumont emphasizes the "early reduction to nonentity of the married woman" in America.[36] When Harriet Martineau visited America in 1834–1837, she came to similar conclusions about American women, except that she saw no difference between the single and married woman. Since there were no real alternatives to marriage, she said, the oppression obviously extended to the single woman as well.[37]

While American culture emphasized individualism and competition, American women were conditioned to accept a passive and submissive role and were taught that it was sanctioned by God and nature. Colonial women read the Marquis of Halifax's book, *The Lady's New Year's Gift, or Advice to a Daughter* (1688), which emphasized submission and advised wiles as the only way of dealing with marital difficulties. A wife must never question her husband's authority, admonished Halifax, even if he is an adulterer, a drunkard, or an idiot.[38] Over a century later the advice was the same. Samuel K. Jennings wrote in *The Married Lady's Companion* (1808) that the wife must adapt herself to her husband, whatever his peculiarities, and he reiterated the Pauline doctrine of submission.[39] William A. Alcott's *The Young Wife* (1837) insisted that woman was created to be "man's assistant": "The very act of entering into the married state is, on the part of the woman, a concession. . . . and submission."[40] This advice continued throughout the nineteenth century, though later it was disguised as medical information. Dr. E. A. Clarke's *Sex in Education* (1873) claimed that mental effort damaged a woman's reproductive organs and thus endangered the human species. In 1883 Dr. George Austin wrote in *The Perils of American Women* that, since woman's part in the reproductive act is passive, she is by nature more passive than man.[41]

Although strong voices were raised in America against this view of women, beginning with Tom Paine, Thomas Branagan, and Charles Brockden Brown at the end of the eighteenth century and including nineteenth-century feminists like Lucy Stone, Elizabeth Cady Stanton, and Susan B. Anthony, they did not represent the view by which most nineteenth-century men and women were guided in their daily lives.[42]

THE MALE PERSONA

While the American woman has been conditioned to accept unreal restrictions on her abilities, the American man has been encouraged to believe that he is all-powerful. Of course, this masculine belief in the power of the individual has proved to be a snare and a delusion for many men. Despite the emphasis on self-reliance, the majority of men have *not* been able to achieve unlimited success on their own.[43] Yet the myth of the individual remains strong, and a man finds it hard to accept failure. He creates instead a false image of himself, a persona who possesses all of the qualities of greatness that the myth of the individual tells him he should possess.

One of the best ways to measure this tendency is to examine the folk heroes that Americans have chosen for themselves. From Davy Crockett and Daniel Boone through the long list of Western badmen, they are all larger-than-life, falsely inflated supermen. Whether they are fighting Indians or bears, the feats of Daniel Boone and Davy Crockett are stupendous. And the Western gunfighter—Billy the Kid, Wyatt Earp, Wild Bill Hickok—assumes the same mammoth proportions. Such men were hardly heroes, but, as Kent L. Steckmesser points out, Western heroes were given epic proportions in order to fit the American ideal image. Kit Carson is described as a Hercules; in fact, he was 5' 6" tall, weighed 135 pounds, and was said by his contemporaries to be "short and wiry." However false and exaggerated these legends may be, they are valuable "as a record of American aspirations and traditions."[44]

These figures were admired not only by little boys reading dime novels. Such political figures as Sam Rayburn and Dwight D. Eisenhower have admitted their admiration for Western badmen. Rayburn, who grew up in Texas, revealed that his hero was a Texas gunman, John Wesley Hardin, who killed his first man at the age of eleven and by eighteen had twenty-seven murders to his credit. Eisenhower admired Wild Bill Hickok, using him in a radio speech in 1955 as a model of American manhood. Hickok was in reality a mean killer who began his career as one of Quantrill's raiders during the Civil War, burning and sacking towns and massacring their inhabitants.[45] Of course, Hardin and Hickok are admired not for the men they really were but for the persona that each projects. The American folk hero, whatever he may have been in actuality, represents a strong, larger-than-life, ideal figure.

In her perceptive analysis of the American character, Constance Rourke notes the tendency of American legendary characters to be overblown, exaggerated figures and points out that this ideal image of the self is often the result of anxiety and self-doubt. The American legendary character, writes Rourke, was obsessed with strength and triumph and "seemed obliged to shout their symbols as if after all he were not wholly secure in their possession." The Yankee and the backwoodsman, for example, were ideal figures participating in a masquerade, and the qualities they adopted were designed to give them confidence and self-esteem.[46]

When the image of the individual is disproportionately large, there is no room for the individuality of other people. The individual who is so intent on establishing his own persona cannot look outward. Thus, as Constance Rourke also observes, American legendary characters were all *solitary* male figures, without wife, family, or any other human relationships: "They appeared always as single figures, or merely doubled and multiplied, never as one of a natural group, never as part of a complex human situation, always nomadic." These legendary characters became "emblems of the national life." The "American Narcissus," says Rourke, looked at himself in this unreal, inflated, isolated figure and saw what he wanted to see—an ideal picture of himself.[47]

The American myth of the individual has encouraged the development of narcissism, not in the psychological sense of an individual's unsuccessful resolution of an early failure in identity,[48] but in the cultural sense that Rourke describes. American culture assumes that the male individualist will achieve by himself and for himself. The narcissism of the American Dreamer lies in his acceptance of this mammoth image of himself. The persona that he creates for himself enables him to reconcile his personal shortcomings with the myth of American individualism: he sees himself as all-powerful and all-encompassing. And he sees only himself.[49]

Historically, the most cogent example of what happens to the woman when the male image is overdrawn is found in the legend of Daniel Boone. In 1784 John Filson published stories about Daniel Boone in *The Discovery, Settlement, and Present State of Kentucke*. In creating the image of a legendary Boone, Filson (and the stories that have followed) left out a very important fact of Boone's life: Mrs. Boone. Rebecca Boone was a strong, capable person, a good markswoman who brought in the game when Boone was ailing, and a competent scout who was able to lead her eight children through Indian territory from Kentucky to Carolina when Boone was held captive by the Indians and believed dead. Yet she is mentioned only peripherally in Filson's account, and today one would not even know that she existed.[50]

OTHER NONPERSONS IN AMERICAN HISTORY

If Rebecca Boone was a casualty of American individualism, it is important to recognize that the denial of her existence was not simply a matter of male-female relationships. Individualism has had the same effect on other persons, both as beings whose individuality has been sacrificed to the individualism of another person and as members of groups not seen as central to America's drama.

Perhaps the best way to understand the consequences to other people of the American emphasis on individualism in the nineteenth century is to examine one of its most significant expressions at that time: the phenomenon of manifest destiny.[51] The individual pioneer and frontiersman had been moving westward onto Indian land since the seventeenth century, and nineteenth-century Americans evolved a theory to justify this encroachment and such government acquisitions as Oregon, California, and Texas. The expanding American nation in the nineteenth century was an extension of the expanding individual—individualism writ large. What had begun as a movement of individuals became government policy.[52] Most Americans would have agreed with journalist Samuel Bowles, who after a trip west wrote in 1869: "We should stop making treaties with tribes. . . . We know they are not our equals; we know that our right to the soil, as a race capable of its superior improvement is above theirs." The Indian, said Bowles, is "the victim of our destiny. . . . It is his destiny to die."[53]

A corollary of manifest destiny is, of course, the belief that the other guy, the victim of your destiny, does not count. This is the other side of American individualism, the side that is visible only if we look at individualism not from the point of view of the individual but from the point of view of the "other"—the person or persons whom the individual sees as either useful to or standing in the way of his expansion.

On a national level, this disregard for other people is evident in American policy toward the Indians, which in the nineteenth century was at best de facto extermination.[54] Americans wanted the land, and it soon became clear that the best way to acquire it was to get rid of the Indians. In fact, Americans sought independence from England in 1776 not only because of the familiar cry of "taxation without representation" but also because of frontier dissatisfaction with Britain's policy of protection of Indian lands.[55] To most Americans, the Indians were simply expendable nuisances, not people at all. This attitude is apparent in Theodore Roosevelt's 1889 description of the settlement of the United States:

> The white settler has merely moved into an *uninhabited* waste; he does not feel that he is committing a wrong, for he knows perfectly well that the land is really owned by no one. . . . The settler and pioneer have at bottom had justice on their side; this great continent could not have been kept as nothing but a game preserve for squalid savages.[56]

Looked at from the Indian's point of view, Roosevelt's use of the word "uninhabited" strikes a particularly jarring note. It points up the American failure to see the Indian as a real presence. For nineteenth-century Americans intent upon realizing their own potential as individuals and as a nation, the Indian was outside civilization and outside history—an abstraction, not a real person. He had no independent existence at all.[57]

It was not only as a consequence of manifest destiny that American individualism led to this disregard for the personhood of others. Another significant group of nonpersons in nineteenth-century America, American Negroes, also remained outside society. Whether slave or free, they were prohibited from participating in American individualism. As Winthrop Jordan points out in his mammoth study, *White*

Over Black: American Attitudes Toward the Negro, 1550–1812 (1968), whites did not include blacks in their definition of Americans.[58]

Whereas the Hispanic slave tradition encouraged manumission, Americans passed laws against it, thus making it more difficult for free blacks to enter society.[59] In fact, historians have found that political democracy actually promoted discrimination against Negroes. As whites in America gained more individual rights, the rights of blacks became more and more restricted; periods of greater emphasis on rights and social mobility among whites (e.g., the Jacksonian era) coincided with periods of increased hostility and legislation against blacks.[60] Jordan concludes that a belief in Negro inferiority was valuable to whites in a fluid social structure because it helped to promote their own social mobility. A white man on the make found Negroes useful in his efforts to pull himself up by the bootstraps, and the exclusion of Negroes provided an assurance of social order.[61] Carl Degler explains that whites in constant competition among themselves used the inferiority of blacks to assure their own place:

> In thus drawing invidious distinctions between black and white, the whites not only removed a possible economic and social rival, but automatically placed a floor under their own slippery status in a loosely structured society in which mobility was at once a value and a threat, and individualism a constant goad.[62]

Although this complex problem cannot be explored fully here, it is apparent that in the nineteenth century there was a direct correlation between American individualism and the degradation and exclusion of blacks, who were not seen as individuals in American society.

INDIVIDUALISM AND THE OTHER

Like Indians and blacks in nineteenth-century America, women as a group were excluded from participation in the

American Dream. The nineteenth-century individualist was white, and he was a man. The American cultural ideal has been the unencumbered expanding white male individualist. However illusory the promise of America may have proved to be for many men, the dominant image for the white American male was that of a larger-than-life superhero whose world was wrought for himself and by himself.

What then of the other people in society, those whom the individualist sees as other than himself, either because they belong to a group defined as outside American individualism or simply because they are "other"? If members of other groups are not seen as individuals, and if, as Benjamin Franklin said, everything—even friendship and marriage—is to be measured by its usefulness to the individual, other people can be seen only in relation to oneself.[63] Or, in the words of Ralph Waldo Emerson, whose individualism was central to nineteenth-century American thought, other people can be regarded only as "feeders and coadjutors" of the self.[64]

In the world of the inflated self, other people do not really count. They exist only as objects to be ignored or destroyed (if they are undesirable) or to be made use of or absorbed into the self (if they are desirable). When an individual magnifies his own individuality to the extent that he sees all phenomena as relating to himself, there is no room for the independent existence of other people.

It is this consequence of American individualism that helps to explain the role of women in nineteenth-century literature. As Simone de Beauvoir pointed out in *The Second Sex* (1949), woman historically has been regarded as the other in society.[65] Thus, in a nation of individuals, in a society that does not grant personhood to others, woman—the traditional other—will be regarded as a nonperson. And it is as such that she is reflected in nineteenth-century American literature. To the extent that an American author accepts this inflated image of the male figure, his image of women is proportionately diminished. And, conversely, as an author recognizes the falsity of the masculine persona, his women characters are more fully drawn.

17

METHOD AND SELECTION

In the ensuing chapters, I shall examine the works and personal attitudes of major nineteenth-century American writers. Although my method is not psychological, I have felt it necessary to look at the attitudes expressed not only in an author's works but in his life as well. Therefore, wherever the material is available, I have examined journals, letters, and private actions in an attempt to understand the relationship between an author's private beliefs and attitudes and the attitudes expressed in his public works. This approach is necessary because my thesis is based on *attitudes*—attitudes toward American individualism, attitudes toward the male individual and the other, and, ultimately, attitudes toward women. I have had to determine how deeply and sincerely those attitudes were felt. Thus, in dealing with an author's attitude toward women, for example, I have examined his portrayal of women in his work, and then I have looked at his relationship with the principal women in his life—his wife, friend, or mother. How a writer viewed the real women in his life is, I think, an essential part of any analysis of his attitude toward women.

Although any choice of authors must be subjective, it was necessary to limit this study, and I have chosen to focus on those who have long been regarded as classic American writers. Since this is a study of cultural influence on literature, it seemed logical to explore the writers that our culture has deemed its best representatives. There were many women writers of women's fiction in the nineteenth century who were popular in their day, and their central characters were always women. But, for the most part, they and their works have not maintained their prominence.[66] Other women writers of greater stature who created some strong female characters—Harriet Beecher Stowe, Sarah Orne Jewett, Mary E. Wilkins Freeman—have, rightly or wrongly, thus far been denied a place in the canon of classic nineteenth-century fiction. The principal male writer that I have not considered, William Dean Howells, was excluded from this study for the same reason: although he created a number of interesting women, his works have not been unqualifiedly admitted to the roster of American classics.

I begin with an examination of the American Transcendentalists because it was they who fully articulated the American belief in the self and translated this cultural attitude into literary terms. The middle section of the book deals with three novelists—Cooper, Melville, and Twain—who exemplify the tendency of American writers to disregard the female person. The final chapters look at two writers—Hawthorne and James—whose ability to portray women of substance sets them apart from other nineteenth-century American authors and coincides with their deviation from the common American belief in individualism.

PART ONE
PART ONE

**AMERICAN LITERATURE AND THE
AMERICAN MYTH**

■ CHAPTER 2 ■

■ CHAPTER 2 ■

TRANSCENDENTALISM AND THE SELF: RALPH WALDO EMERSON

I am always environed by myself: what I am all things reflect to me.

Ralph Waldo Emerson[1]

Transcendentalism in America has never been clearly defined even by the New Englanders who were its most famous practitioners. Yet there is one aspect of Transcendentalism that any student of American thought would have to agree is one of its principal characteristics: a preoccupation with the importance of the self. Even if one believes that deep beneath the vigorous protestations of self there flowed dark rivers of uncertainty and doubt, the message and major emphasis of the Transcendentalists was unquestionably the assertion of the primacy of the individual. For Emerson and Whitman, as Quentin Anderson points out in *The Imperial Self*, the whole world was within: both of these writers created an "inward empire in which assumptions about the world, horizontal relationships, counted . . . only as material for the self."[2] The same can be said of Henry Thoreau, whose ideal was a society of one and whose life work was the creation of his own journal.

Although the present work is primarily concerned with American fiction writers and their failure to portray fully developed women, I have begun with the Transcendentalists, who, though not writers of fiction, are valuable as a means of understanding how the American conception of the inflated male figure has been seen by American literary artists. In the work of Emerson and Thoreau one can clearly see the literary translation of American individualism—the self expanding and absorbing until there is no room for the selfhood of others. And in the writings of Margaret Fuller, who as a Transcendentalist and a woman was herself both the self and the other, one can see how this dual role affected the conception of the Transcendental self and the question of otherness.

Although Emerson and Thoreau came to prominence as rebels, they are nevertheless in the mainstream of American thought, that is, in the tradition of American individualism. Their affinity with American thought is evidenced by the frequency with which they continue to be quoted and copied, the perpetual reprinting and anthologizing of their works, and their persistent appearance on high school and college syllabi. Emerson, who outlived his rebel image to become the Sage of Concord during his lifetime, has been quoted for over a hundred years as an American Confucius on calendars, in businessmen's journals, and in popular magazines. Yet, if Emerson and Thoreau were rebels at all, they were rebels not against Americanism but against Anglo-European traditions that Americans had already overthrown. These traditions were predicated on a dependence upon limitations external to the individual—birth, convention, social relationships, authority—that Americans had denied. The Transcendentalists gave literary expression and sanction to the attitudes that the American people had already evolved in their everyday pursuit of individual power and wealth.[3]

Emerson's first published work, "Nature" (1836), established his concern with the self. He begins with an appreciation of nature, but it soon becomes apparent that his essay is not a hymn to the glories of the natural world in the tradition of the nineteenth-century nature worshippers but rather a glorification of the individual man. Emerson emphasizes that man must not make the mistake of looking at himself as only one aspect of nature. Such a view will lead him to compare himself with the grandeur of nature and consequently to regard himself as minute and insignificant. Instead, Emerson says, man should see nature as a reflection of himself: "The whole of nature is a metaphor of the human mind."[4] Emerson's conception of man's relation to nature is vividly illustrated by a dream he recorded in his journal in 1840:

> I dreamed that I floated at will in the great Ether, and I saw this world floating also not far off, but diminished to the size of an apple. Then an angel took it in his hand and brought it to me and said, "This must thou eat." And I ate the world.   (*JMN*, 7: 525)

Emerson's published essays support this view of man as the center of the universe. According to him, the individual has the ability and the obligation to mold the world to his will, for man, not nature, is dominant (*Works*, 1: 10, 40). That Emerson means not only the extraordinary man or the poet becomes clear at the end of "Nature," where his exhortation to "build therefore your own world" is made implicitly applicable to the democratic man:

> All that Adam had, all that Caesar could, you have and can do. Adam called his house, heaven and earth; Caesar called his house Rome; you perhaps call yours, a cobbler's trade, a hundred acres of ploughed land, or a scholar's garret. Yet . . . your dominion is as great as theirs.
> (*Works*, 1: 76)

In his Phi Beta Kappa address the following year, Emerson refined his individualism. Although the lecture is addressed to the "American Scholar," whom Emerson urges to free himself of European traditions and standards in literature, he envisions his advice being applied to the American nation as a whole. The address concludes with an exalted picture of a nation of individuals, each acting for himself and governed only by the dictates of his own nature (*Works*, 1: 115).

Obviously, the most valuable trait for any individual is self-reliance. "Trust thyself," Emerson writes in his essay "Self-Reliance" (1841); "Nothing is at last sacred but the integrity of your own mind" (*Works*, 2: 47, 50). For Emerson, self-reliance meant trusting to one's self and one's own instincts independent of tradition, conventional religion, government, circumstances of birth, or even emotional entanglements.

Despite Emerson's insistence on the grandeur of the self, this philosophy in practice necessarily involves the pettiness that is inherent in any systematic refusal to learn from others. When Emerson traveled to Europe after the death of Ellen Tucker, his first wife, and after his resignation from the pulpit, he found very little of real interest to him in the intellectual life of Europe, except for Thomas Carlyle, whose self-assertion matched his own. Paris especially disappointed him, and he wrote home to his brother William of his boredom: "A lecture at the Sorbonne is far less useful to me than a lecture I write myself. . . . Je préfère mon inkstand."[5] He felt no interest in the political, social, and economic conditions of the countries he visited, and it was during his trip home in 1833 that he formulated the concept that he was to repeat many times: "A man contains all that is needful to his government within himself. He is made a law unto himself. . . . God is in every man" (*JMN*, 4: 84).[6] One might be tempted to say that Emerson's lack of interest in Europe was owing to his recent bereavement were it not for the fact that this insularity became the prevailing attitude throughout his life. The relationship between Emerson's philosophy and the events of his life was a close one, but before we examine that relationship, we must have a clear understanding of his philosophy.

Implicit in Emerson's ideas is the provincialism and narrowness of the self-interested person. In reacting against the restrictions of Anglo-European tradition and authority, the American individualist is limited by the interests of the self.

According to Emerson, the individual need not concern himself with the institutions of society because, as representatives of the outside world, they would interfere with the development of the self. In "Self-Reliance," Emerson declares that "no law can be sacred to me but that of my own nature," and he insists that the individual must not rely on external conditions of society like religion, the arts, property, or government (*Works*, 2: 50). In the "Divinity School Address" (1838), Emerson says that he can accept only what is in accord with himself. Other people, other traditions, however wise, can serve only to stimulate his own thinking; they can teach him nothing (*Works*, 1: 127–133; 2: 61).

If the institutions of society are unnecessary for the individual and an infringement upon the self, literature itself is valuable only insofar as it is useful for the individual. In the Phi Beta Kappa address (1837), Emerson tells the assembled scholars that books are not necessary for knowledge because knowledge is already in one's mind. Moreover, when we read books, we see only our own thoughts. One can read nature directly, without books (*Works*, 1: 87–94). In the later essay "Nominalist and Realist," Emerson writes that he reads only to find his own thoughts: "What is done well I feel as if I did; what is ill done I reck not of" (*Works*, 3: 231–233).

For Emerson, the individual is also the key to all history. In 1839 he wrote in his journal: "There is no history; There is only Biography. . . . You can only live for yourself. . . . The new individual must work out the whole problem of science, letters, & theology for himself[,] can owe his fathers nothing" (*JMN*, 7: 202). Such a claim for the powers of the individual is obviously a narrow one. The reader thinks of the rebellious adolescent, whose search for self drives him into a don't-try-to-tell-me-anything stance. As a phase of growth, perhaps, such an attitude is necessary to the development of self-awareness and individual identity. But as a permanent philosophy and way of life, it can only be insulating and self-restricting.

When Emerson says there is no history, only biography, he means not only that every man is capable of evolving the facts and truths of the world in his own person ("Of the universal mind each individual man is one more incarnation" [*Works*, 2: 8–10, 3–4, 63]) but also that history itself is determined by individuals. In "Self-Reliance" he tells us that "all history resolves itself very easily into the biography of a few stout and earnest persons" (*Works*, 2: 61), and his collection of lectures, *Representative Men* (1850), explores the specific lives of some of them. The lessons to be derived from these lectures are: one should rely on one's own instincts; one should act by asserting the will; and one should not concern oneself with tradition or the opinions and concerns of others. Swedenborg, Emerson says, represents the highest form of man— the mystic—because he is able to divine what is right without relying upon his experience in this world (*Works*, 4: 93, 95). It is important to recognize, however, that, although Emerson ranks the mystic as the highest form of man, he does so not because mysticism per se is valuable but because mysticism makes it easier for the individual to transcend the experience of the world. Thus the mystic need not feel the qualms that might affect ordinary men concerning the essential rightness of the inner vision. The mystic *knows* he is right.[7]

For Emerson, the strong, self-reliant individual is the ideal man, whether he is dealing in ideas or armies, real estate or railroads. In the introductory essay to *Representative Men*, he affirms that all men have the potential to be great: "There are no common men" (*Works*, 4: 31). As he declared in a speech at Dartmouth in 1838, the value for him of great men like Plato, Milton, and Shakespeare is that they show us we can be great too (*Works*, 1: 161). And the best measure of civilization in any country, according to his essay "Civilization" (1862), is the strength and self-reliance of its men (*Works*, 7: 31–32).

Emerson's view of the individual leaves no room for the individual's relationship to other people. His message is that the individual should insulate himself from others as much as possible. Society, Emerson says, is crippling and diminishes the individual (*Works*, 2: 199; 7: 9). In his lecture on "Literary

Ethics" (1838), Emerson told his audience of students that if they would be great, they must be solitary (*Works*, 1: 173). More than twenty years later, he was still advising solitude. The man of genius must remain "independent of the human race," protecting himself by self-reliance: "Each must stand on his glass tripod if he would keep his electricity" (*Works*, 7: 6).

In "Self-Reliance" Emerson spells out very clearly what the individual's attitude must be toward other people. He must elevate himself above the demands of the world outside himself: "Friend, client, child, sickness, fear, want, charity, all knock at once at thy closet door and say,—'come out unto us.'" But "keep thy state; come not into their confusion" (*Works*, 2: 72). Emerson makes no exceptions for close relatives: "I shun father and mother and wife and brother when my genius calls" (*Works*, 2: 51). What if the individual should cause his friends pain? Emerson's answer is clear: "I cannot sell my liberty and my power, to save their sensibility" (*Works*, 2: 74). In the essay "Experience" Emerson warns that other people will drown the individual if he gives them "so much as a leg or a finger" of sympathy: "The great and crescive self, rooted in absolute nature, supplants all relative existence and ruins the kingdom of mortal friendship and love" (*Works*, 3: 77, 81).

Emerson deals with other people in the same way that he deals with everything else that is outside the individual. Other people have no existence, no substance, except as they are absorbed into or made use of by the self. In his "Lecture on the Times" (1841) Emerson explicitly tells his audience that nothing is real but the self: "All men, all things . . . are phantasms and unreal beside the sanctuary of the heart" (*Works*, 1: 279). "The Transcendentalist," a lecture given in the same decade, asserts that the "mind is the only reality"; other people are only "reflectors" (*Works*, 1: 333). And in a later essay, "Culture" (1851), Emerson gives us a clue as to the function of these unreal phantasms and reflectors in the life of the transcendental self:

> I must have children, I must have events, I must have
> a social state and history, or my thinking and speaking
> want body or basis. But to give these accessories any
> value, I must know them as contingent and rather showy
> possessions, which pass for more to the people than to
> me.   (*Works*, 6: 158)

In all of his essays and lectures Emerson never treats other
people as though they had any value in their own right. They
are important, he remarks in his *Society and Solitude* lectures,
only because they can provide inspiration and fire the individual to performance (*Works*, 7: 10–12, 347–348). All ac-
quaintances, even friends, are principally valuable for the
way in which they can serve the self. The individual can absorb and use the friend's knowledge and wisdom, making it
his own. In the early essay "Nature," Emerson writes that
a friend should be absorbed until he becomes an "object of
thought" (*Works*, 1: 46). Friends are also valuable as a reflection of the self:

> In the last analysis love is only a reflection of a man's own
> worthiness from other men. Men have sometimes ex-
> changed names with their friends as if they would signify
> that in their friends each loved his own soul.
>   (*Works*, 2: 212)

Although at times Emerson may warn against self-love
and urge concern for others, it is only to point out the importance of other people for the self. In *Representative Men*
he admonishes that "we must not contend against love" or
deny the existence of other people, but the reason he offers, is
that other people can be useful to us: "Other men are lenses
through which we read our own minds" (*Works*, 4: 5). In his
journal in 1861 he wrote: "A wise man, an open mind, is as
much interested in others as in himself; they are only exten-
sions of himself" (*Journals*, 9: 298). Thus, in Emerson's philosophy, everything comes back to the self. Whatever is out-

side the self has no function except as it is related to the self (*Works*, 2: 214–215).

How does Emerson justify this total reliance on and concern with the self? The individual, he claims, has higher goals than earthly relationships to think about. Earthly love is only a training ground for higher love (*Works*, 2: 182–183). In the essay "Nature" Emerson explains that when the individual is able to partake of the Universal Being, all earthly relationships become unimportant: "The name of the nearest friend . . . is then a trifle and a disturbance. I am the lover of uncontained and immortal beauty" (*Works*, 1: 10). Beside the infinite, all finite objects seem unimportant. This sentiment sounds very fine, but when we think about what Emerson means by the Universal Being, we see his philosophy in a new light. For Emerson, the Universal Being is within. When the individual withdraws from society to commune with Nature, what he sees is himself (*Works*, 1: 10). Thus, when Emerson states that the individual must devote himself to higher things and cannot be distracted by trifles, what he means, ultimately, is that those higher concerns are the self.

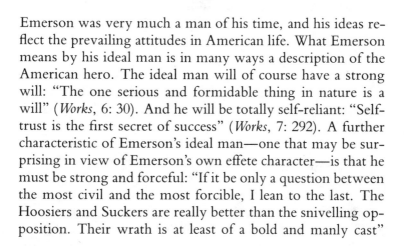

Emerson was very much a man of his time, and his ideas reflect the prevailing attitudes in American life. What Emerson means by his ideal man is in many ways a description of the American hero. The ideal man will of course have a strong will: "The one serious and formidable thing in nature is a will" (*Works*, 6: 30). And he will be totally self-reliant: "Self-trust is the first secret of success" (*Works*, 7: 292). A further characteristic of Emerson's ideal man—one that may be surprising in view of Emerson's own effete character—is that he must be strong and forceful: "If it be only a question between the most civil and the most forcible, I lean to the last. The Hoosiers and Suckers are really better than the snivelling opposition. Their wrath is at least of a bold and manly cast"

(*Works*, 6: 65). Though not rugged and physically strong himself, Emerson shared the American reverence for masculine strength, and his writings betray a particular affection for the adjective "manly."[8] Speaking contemptuously of conservative natures as "invalid and effeminate," he asserts in the essay "Fate" in the 1850s: "Strong natures, backwoodsmen, New Hampshire giants, Napoleons, Burkes, Broughams, Websters, Kossuths, are inevitable patriots" (*Works*, 6: 13). Thus, for Emerson, strength is equated with patriotism. The strong man, the assertive individual, was as American to him as film actor John Wayne was to later generations of Americans.

It is significant also that, although Emerson was critical of materialistic values, the ultimate goal of his strong, forceful, self-reliant individual is to be rich and powerful. In fact, Emerson sees the pursuit of wealth as an obligation. In the essay "Wealth" (1851) he maintains: "The manly part is to do with might and main what you can do" (*Works*, 6: 94). The pursuit of wealth is necessary for civilization; if people did not strive for wealth, there would be no progress:

> The pulpit and the press may have many commonplaces denouncing the thirst for wealth; but if men should take these moralists at their word and leave off aiming to be rich, the moralists would rush to rekindle at all hazards this love of power in the people, lest civilization be undone. (*Works*, 6: 95–96)

That Emerson was as impressed by monetary success as he was by power is evident in the kinds of examples he offers of self-reliant individuals. In the essay "Power" (1851) he describes life as "a search after power." After detailing the virtues of the strong individual, he uses the example of the real estate entrepreneur, thus making very American his exemplary man: "A feeble man can see the farms that are fenced and tilled, the houses that are built. The strong man sees the possible house and farms. His eye makes estates as fast as the sun breeds clouds" (*Works*, 6: 56, 58–59). In "Uses of Great Men" (1845), when Emerson wants to give an example of the type of great man who stands out above the anonymous masses in the city, he thinks of the railroad (*Works*, 4: 4). And when he lists the great men to come, his list is hardly transcendental: "a great salesman, then a road-contractor, then a student of fishes, then a buffalo-hunting explorer, or a semi-savage Western general" (*Works*, 4: 19). With the exception of the student of fishes (Thoreau perhaps?), Emerson's idea of great men clearly corresponds to the nineteenth-century American image of success. Notwithstanding the high-sounding rhetoric with which he managed to cloak much of his writing, Emerson was distinctly in tune with American ideas of wealth and power.

We have seen how Emerson embraced the success myth and the concept of the American hero. He also accepted the belief in manifest destiny and enthusiastically shared his country's faith in progress. Speaking of the settlement of America, he writes in "Fate":

> Cold and sea will train an imperial Saxon race, which nature cannot bear to lose. . . . All the bloods it shall absorb and domineer: and more than Mexicos, the secrets of water and steam, the spasms of electricity, the ductility of metals, the chariot of the air, the ruddered balloon are awaiting you.   (*Works*, 6: 32)

Some of Emerson's pronouncements also look forward to the survival-of-the-fittest doctrine of Social Darwinism. His emphasis on the self-reliant individual and disregard for others provide an excellent rationale for the robber-baron psychology. In the 1850s he wrote: "The strongest idea incarnates itself in majorities and nations, in the healthiest and strongest" (*Works*, 6: 13–14). Emerson's theory of compensations helped him to justify whatever unpleasant means might be necessary for Americans to fulfill their destiny. Of the California gold rush, for example, he wrote that it did not matter what immoral means were used; the function of the gold rush was to hasten the settlement and civilizing of the West (*Works*, 6: 255).

Throughout his life, Emerson wrote about Americans as the chosen people. In 1844 he confided to his journal: "The idea which I approach and am magnetized by,—is my country" (*JMN*, 9: 66). In "The Young American," a lecture given to a Boston Mercantile Association in the same year, Emerson outlined the promise and challenge of America and spoke of "the Spirit who led us hither and is leading us still." Urging the young businessmen to accept the challenge of "the development of our American internal resources, the extension to the utmost of the commercial system," he concluded with a prophecy of America's future as a "new and more excellent social state than history has recorded" (*Works*, 1: 391, 395). Twenty years later Emerson was still extolling the greatness of America's destiny. In 1863 he declared in "The Fortune of the Republic" that America existed for the regeneration of the world.[9] And after the Civil War he wrote in his journal that America's superior political institutions would make it "the leading Guide and Lawgiver of the world" (*Journals*, 10: 195).

In adopting this view of America as the destined leader of the world and the rightful owner of the continent,[10] Emerson accepted the disregard for others that necessarily accompanied such an enthusiastic belief. Although critical of specific instances of white mistreatment of the Indians (e.g., the 1838 removal of the Cherokees), he accepted without question the theory that it was America's destiny to displace the Indian. In 1826 he wrote in his journal:

> It is the order of Providence that great objects must be purchased by great sacrifices. . . . It seems to be out of a sort of obedience and acknowledgement of this high and melancholy necessity . . . that America has yielded up her vast indigenous family tribe after tribe to the haughty Genius of Civilization.   (*JMN*, 2: 14)

Not only the Indian, but all others who stood in the way of American expansion were unlamented victims of the nation's destiny. In 1844 Emerson wrote that Americans would eventually overrun the Texas territory, as well as Mexico and

Oregon, and "it will in the course of ages be of small import by what particular occasions and methods it was done" (*JMN*, 9: 74).

Merging the concept of manifest destiny with a belief in the survival of the fittest, Emerson was able to explain very comfortably the exclusion of peoples who did not fit into his view of America. In 1840 he wrote in his journal of the black race: "It is plain that so inferior a race must perish shortly like the poor Indians." And, maintaining that the Indians had disappeared because there was no place for them, he concluded: "That is the very fact of their inferiority. There is always place for the superior" (*JMN*, 7: 393).[11]

This attitude toward others helps to explain Emerson's strong militancy during the Civil War. Although at first he refused to be drawn into the abolitionist fight, insisting that he had to devote himself to his own work, by 1850 the cause had won his sympathy, and by 1858 he was a zealous abolitionist. With a total disregard for the human qualities of Southerners as people, he urged the pleasures of destroying such a terrible foe. For Emerson, the war was wholly an abstraction. He wrote of the glories and uses of war and described how war organized society and brought out the genius of all men, making them more manly and self-reliant (*Journals*, 9: 301, 362, 492–494, 512). At the end of the war, he expressed his satisfaction that the rebels had been "pounded . . . into a peace," complaining only that Grant's terms were too easy (*Journals*, 10: 93–94).[12]

Emerson demonstrates in his public writings a concern with self and a disregard for other people that more than match the attitudes of the American cultural hero. Moreover, for Emerson, this attitude was not simply a public stance. In his private life, too, he attempted to maintain the same self-oriented insularity that he advised in his lectures and essays. Emerson was, of course, extreme in his preoccupation with self. Not everyone who subscribed to American individualism practiced the same reserve in relation to other people. However, Emerson does provide us with a clear example of the consequences to human relationships of an exaggerated emphasis on the self.

Emerson's biographers have theorized that his philosophy developed out of a personal inability to commit himself to others because of various psychological fears. Phillips Russell says that the young Emerson built a shell around himself to make up for a lack of physical abilities and that without such a shell he might have gone insane like his brother Edward.[13] Ralph Rusk explains that Emerson transmuted the "unhappy emotional experiences" of his own life (his inability to make friends, his personal tragedies) into a "satisfying theory of the proper conduct of one's life."[14] Emerson's most recent biographer, Gay Wilson Allen, probably comes closest to the truth when he concludes that Emerson's self-orientation was a form of self-protection, a "striving for emotional invulnerability."[15] Clearly, Emerson's life experience, whether it determined or only confirmed his philosophy, was closely related to his extreme individualism.

Whatever the reason for Emerson's insularity, the result was the same: in his private life Emerson was either unable or unwilling to commit himself to other people. In 1838 he wrote in his journal that he wished he had been more expressive in his relations with his first wife, Ellen, and with his brothers, Charles and Edward, all now dead, and he resolved that in later relationships he would not be so cold (*JMN*, 5: 456). Yet a few years later he admitted that he could not express himself to his second wife, Lidian, and Lidian often complained of his coldness (*JMN*, 7: 471).[16] When his son, Waldo, died in 1842, Emerson wrote to Caroline Sturgis: "I chiefly grieve that I cannot grieve; that this fact takes no more deep hold than other facts. . . . Must every experience . . . only kiss my cheek like the wind & pass away?" (*Letters*, 3: 9). The next year he confessed in his journal of a great inability to communicate with others: "It is a pathetic thing to meet a friend prepared to love you, to whom yet, from some ineptitude, you cannot communicate yourself" (*JMN*, 8: 365).

As these comments indicate, Emerson was sometimes troubled by his lack of feeling for people. He wrote of himself in 1840: "None knows better than I—more's the pity—the gloomy inhospitality of the man, the want of power to meet and unite with even those whom he loves in his 'flinty way'" (*Letters*, 2: 350–351). Emerson's philosophy may represent in part an attempt to create a system that explained and allowed him to accept his own limitations. As Margaret Fuller noted in her 1842 journal, Emerson seemed entirely to have "dismissed" the idea of tragedy and feeling, but he needed constantly to urge himself to accept this quality in himself: "Whenever in his journal he speaks of his peculiar character & limitations he has written in the margin 'Accept.'"[17]

It is also possible that Emerson was deeply affected by the experiences that he claimed did not touch him. He may have had to work very hard to maintain the unruffled exterior that he presented to the world; he may even have been fooling himself when he claimed that he had never felt pain.[18] His journals and letters contain occasional statements of depression; though far outweighed by his overwhelming optimism, these statements indicate that he was not untouched by life. After the deaths of Ellen, Charles, and Waldo, Emerson was particularly vulnerable to negative thoughts. Five days after Ellen died, in February 1831, he asked God to be merciful and "repair this miserable debility in which her death has left my soul" (*JMN*, 3: 226). Two years later he had to exhort himself not to be downhearted: "Be cheerful. What an insane habit is this of groping always into the past" (*JMN*, 4: 77). When his brother Charles died in 1836, Emerson again was hard hit. Ralph Rusk suggests that this loss was so severe that it threatened the whole structure of Emerson's philosophy.[19] His letters hint at this grief. He wrote to Abel Adams that in losing Charles, "I have lost all of my society," and he confided to Harriet Martineau: "I can gather no hint from this terrible experience. . . . I grope in greater darkness" (*Letters*,

2: 23, 24). But the greatest blow, perhaps, was the loss in January 1842 of Emerson's first child, the blue-eyed "darling boy," Waldo. Emerson wrote in his journal two months later: "I comprehend nothing of this fact but its bitterness. Explanation have I none, consolation none" (*JMN*, 8: 205).

Yet, after each of these lapses, the evidence for which is deeply buried in Emerson's otherwise monochromatic writing, Emerson seemed to return quickly to his previous mode, reiterating in his public and private writing that all that mattered was the Universal Truth—that when events were looked at in the larger scheme of things, there were compensations for all apparent evils. In 1835 he wrote in his journal that when Ellen died, "the air was still sweet, the sun was not taken down from my firmament, and however sore was that particular loss, I still felt that it was particular, that the Universe remained" (*JMN*, 5: 19–20). He expressed the same confidence in his poem about Waldo's death, "Threnody."[20] And in the essay "Experience" he wrote: "In the death of my son, now more than two years ago, I seem to have lost a beautiful estate,—no more" (*Works*, 3: 48). In 1839 he cautioned that "the compensations of calamity are not to be found by the Understanding suddenly but require years of time to make them sensible." In a possible reference to his decision to resign his pastorate after his first wife's death, he continued: "The death of a dear friend, wife, brother, lover, seems an unmixed loss, but it commonly operates revolutions in the way of life" (*JMN*, 7: 200–201). Here, apparently, was Emerson's way of dealing with tragedy: he was able to hide the pain—perhaps even from himself—by converting the experience into a grand generalization.

It is interesting to note that the occasional cries of pain, the doubts, the negative thoughts that creep into Emerson's private journals and letters are carefully kept out of his lectures and essays. The image that Emerson created for the public was a persona that never faltered, a man who possessed the inner strength of a spiritual Davy Crockett and the unflagging optimism of the Horatio Alger hero. Emerson maintained this image not only in the public world but in his private world as well. A passage from his journal in 1838 gives us an idea of how Emerson presented himself to his friends:

> I told J[ones] V[ery] that I had never suffered, and that I could scarce bring myself to feel a concern for the safety and life of my nearest friends that would satisfy them: that I saw clearly that if my wife, my child, my mother, should be taken from me, I should still remain whole. . . . I should not grieve enough, although I love them. But could I make them feel what I feel—the boundless resources of the soul,—remaining entire when particular threads of relation are snapped,—I should dismiss forever the little remains of uneasiness I have in regard to them. (*JMN*, 7: 132)

That Emerson himself came to believe in this persona is apparent from statements like this one from his journal in 1860: "I reached the other day the end of my 57th year, and am easier in my mind than hitherto. I could never give much reality to evil and pain" (*JMN*, 9: 273).

What happens to human relationships when a philosophy that does not recognize the reality of other people is put into practice in a world where other people obviously exist? Emerson's friend James Eliot Cabot reveals in his biography of Emerson that it was impossible for any friend of Emerson's to have a satisfying relationship with him. Cabot himself, Bronson Alcott, Ellery Channing, Henry James, Sr., Jones Very, Margaret Fuller—all became impatient at Emerson's practice of going only so far and then no farther in his personal relationships. Ellery Channing declared that Emerson was "a terrible man to deal with . . . he cannot establish a personal relation with any one."[21] Cabot describes how Emerson would refuse to discuss ideas that were not his own: "If you urged them upon him, he would receive your remarks in gracious silence, or answer at cross purposes." And

Henry James, Sr., looking back on his friendship with Emerson, complained that "Emerson always kept one at such arm's-length, tasting him and sipping him and trying him, to make sure that he was worthy of his somewhat prim and bloodless friendship." [22]

From Emerson's point of view, other people were often simply a source of annoyance. In 1835, when he was engaged to Lidian, he wrote in his journal: "If a conversation be prolonged which is not exactly in my key, I become nervous. . . . Society suffocates . . . and irritates" (*JMN*, 5: 48). Over thirty years later he was saying the same thing: "Society is compulsory and wasteful to the individual" (*Journals*, 10: 170).

Yet, despite his insistence upon solitude, Emerson throughout his life surrounded himself with other people. Not only relatives and friends filled the house in Concord; Emerson seemed to hold a perpetual open house for writers, thinkers, and interested persons of all kinds who came to him for conversation and inspiration. At first this attitude seems paradoxical. One asks whether Emerson really meant it when he said he wanted solitude. Why did he encourage people to come to him if he really wanted to be left alone? I think the answer is suggested by a passage in the essay "Domestic Life" (1859): "There is no event greater in life than the appearance of new persons about our hearth, except it be the progress of the character which draws them" (*Works*, 7: 128). When Emerson said that he must have society on his own terms, he meant that he wanted people to come to him as a central figure, to contribute to the expansion of his self.

Emerson apparently liked to be with people only when he could make use of them for his own development. In a letter to his brother William in 1836 he praised Margaret Fuller (whom he had just met), not for her personal qualities, but because she contributed to his own growth. With a very intelligent person, he remarked, "you stretch your limbs and dilate to your utmost size" (*Letters*, 2: 32). When he learned of her death in 1850, he regretfully wrote in his journal: "I have lost in her my audience" (*JMN*, 11: 258). Of his friend

Alcott, Emerson noted: "When I go to talk with Alcott, it is not so much to get his thoughts as to watch myself under his influence. He excites me, and I think freely."[23] Emerson had no qualms about regarding people in this way. In a letter to Margaret Fuller in 1842 he clearly stated his need to use others for the betterment of himself, establishing a credo for his personal life that literally followed the advice of his lectures and essays: "Lidian sometimes taxes me at home with an egotism more virulent than any against which I rail. Perhaps she is right. . . . Each must build up his own world, though he unbuilt all other men's for his own materials" (*Letters*, 3: 20).

Lidian tried very hard to bring Emerson to make more of a human commitment to her. In an 1841 letter to her he referred to what must have been an accusation of hers that he had no regard for people and things outside himself, and he admitted that he tended to "postpone persons and things in my high times" (*Letters*, 2: 427). In 1842, when he was lecturing in Providence, he wrote to Lidian, complaining that she had not written to him, and asked: "Well, is this to punish my philosophy?" (*Letters*, 3: 12). Apparently he meant that she had not written to him because his philosophy led her to believe that he did not care for her or the children and thus would not want news of them. Since this letter was written less than a month after Waldo died, the reference to his philosophy may be specifically linked to Emerson's optimistic attempt to make all tragedies appear for the best and his insistence that nothing really touched him. In this real tragedy it is easy to see how such a philosophy would make the boy's mother feel that Emerson did not care for any of them. The following year Lidian's pain is recorded in Emerson's journal: "Dear husband, I wish I had never been born. I do not see how God can compensate me for the sorrow of existence" (*JMN*, 8: 365). Emerson makes no discernible comment on the entry, but a few pages later he writes: "Persons are fine things, but they cost so much! for *thee* I must pay *me*" (*JMN*, 8: 370).

Sometime between 1840 and 1845 Lidian wrote a satirical comment on the Transcendentalist philosophy, calling it her "Transcendental Bible." It gives us an idea of the cost to human relations of the insistence on the primacy of the self:

> Loathe and shun the sick. They are in bad taste, and may untune us for writing the poem floating through our mind. . . .
>
> Despise the unintellectual, and make them feel that you do by not noticing their remark and question lest they presume to intrude into your conversation. . . .
>
> It is mean and weak to seek for sympathy; it is mean and weak to give it. . . . Never wish to be loved. Who are you to expect that? Besides, the great never value being loved. . . .
>
> If you scorn happiness (though you value a pleasant talk or walk, a tasteful garment, a comfortable dinner) if you wish not for immortal consciousness (though you bear with impatience the loss of an hour of thought or study) if you care not for the loss of your soul (though you deprecate the loss of your house) . . . if you care not that a benign Divinity shapes your ends (though you seek a good tailor to shape your coat) if you scorn to believe your affliction cometh not from the dust (though bowed to the dust by it) then, if there is such a thing as duty, you have done your whole duty to your noble self-sustained, impeccable, infallible Self.[24]

When looked at from the point of view of the other, the Transcendental Self leaves much to be desired. What the insular individual may see as a glorious pursuit of the ideal self becomes a cold, unfeeling, even materialistic selfishness.

Margaret Fuller's 1842 journal, which she kept while visiting the Emersons in Concord, contains a revealing passage regarding Emerson's relationship with Lidian. Fuller tells how Lidian burst into tears on two instances when it seemed that Emerson was spending time with Fuller that she herself could not claim. Fuller notes how Emerson remained serene and silent, never offering a word of reassurance. Later

Lidian complained to Fuller of his coldness. Fuller wrote: "I think she will always have these pains, because she has always a lurking hope that Waldo's character will alter, and that he will be capable of an intimate union; now I feel convinced that it will never be more perfect between them two."[25]

That Lidian was never able to obtain a more complete relationship with Emerson is implied in a letter he wrote to her from London in 1848. She apparently had asked him to write more warmly, to commit himself more fully. He replied that he never could: "Ah you still ask me for that unwritten letter always due, it seems, always unwritten . . . by me to every sister and brother of the human race." Emerson goes on to explain why he cannot write such a letter. He has a higher calling and cannot deal with mere earthly involvements:

> The trick of solitariness can never leave me. My own pursuits and calling often appear to me like those of an "astronomer royal" whose whole duty is to make faithful minutes which have only value when kept for ages, and in one life are insignificant.   (*Letters*, 4: 32)

Faced with such grandiose proclamations in her daily life, it is not surprising that Lidian commented in April of the year that Waldo died, "Save me from magnificent souls. I like a small common-sized one" (*JMN*, 8: 242).

Given Emerson's inflated view of the self and his consequent failure to recognize the independent existence of other people, what was his view of women, the institutionalized other? It is evident from both his public and private writings that Emerson was unable to see women as individuals like himself.

Even in his own marriages, Emerson tended to think of his wife more as an abstraction than as a real person. Ellen Tucker, to whom Emerson was married for eighteen months

before she died of tuberculosis in 1831, was his "beautiful angel." As Phillips Russell points out, Emerson's writing about
Ellen reveals no closeness. He apparently worshipped her
"from a distance; as if she were a goddess."[26] Although Gay
Wilson Allen is probably right that Ellen "thawed his emotions" more than anyone else, her loss cannot be the reason
for his failure to commit himself to people in later years.[27]
One wonders how fully he would have been able to give
himself even to Ellen had she lived. Before he met Ellen, he
complained of his inability to feel: "I have not the kind affections of a pigeon." And he described himself as "ungenerous
& selfish, cautious & cold" (*JMN*, 1: 134). Soon after her
death, he noted that now she would know the "selfishness"
that he had concealed from her in life (*JMN*, 3: 226–227).
And in later years he reproached himself that his attitude toward her had been governed too much by "coldness & pru-
dence" (*JMN*, 5: 456). Emerson referred to Ellen as "the angel who walked with me in my younger days" and thought
of her as an example of the true role of woman—an angel to
be revered by man and to guide him to "honor and religion"
(*JMN*, 8: 381). Emerson apparently loved Ellen as much as
he was capable of loving anyone, but it was the love of veneration. By making a real woman into an angel, an abstraction,
Emerson was able to keep himself intact.

If Ellen was his "beautiful angel," Lidian was his "good
angel." A mature woman of thirty-one when she met Emerson, with a strong personality and "inexhaustible originality,"[28] she considered herself privileged to be married to such
a great man and at first believed Emerson's own estimate of
himself.[29] (She said of his Phi Beta Kappa speech that it was
"God's truth—fitly spoken.")[30] Lydia Jackson relinquished
her identity when she married Emerson, not only giving up
her last name but allowing him to change her first name as
well. It has been suggested that Emerson made the change
because he thought that the name Lidian would sound better
with the surname Emerson, but his comments at the time reveal that he simply preferred the name Lidian.[31] I believe that
Emerson changed Lydia's name because he was marrying not

Lydia Jackson but himself; to rename her was a way of making her a part of himself. That he chose the particular form he did, adding an *n* sound at the end, may have been a way of changing her into Ellen, the part of himself that he had lost four years before and whose name Lidian agreed to give in full to their first daughter (Emerson commented that she "magnanimously makes my gods her gods" [*JMN*, 7: 170]). Lidian later rebelled against Emerson's ideas,[32] but he never saw her as an independent being; she existed only in relation to himself. For Emerson, Lidian personified Goodness and Christian Love, and his favorite name for her was Asia, which to him meant femininity, Christianity, and all that he regarded as intuitive and static, without will or reason. (The concept of Europe he saw as masculine, active, and creative, "a land of arts, invention, trade, freedom" [*Works*, 4: 52, 62]).[33]

Emerson's concept of women in general was not very different from the way in which he regarded Ellen and Lidian. Just how limited that view was is apparent in his acceptance of all the contemporary stereotypes about women. He ascribed certain fixed characteristics to women as opposed to men. Man is the Head; woman, the Heart. Man is the Intellect; woman, the Affections. The purpose of marriage, he said in an 1837 lecture, is the union of intellect and affection.[34] Moreover, man is strong; woman is weak: "A woman's strength is not masculine but is the irresistible might of weakness" (*JMN*, 5: 505). Not only does Emerson maintain that women have weak wills and are capricious and unstable (*JMN*, 4: 256–257), but he equates femininity with defectiveness, as is apparent in his tendency to label as "effeminate" people whom he also describes as "the halt, the blind, and the invalid" (e.g., *Works*, 6: 13). That Emerson associated femininity with invalidism is not surprising, given his own experience with women. His first wife was dying of tuberculosis throughout their short marriage, and his second wife complained of chronic ill health. Even his independent friend Margaret Fuller suffered from incapacitating headaches. Since much of the female invalidism of the nineteenth century was obviously induced by cultural restrictions and conditioning,[35] Emerson cannot be judged too harshly for accepting what seemed to be a well-substantiated fact. However, his leap from physical weakness to weakness of character is not so easily excused.

Another aspect of Emerson's man–woman dichotomy is the contrast between reason and intellect. Men are reasoning beings; women act by instinct. A few years after his marriage to Lidian, Emerson, struck by something she had said, wrote in his journal: "I, as always, venerate the oracular nature of woman. The sentiment which the man thinks he came unto gradually through the events of years, to his surprise he finds woman dwelling there in the same, as in her native home" (*JMN*, 7: 96). Almost thirty years later he still considered women to be unthinking and instinctive: "Man's conclusions are reached by toil. Woman arrives at the same by sympathy" (*Journals*, 10: 171). Given Emerson's high opinion of intuitive knowledge, one might interpret this view as a compliment. However, Emerson clearly associates women's intuition not with intuitive reason but with unthinking instinct. And what it reveals most of all is Emerson's failure to see women as people. If one venerates a woman, one cannot regard or treat her as a person. Moreover, to say that a woman is intuitive can also be a way of explaining how someone whom you do not consider to be very intelligent is able to make astute observations. If we think about what it means to say that women are intuitive, unreasoning creatures, we can only conclude with Emerson that they are neither very perceptive nor very intelligent. Thus when writing about Plato in his journal in 1845, Emerson commented: "Yet to women his book is Mahometan" (*JMN*, 9: 184).

If women are not very intelligent, neither are they very creative. Emerson regards man as creative; woman is passive. This view of the sexes is spelled out very graphically in the sexual language Emerson uses when he attempts to explain the difference between the great man and his imitators. A great man like Luther, Montaigne, or Pascal "utters a thought or feeling in a virile manner," Emerson entered in his journal in 1859. The great man is usually followed by "any number of spiritual eunuchs and women, who talk about that thought. . . . Each of these male words . . . delight and occupy them. . . . Great bands of female souls who only receive the spermatic *aura*" (*JMN*, 14: 277). That Emerson was still thinking in these terms at the age of fifty-six after having been closely connected with some of the most creative women thinkers of his time (Margaret Fuller, Harriet Martineau), after having taken a stand in support of the women's rights movement, and after having read and praised the works of leading nineteenth-century European women writers (George Sand, Madame de Stael) indicates how deeply imbedded the stereotype was in his mind. It also shows how unwilling he was to accept ideas that did not fit into his own scheme of things.

In Emerson's view of life, the best place for women was in the home. In the 1838 lecture "The Heart," Emerson quotes from Felicia Hemans's poem "To Corinna at the Capitol" to illustrate this point:

> Happy, happier far than thou,
> With the laurel on thy brow,
> She who makes the humblest hearth
>   Lovely but to one on earth.
>
> (*Lectures*, 2: 283)

In 1841, on considering the question of women testifying at trials, Emerson commented in his journal that such action would be a "misplacement of our good Angel." She should remain in the home, "that shrine of sanctity, sentiment, and solitude" (*JMN*, 8: 85). Linked to this conviction that women belong in the home is the belief that, whereas man is an explorer and adventurer, woman is the keeper of civilization. Emerson's acceptance of this traditional view of women is clear from his many references to women as the civilizers of society, the regulators of fashion, taste, and manners (*Works*, 7: 24; *Journals*, 10: 172). Maintaining that women are constitutionally concerned with appearances, he writes in the essay "Manners" (1841–1842) that their function is to fill man's "vase with wine and roses to the brim," thus making his life more civilized (*Lectures*, 2: 302; *Works*, 3: 150). He also writes in "Manners" that fashion and manners are unimportant to the true spirit and describes fashion as "a word of narrow and often sinister meaning" (*Works*, 3: 122). Thus, despite the pleasantness of women's role, it is an insignificant one.

It should be apparent that Emerson, like most of his contemporaries, viewed women only in relation to man. The two principal functions that woman might have were "the comforter in the home and softener of man" or the goddess who inspired man to honor, morals, and religion. For her to function in the latter way, man must observe woman "reverentially" and be guided by the "bright revelations of her best nature" (*JMN*, 8: 300–381; *Works*, 3: 150). In either role, woman is ministering angel for man, and Emerson liked to see her as such (See *JMN*, 7: 260).

Emerson must have noticed that there were women who did not fit into the category that he had assigned them, women who manifested traits that were not "feminine." Unfortunately, when Emerson did make such observations, he did not re-examine his categories. Rather, he assumed that the fault lay in the woman. He evaluated a woman's success as a woman by how faithfully she lived up to his ideal characteristics for her. For example, from his premise that affection was "the basis of the nature of Woman," he concluded that "women are charming by their submission to it" (*Lectures*, 2: 281). Women who did not demonstrate the characteristics Emerson admired in women he condemned as masculine (*JMN*, 8: 380–381). When asked to speak at a women's convention in 1855, he concluded by telling his audience of women that they should not try to act like men but should remain feminine: "A masculine woman is never strong, but a lady is" (*Works*, 11: 425).

A woman who exhibits masculine characteristics is somehow overstepping her role, but a man who contains feminine traits is a higher form of man. Thus, in *Representative Men* Emerson's praise of Plato is inspired partly by Plato's ability to combine in himself both the feminine principle symbolized for Emerson by Asia and the masculine principle represented by Europe (*Works*, 4: 52). In his journal in 1842 Emerson proposed that the "highly endowed man . . . is a Man-woman and does not so much need the complement of Woman to his being" (*JMN*, 8: 175). About the same time, he wrote: "Always there is this Woman as well as this man in the mind; Affection as well as Intellect" (*JMN*, 8: 230). Obviously, Emerson could not conceive of a woman becoming such a Man-woman because he did not view woman as an independent being. Although he could see himself or any great man in this self-reliant role, he could see woman only in her relation to man.

The phrase from Emerson's 1840 journal that might be quoted in support of a man-woman of either sex—"Hermaphrodite, is then the symbol of the finished soul"—must be looked at in the context of the entry in which it appears. It is taken from a conversation in which others attempted to apply this principle to women. Emerson, impatient with them, criticizes as masculine the women who took part in the discussion: "Much poor talk concerning woman which at least had the effect of revealing the true sex of several of the party who usually go disguised in the form of the other sex" (*JMN*, 8: 380–381).

Despite Emerson's emphasis on self-reliance and insistence upon high goals, then, it is clear that his philosophy was not intended to apply to women. The Transcendental Self could only be a man. In fact, one of the arguments Emerson uses for self-reliance is that a man will be better able to take care of a woman, "for how can he protect a woman, who cannot protect himself" (*Works*, 7: 7). Emerson does not expect women to have the same high goals as men. In 1842 he wrote in his journal (he later used the passage in "Domestic Life") that it was a shame that so many men had low aspirations and settled too early on trifles. Of women, however, he said that it was only "reasonable" that they should settle early on love and marriage (*JMN*, 8: 291; *Works*, 7: 123–125).

Emerson recognized that there were unmarried women, or women without men, but he could not consider them to be independent beings. Even they could be seen only in relation to men, as muse or goddess: "The true Virgin will raise herself by just degrees into a goddess admirable and helpful to all beholders" (*JMN*, 4: 103). At one point in his journal he commented on the problem he had encountered in talking to women about his philosophy (the lady mentioned is probably Margaret Fuller, whom he had quoted two pages earlier in the journal):

> In conversing with a lady it sometimes seems a bitterness and unnecessary to insist as I incline to do, on this self-sufficiency of man. . . . We talk of courses of action. But to women my paths are shut up and the fine women I think of who have had genius ard cultivation who have not been wives but muses have something tragic in their lot. (*JMN*, 5: 409–410)

If women must be wives or muses, what then was Mary Moody Emerson, the paternal aunt with whom Emerson had corresponded since childhood and who exerted a powerful influence on his development? No one's wife, Aunt Mary was a strong-willed, independent woman upon whom Emerson's mother called from time to time to help out with her "fatherless children." She apparently was fond of her nephews and ambitious for them. However, when she disapproved of someone, she made no bones about it; Emerson and most of her relatives were afraid of her sharp tongue and caustic wit. Emerson's daughter Ellen tells of how Emerson and his mother "trembled" and marveled when Lidian answered her back.[36] Aunt Mary obviously was no goddess, but she was Emerson's earliest muse. He called her a "sibyl" (*Letters*, 5: 326) and tested out his ideas in his letters to her. Despite her irascible nature, Emerson was able to smile at her outrageous behavior. He also asserted his independence from her, both in his life and in his religion. But he respected her originality and called her a "genius" from whom any intelligent young man could learn. "By society with her," he said, "one's mind is electrified and purged" (*JMN*, 7: 442; *Works*, 10: 380–381, 404). Her principal importance for Emerson was the effect that she had on him. And it was her writings that he valued, he told his brother William after her death, not her presence (*Letters*, 5: 326). Thus he was able to encompass even the formidable Mary Moody Emerson in his philosophy by reducing her to an abstraction that was valuable only as it served the needs of the self.

How did Emerson reconcile his attitude toward women with his support of the women's rights movement? Apparently he felt able to support the call for the vote and to concede political and civil wrongs, but he could not bring himself to advocate rights that would take woman out of the home or give her autonomy as a human being. His comments reveal a fundamental inability to see woman except in her relation to man. In 1850 he wrote to Paulina W. Davis, who had asked him to take part in a convention: "I should not wish women to wish political functions, nor, if granted, assume them." Indicating that a woman is to be judged by how faithfully she lives up to man's concept of her, he continued: "I imagine that a woman whom all men would feel to be the best would decline such privileges if offered, and feel them to be rather obstacles to her legitimate influence" (*Letters*, 4: 229–230). A woman's "legitimate influence," apparently, was the use of her feminine qualities to obtain what she wanted. Writing in his journal in 1851, he observed apropos of a women's rights convention held in Worcester that the real solution would be for all women to be healthy and beautiful. Then they would have no need to fight for their rights because all men would do their bidding. "A sound and beautiful woman," a Venus, he said, magnetizes men (*JMN*, 11: 444).

All of Emerson's ideas on women are contained in his speech to the women's rights convention in Boston in 1855. Describing women in conventional terms as unthinking, sentimental, weak, and uncreative, he told the assembled women who had come to hear the great man's wisdom that woman is the sail and man the rudder; if women try to steer, there will be trouble. "The life of the affections is primary to woman," he admonished; she is the "Angel in the parlor," whose function is to "embellish trifles." There was no reason why women should not vote, Emerson declared, and he listed the objections that had been made: women are ignorant of affairs; they are impractical, too emotional, too idealistic. Without denying any of these stereotypes, he acknowledged only that they should not prevent women from voting. Many men are ignorant and emotional, he realized, expressing a hope that the idealism of women would counterbalance the "brutal ignorance and mere animal wants" of the "intemperate" immigrant vote.

Emerson's condescending attitude throughout the speech attempts to make womanhood appear so beautiful that no woman would be brave enough to deny it. But the implication of his words is that women *are* inferior and should trust in man's better judgment and superior knowledge to help them. Voting is a harmless exercise; votes from many different types of people cancel themselves out anyway. If woman really wants something done, her best resource, and the one best suited to her temperament and abilities, is to rely on a good man: "Woman should find in man her guardian." Emerson concluded by assuring his audience that "whatever the woman's heart is prompted to desire, the man's mind is simultaneously prompted to accomplish" (*Works*, 11: 403–426).

Here, then, is the "legitimate influence" of woman; she must rely upon the good will of men and remain dependent upon them. There is no evidence that Emerson's opinion of women's rights ever changed. A speech on women written after the Civil War but apparently never delivered repeats the same arguments: women are the civilizers; they represent love and religion; and they might as well have the vote because they could not make worse choices than many men (*Works*, 11: 627–630). In May 1869, in a speech before the New England Women's Suffrage Association, Emerson concluded his very general remarks with a declaration that the rights of women should not be denied.[37] Later in the same year he sent a letter to the Essex County Women's Suffrage Association, indicating that, although he sympathized with the efforts of women, he could not really conceive of what true equality would mean.[38]

Throughout his life, Emerson maintained the same view of women. If man is the center of the universe, woman, in her traditional role of other, is one of the feeders and reflectors of man. Man is the sun; woman the moon (*JMN*, 5: 179). Man is the subject; woman the object.

Emerson, who referred to himself as an "icicle" in social relationships (*Letters*, 2: 438), is an extreme example of the insular individual, but his failure to relate to other people is an indication of the ultimate consequences of the emphasis on individualism. The man who accepted this overwhelming view of the self could not see other people as individuals. Consequently, he would not see women—whom, by definition, he would regard as the other—as independent human beings. He could see all others only in relation to the self.

Emerson's philosophy reflects the problem confronting any man who subscribed so completely to the myth of American individualism. Believing that he could do anything, but learning that in reality he had limitations, he had to create a false image of himself, a persona who was the marvelous being that he believed he should be. Like the American Narcissus, he saw himself as a giant among giants. And, since the most important goal for him was development of the self, he had to see other people as fodder for giants.

■ CHAPTER 3 ■

■ CHAPTER 3 ■

THE GENDER OF AMERICAN INDIVIDUALISM: HENRY DAVID THOREAU AND MARGARET FULLER

Has my song
My most creative, poised and long
Genius-unfolding song
No existence of its own?

Margaret Fuller, 1844[1]

When Emerson declared in 1833, "I am thankful that I am an American as I am thankful that I am a man,"[2] he made a statement that the American individualist would heartily agree with. While evolving his theories of Transcendentalism, Emerson could be comfortable in the knowledge that American culture provided the right climate for the individual growth and expansion that he advocated. And as a man, he could take for granted that the individualism of his society applied to him. Since it is my contention that an author's relationship to American individualism determines his conception of women, I shall examine what happened to the Transcendental concept of the self when it was put into practice by two Americans writing in the Emersonian tradition. For Henry

55

David Thoreau, Transcendentalism coincided with the masculine tradition of American individualism. But for Margaret Fuller, the Transcendental doctrine of the self was incompatible with American culture.

Henry David Thoreau took Emerson's philosophy and attempted to put it into practice in a way that Emerson, with his family and social commitments, could not. Like Emerson, Thoreau was primarily dedicated to the expansion of the self. Maintaining that the self contains all that it is necessary to know, Thoreau tried to infuse self-exploration with all the excitement of an adventure. Explore "your own streams and oceans," he urges in *Walden*; "Explore thyself."[3] Thoreau's principal goal in life was to record and order his own thoughts and experiences in his published works and, ultimately, in his own voluminous Journal. As Leon Edel notes, "All of Thoreau's writings represent a continuous and carefully documented projection of the self."[4]

What is interesting about Thoreau's statement that "my Journal should be the record of my love" is that there is no *beloved* in the Journal.[5] When people are mentioned in the Journal, they are being observed or commented upon as though they were part of the natural scenery. Except for occasional references to Ellery Channing, there is no record of any real interaction between Thoreau and other people. The discussions of friendship notwithstanding, no other person attains individual status. The only real person in the Journal is Henry David Thoreau, and the love story recorded is a love of self. Thoreau wrote in 1851: "May I love and revere myself above all the gods that men have ever invented" (*Journal*, 2: 390).

Obviously, other people did exist in Thoreau's world. He lived with his family most of his life, and he numbered among his friends the Emersons, Bronson Alcott, Ellery Channing, Mary Moody Emerson, and Lucy Brown, as well as numerous other residents of Concord. Yet they appear in the Journal only peripherally, and even then more as observable phenomena than as separate beings.

The people in *Walden* are portrayed in the same way. The only suggestion of interaction is in the description of the visits of the poet (Ellery Channing) (*Walden*, pp. 247–249, 295). Other people—the Canadian woodchopper, for example, and John Field, the Irishman—are interesting phenomena to be observed and commented upon just as Thoreau observed and commented upon the phenomena of the natural world. In fact, Thoreau tells us that this was how he viewed people: "As I walked in the woods to see the birds and squirrels, so I walked in the village to see the men and boys" (*Walden*, p. 185).

Thoreau regarded people in the same way that Emerson did: they had no independent existence for him but were valuable only in relation to the self. As he observed in 1851, "There is many a coarsely well-meaning fellow, who knows only the skin of me. . . . I get the whole good of him and lose nothing by it" (*Journal*, 2: 285; 7: 48). Thoreau used other people to contribute to the expansion of his self. In 1840 he compared his friend with an echo, commenting that "the sympathy of a friend gives plainness and point to my speech" (*Consciousness*, p. 199). In Perry Miller's words, Thoreau sought "to arrange experience so that both the labors of other men and the affections of women . . . would minister to his egotism."[6]

Asserting that the individual must step to his own music (*Journal*, 2: 316), Thoreau conceived of the self as a separate and distinct entity. In 1840 he described his sense of himself as a planet (*Consciousness*, p. 149). Withdrawing into his own consciousness, Thoreau saw himself as totally divorced from all that surrounded him:

> If with closed ears and eyes I consult consciousness for a moment, immediately are all walls and barriers dissipated, earth rolls from under me, and I float, a subjective, heavily-laden thought . . . eternity and space gambolling familiarly through my depths. I am from the beginning, knowing no end.　　　　　(*Journal*, 1: 53–54)

It should be clear from this passage that Thoreau's self can be maintained only by closing out the external world. His idea of the pure self directly opposes the concept of social relationships.[7] Thoreau believed that each person should be "as inaccessible as a star" (*Consciousness*, p. 216). In order to maintain the sanctity of the self, Thoreau had to establish this distance between himself and other people. Relationships with others were a waste of time; they threatened the integrity of the self and interfered with the expansion of the individual soul. Throughout his writings, Thoreau expressed a contempt for social relationships. "What men call social virtues," he wrote in his Journal in 1852, "is commonly but the virtue of pigs in a litter" (*Journal*, 4: 397; 10: 350).

There are indications in the Journal that Thoreau wished to be closer to other people than he would admit openly. Occasionally in the passages on friendship from the 1840s and 1850s, he seems to be searching for human contact. For example, there is this rather wistful entry in June 1855: "What if we feel a yearning to which no heart answers? I walk alone. My heart is full. . . . I knock on the earth for my friend. I expect to meet him at every turn; but no friend appears" (*Journal*, 7: 416–417). Other passages in the Journal suggest that Thoreau strongly felt the loss of friendship. Writing in 1857 of a friendship decaying, he said: "Morning, noon, and night, I suffer a physical pain, an aching of the heart which unfits me for my tasks" (*Journal*, 9: 276–278).

This aspect of Thoreau's feelings is never allowed to enter the published work, however. If the image of a solitary Thoreau is maintained in the Journal, it is even more strongly insisted upon in his published work. In *Walden*, for example, one is apt to pass over Thoreau's mention of the fact that he left the woods every day or two to visit friends (*Walden*, p. 185). Nor would one suspect from the self-reliant self-portrait that Thoreau went home often, enjoyed frequent dinners with the Emersons and other friends, and received a visit every Saturday from his mother and sisters bearing freshly baked doughnuts and pies.[8] The impression that Thoreau intended to convey of himself in *Walden* is one of independent solitude. He felt lonesome in the woods only once, he claimed, soon after arriving at Walden, but he quickly recovered from that "slight insanity" (*Walden*, p. 146). It is "wholesome to be alone," he asserts; "I love to be alone" (*Walden*, p. 150). Thoreau created a persona for the reader (and for himself), a persona who lives alone and likes it. At the beginning of *Walden* he suggests that every man might be better off if he got into a large box, bored a few holes in it for air, and hooked down the lid (*Walden*, p. 32).

Although in his Journal Thoreau occasionally expressed a longing for human relationships, he shared Emerson's feeling that he could accept society only on his own terms. What troubled Thoreau was not simply that he had no friend but that he had no friend who was sufficiently interested in him: "One talks to me of apples and pears, and I depart with my secret untold. His are not the apples that tempt me" (*Journal*, 7: 317). Thoreau did not want a friend with an individuality of his own. "Echoes are almost the only kindred voices I hear," he wrote in 1853 (*Consciousness*, p. 199). What he wanted in a friend was a confirmation of the self.

Thoreau's contemporaries, even those who might be faulted for a similar egotism, commented on his self-orientation. Ellery Channing remarked that Thoreau "made no account of love."[9] Walt Whitman concluded that "Thoreau's great fault was disdain—a disdain for men. . . . He couldn't put his life into any other life—realize why one man was so, and another man was not so."[10] This inability, or unwillingness, to put himself in another's place was the result of a self-absorption that negated the significance of other people. Emerson once commented of Thoreau that he was totally uninterested in what other people think:

> It is curious that Thoreau goes to a house to say with little preface what he has just read or observed, delivers it in a lump, is quite inattentive to any comment or thought which any of the company offer on the matter, nay is merely interrupted by it, and when he has finished his report departs without precipitation.[11]

This entry appears in Emerson's journal right after a passage entitled "Monochord," in which he discusses people "whose world is only large enough for one person." Apparently Emerson, himself accused by friends of this lack of interest in others' ideas, perceived the same quality in Thoreau. It is interesting to try to imagine these two very self-absorbed men attempting to carry on a conversation, each one intent solely upon what he himself had to say. In 1853 Thoreau complained of Emerson's own self-absorption: "Talked, or tried to talk, with R. W. E. Lost my time—nay, almost my identity" (*Journal*, 5: 199).

In Thoreau's world, other people interfere with the expansion of the self. The heartaches that involvements with other people inevitably bring "impede the current of my thoughts," he complained; "they unfit me for my tasks" (*Journal*, 9: 276–278). In *Walden* Thoreau insists that it is better to travel alone: "He who travels with another must wait till that other is ready" (*Walden*, p. 80). Other people only hold back the individual. In 1854 he describes the debilitating effects on the self of being with other people when conditions in his attic had forced him to sit downstairs with the family in the evenings for a month: "I must cultivate privacy. It is very dissipating to be with people too much" (*Journal*, 6: 415–416). And in *Walden* he declares that he loves to be alone because company is wearisome: "I never found the companion that was so companionable as solitude" (*Walden*, p. 150). For Thoreau, other people have no importance. He compares them with gnats that fly around his face so closely that they cannot really be seen (*Journal*, 3: 460–461).

Certainly other people have less reality for Thoreau than his own thoughts. In 1850 he proclaimed to Harrison Blake that actual events were "far less real than the creations of my imagination." On his return from Fire Island, where Margaret Fuller, her husband, and son were drowned in a shipwreck, Thoreau said of a button he had torn from her husband's body on the shore: "All the life it is connected with is less substantial to me, and interests me less, than my faintest dream. Our thoughts are the epochs in our lives: all else is but as a journal of the winds that blew while we were here."[12] In 1852 Thoreau described his thoughts as separate entities: "They have a certain individuality and separate existence, aye personality" (*Journal*, 2: 217). This is more than one can say of other people in Thoreau's world. For Thoreau, nothing and no one outside the self has existence, except in relation to the self. On the inside back cover of Volume 3 of his Journal, Thoreau scribbled a description of himself that says it all: "Though I should front an object for a lifetime, I should see only what it concerned me to see" (*Consciousness*, p. 218).

Thoreau maintained that the individual can learn nothing from others. "One generation abandons the enterprises of another like stranded vessels," he wrote in *Walden*, continuing: "The old have no very important advice to give the young" (*Walden*, pp. 9–12). Moreover, the preceding generations are not alone in their inability to teach us anything. No one can "say what prospect life offers to another" (*Walden*, p. 11). Parents, friends, relations cannot guide us. The divinity, Thoreau said, is within each man (*Journal*, 1: 239; 3: 119).

How does Thoreau justify such a total dependence on the self? Like Emerson, he believed he had a higher mission in life, and that mission involved the development of himself. In 1841 he wrote: "My Journal is that of me which would else spill over and run to waste. . . . I must not live for it, but in it for the gods" (*Journal*, 1: 206–207). Thoreau associated himself with a higher truth, the truth that sees beyond mere earthly particularities. For him, the truth of the universe was within: "I cannot attach much importance to historical epochs—or geographical boundaries—when I have my Orient and Occident in one revolution of my body" (*Consciousness*, p. 155). And in 1854 he asserted that there was nothing extraneous to himself: "This earth which is spread out like a map around me is but the lining of my inmost soul exposed" (*Journal*, 6: 194).

This last Journal entry gives an idea of what nature meant to Thoreau. Like Emerson, Thoreau preferred nature to human society, and for the same reason: in nature Thoreau felt better able to expand to his full size. In society, he said, "I am almost invariably cheap and dissipated." But alone in the woods "I come to my self. . . . I am not thus expanded, recreated, enlightened, when I meet a company of men" (*Journal*, 9: 208–210). Of course, the reason the individual cannot expand thus in company with other people is that other people put demands on him that restrain his growth. Alone in the solitude of nature he is able to imagine himself as big as nature itself—and there is no other self there to contradict him. If, as Thoreau said, he always saw himself "in the rear of his eye" (*Consciousness*, p. 162), when he looked out and around himself, what he saw ultimately was himself. He reflected in 1853: "I love nature partly *because* she is not man, but a retreat from him" (*Journal*, 4: 445). Here, then, is the major value of nature: it is a retreat from mankind in which the individual can expand to mammoth proportions without interference. In 1856, our nation's most revered naturalist wrote: "Man is all in all, Nature nothing, but as she draws him out and reflects him" (*Journal*, 9: 121).

Like Emerson, Thoreau was truly American in his reverence for the self. Moreover, although he is usually presented as a rebel and a critic of American society, he was one of the most nationalistic of our writers.[13] His rebellion was not against America but against the Anglo-European traditions that the American individualist had renounced. And his criticisms of society were from the point of view of that individualist. His famous jailing for nonpayment of taxes, however much it may have been used by 1960s antiwar protesters as an example of courageous rebellion against unjust government policy, actually fits very comfortably into the American tradition of individualists who rail against government control and welfare legislation. Thoreau admired America and shared Emerson's belief in the greatness of his country's destiny. In a passage from his Journal in 1852 he expressed his faith in the splendors of America and his belief that Americans were destined to be the best of men:

At length, perchance, the immaterial heaven will appear so much higher to the American mind. . . . We shall be

> more imaginative; we shall be clearer, as our sky, bluer,
> fresher; broader and more comprehensive in our under-
> standing, like our plains; our intellect on a grander scale,
> like our thunder and lightning. . . . Will not man grow
> to greater perfection intellectually, as well as physically
> under these influences? (*Journal*, 3: 268)

This is Thoreau's version of manifest destiny: the greater natural beauties of the American continent will be reflected in the American people, making them a superior race of men.

Significantly, Thoreau did not apply this same analogy to the Indians, who, after all, were exposed to the natural beauties of America long before whites arrived. Although Thoreau admired the Indians' way of life, their closeness to nature and wild freedom ("The charm of the Indian to me is that he stands free and unconstrained in Nature" [*Journal*, 1: 253]), he nevertheless accepted the conventional American view of the Indian as a victim of America's destiny. Similarly, he admired the self-reliance of the white pioneer. "Our brave forefathers have exterminated all the Indians," he says in *A Week on the Concord and Merrimack Rivers* (1849), and he urges his countrymen to be as strong and courageous as the "sturdy pioneers" who took the land away from the Indians. He describes without comment the displacement of the Indians and the white attempts to convert them to Christianity.[14] Although there is a certain sadness in his occasional references to the fact that Indians once roamed the forests where towns now stand, it is more a nostalgia for a way of life than a sense of the loss of real people.

At a time when young men in America were being urged to "go west," Thoreau, who himself was never able to leave Concord for very long, identified strongly with the westward movement. In the late 1830s he talked of going west with his brother John (*Letters*, pp. 13–17), and even after he gave up the idea, he consistently used the Western adventure as a metaphor for self-exploration: "What does the West stand for? Is not our own interior white on the chart? . . . Be a Columbus to whole new continents and worlds within you. . . .

Start now on that farthest Western way, which does not pause at the Mississippi or the Pacific" (*Walden*, pp. 353–355).

Thoreau's emphasis on self-reliance and individualism is part of the American myth. Although he eschewed a traditional profession, he was not without the ambition for individual achievement that characterizes the American individualist. For Thoreau, the struggle to get ahead took place totally within. He poured his energies into the development of the self just as relentlessly as any commercial self-promoter. Only the symbols of success were different. Thoreau had no use for material goods, but he shared the American respect for success and subscribed to the notion of individual struggle: "Life is a battle in which you are to show your pluck, and woe to the coward. . . . Despair and postponement are cowardice and defeat. Men were born to succeed, not to fail" (*Journal*, 5: 36).

Thoreau accepted this traditional view of life, and the persona that he created for himself fulfilled the criteria of the American hero. Carrying to an extreme the maxim of self-reliance and individualism, he portrayed himself as a sturdy pioneer who sought nothing from anyone. Like Emerson, he constantly used the word "manly" in his emotional life. Writing in 1851 that man should rely on his own resources in the way that animals do in winter, he asserted that "to the healthy man the winter of his discontent never comes." That is, a healthy man is content in his cold insularity (*Journal*, 3: 70). For Thoreau, emotions, human feelings, are a sickness. When he was sick, he noticed a "certain softness" in himself and concluded that if he were sick for any length of time, "some sympathy with mankind and society might spring up." But, he said, such feelings were a weakness and only the result of bad bowels (*Journal*, 3: 106).

Thoreau worked very hard to maintain this persona of total self-reliance. The death of his brother John from lockjaw in January 1842 appears nowhere in the Journal, yet the extent to which Thoreau was affected by his brother's death is apparent in the psychosomatic lockjaw and ill health that incapacitated him for months afterward.[15] He stopped writing in the Journal for a month after John's death, and it was almost three years before he began writing regularly again. Such a personal involvement with tragedy must have made it too difficult for Thoreau to maintain the image that he felt he had to project. But in his published work and in his Journal where he could preserve the persona, the image of himself that Thoreau presented was one of total self-reliance, physical and emotional strength, and optimistic faith in himself and in his country. His persona is as cocky and self-assured as the chanticleer to which he compares himself in *Walden* (p. 94). Each man must "believe that each day contains an earlier, more sacred, and auroral hour," and he concludes *Walden* with an ode to progress: "There is more day to dawn. The sun is but a morning star" (*Walden*, pp. 99, 367).

If we ask how women fit into the world Thoreau created, the answer would have to be not at all. The few references to women in the Journal show that Thoreau held a very conventional opinion of women. They were instinctive and unthinking, their "reason weaker" than man's, and their wills blunted (*Journal*, 2: 116). In 1852 he observed that women everywhere "make it evident that they have but little brains" (*Journal*, 3: 258). When he heard a women's rights lecture in December 1851, he concluded that the speaker was a woman in the "too common sense" and that her arguments were not worth answering (*Journal*, 2: 168). "The society of young women is the most unprofitable I have ever tried," he deplored in the same year (*Journal*, 3: 116). The only woman who is described at length in the Journal, Mary Moody Emerson, is praised not for herself but because she will "provoke good conversation and the expression of what is in you" (*Journal*, 3: 113–114).

The ideal world portrayed in *Walden* has no place for women. The very real mother and sisters whom Thoreau visited almost daily do not appear at all; nor are they mentioned in the chapters on visitors, although they were in fact weekly visitors. The two or three women mentioned in *Walden* are seen only from a distance and are portrayed in the stereotypical role of housewife: Mrs. Collins, Mrs. Field, and the anonymous "uneasy housekeepers" who comment on the cleanliness of Thoreau's sheets (*Walden*, pp. 47–48, 226–227, 169).[16]

Like Emerson, Thoreau regarded women as abstractions, not as real beings. Either they were conventional, flighty creatures governed by their instincts and emotions, or they were strange creatures on a level outside the realm of male life. Thoreau wrote in 1850 that women commanded "a vast amount of veneration—like Nature."[17] Just how thoroughly he had absorbed a stereotyped image of women is revealed in an 1851 passage in the Journal. Criticizing people who fear the influence of a radical book, he said such unthinking people were as "simple as oxen" and compared them to women. The irony is that the book that sparked this tirade against such womanish thinking was written by a woman: Harriet Martineau (*Journal*, 2: 468).

Although women were not admitted into the world of Thoreau's persona, they were undeniably present in his real world. Thoreau lived at home with his mother and father, two sisters, and aunts almost all of his life, and he had a very close relationship with his immediate family. His letters to his mother and father during his six-month absence in 1843, when he was tutor to William Emerson's son on Staten Island, express affection and an eagerness for letters from home. Although he denied feelings of homesickness, he clearly missed his family and was soon back in Concord. He wrote to his mother on August 6, "I think of you all very often," and offered that he "would be content to sit at the back door in Concord under the poplar tree, henceforth forever" (*Letters*, pp. 98–100). His letters to his sisters, Helen and Sophia, are also friendly (though he noted once that he knew Helen did not like sentiment in a letter [*Letters*, p. 27]). The extent of his feeling for his sister Helen is suggested in the emotional outpourings in the unpublished fragment "A Sister," written around the time of her death in 1849. It reads in part:

> A Sister. One in whom you have—unbounded faith— whom you can—purely love. . . . Whose heart answers

to your heart. Whose presence can fill all space. One who is spirit. Who attends to your truth. . . . Whom in thought my spirit continually embraces. Unto whom I flow. . . . Who art clothed in white. . . . Who art all that I can imagine—my inspirer. The feminine of me—Who art magnanimous.[18]

This passage reveals a side of Thoreau that is never permitted into the Journal or the published works. It is a significant indication of the warmth Thoreau was capable of feeling for another person in spite of the insularity of his persona.

Thoreau also had close female friends outside of his family. His letters to Lidian Emerson, who, he wrote to her in 1843, was like an "elder sister" to him (*Letters*, p. 27), were warmly admiring. She represented "woman" to him, he penned on May 22, 1843, and the following month he affirmed: "The thought of you will constantly elevate my life" (*Letters*, pp. 76–79, 87–89). He lived with the Emersons for two years (1841–1843) and stayed with Lidian and the children in 1847–1848 when Emerson was in Europe. Another close friend was Lidian's sister, Lucy Brown, who lived with the Thoreaus for a time. His letters to her are warm and confiding. Finally, it is known that he was in love with a young woman, Ellen Sewall, to whom he proposed in 1840. His suit, like his brother's earlier, was rejected, apparently primarily because of her father's anti-Transcendental bias.

What is one to make of the fact that Thoreau so completely obliterated women from the world he created while remaining closely attached to women in real life? Some critics have looked for psychosexual explanations—latent homosexuality, oedipal fear and hostility.[19] These explanations would have more validity, perhaps, if Thoreau excluded only women. But in fact *all* other people are missing from his ideal world. A more comprehensive explanation for Thoreau's insistence upon solitariness is his wholehearted acceptance of the American myth of individualism. His published and private writings center almost exclusively on himself. He projects the image that was defined by his culture as the hero of American myth: a self-reliant, manly individualist whose main concern is the development of the self.

Thoreau was able to envision a solitary world primarily because, for him, other people could be reduced to abstractions. In a revealing Journal passage in 1851, Thoreau wrote that he liked people best when he was not with them: "I *really* can communicate with my friends and congratulate myself and them on our relation and rejoice in their presence and society oftenest when they are personally absent." He then felt a "remarkable gladness in the thought that they existed. . . . Yet such has never been my actual waking relation to any" (*Journal* 2: 183). By insisting that his relationship with another person involved only that person's image and not the person him/herself, Thoreau was able to avoid the pain that a loss of the other person might bring. How this worked for him is apparent in his comments on the death of his brother John:

> I do not wish to see John ever again,—I mean him who is dead,—but that other, of whom he was the imperfect representative. For we are not what we are, nor do we treat and esteem each other for such, but for what we are capable of being.　　　　　　　(*Letters*, p. 42)

A man who best relates to people when they are absent and who perceives people not as they are but as he conceives of them is dealing not with people but with the image he has created of them.[20]

When other people are treated as images, it is easier to lessen one's grief by universalizing a particular loss, as Thoreau did with John's death:

> Soon the ice will melt, and the blackbirds sing along the river which he frequented, as pleasantly as ever. The same everlasting serenity will appear in this face of God, and we will not be sorrowful if he is not.
>
> 　　　　　　　　　　　　　(*Letters*, p. 41)

This Emersonian response to death is apparent also in Thoreau's remarks on the death of Emerson's son, Waldo. Considering Thoreau's closeness to the Emersons and little Waldo at this time (he was living with the family), his comment seems cold and unfeeling:

> He died as the mist rises from the brook. . . . Neither will Nature manifest any sorrow at his death, but soon the note of the lark will be heard down in the meadow, and fresh dandelions will spring from the old stocks [sic] where he plucked them last summer.   (*Letters*, p. 42)

Anyone who has been close to a five-year-old child cannot help but feel a chill at these words. But for Thoreau, this attitude was necessary in order to preserve the persona that he struggled to maintain. When other people are viewed as abstractions, their deaths cannot touch us. There is no hurt, no threat to the sanctuary of the self.

Thus, by reducing other people to abstractions, Thoreau was able to resolve the paradox that he felt within himself and to keep the self intact. Although the man Thoreau might have needed love and friendship, he strove to create a persona, an ideal self that could "live free and uncommitted" (*Walden*, p. 93) like the prototypical individualist of the American myth.

The self that Thoreau created was so all-encompassing that it had no room for other people. And women, as the traditional other, were needed least of all. For Thoreau, women had no real existence. Thus he was able to imagine a world in which they simply did not exist. Thoreau, like Emerson, conceived of himself as the Man-woman: "Genius is inspired by its own works; it is hermaphroditic" (*Journal* 11: 204).

Emerson and Thoreau were writing in the American tradition, the tradition that glorifies the individual and insists upon the sanctity of the self. Such a philosophy forces the individual to protect himself by projecting a persona that exhibits all of the traits he feels he must live up to. With all of his energies devoted to the development of this inflated self, the American Narcissus can allow no room for the reality of other selves. That Americans have adopted this philosophy wholeheartedly and continue to endorse the writings of Emerson and Thoreau with such enthusiasm indicates how much this belief in the totality of the self remains a part of our culture.

Such a philosophy will be criticized only if one looks at it from the point of view not of the expanding self but of the other, the one who is being absorbed and disregarded by the self. Since American men are conditioned to believe in the myth of the individual, they have not been inclined to question it. But what happens when women look at the philosophy of the self?

One of the most perceptive criticisms of Emerson's philosophy came from a woman, "a stout farmer's wife." Her reaction to one of his lectures is printed as an amusing anecdote by Edward Emerson in his notes to his father's works. Emerson had insisted that the other people in Plato's life were unimportant, that their value came only from the use Plato was able to make of them. The farmer's wife is quoted as having complained that Plato had done a terrible thing when he had, as Mr. Emerson said, "ground his wife and children into paint."[21] The joke for Edward Emerson was that this uneducated woman took literally what Emerson had intended only as a metaphor. Yet the perceptiveness of her comment is that she was able to see the literalness of the metaphor. When one is the other—in this case the wife—one is apt to resent being told, however elegantly, that one's function in life is to be used by another person.

The male listeners in the audience could of course identify with Plato, as Emerson intended them to. They would take for granted that the woman was to be used for the glorification of the great man. The man hearing this philosophy expressed can see a place for himself in it. When he is told,

"Expand the self, absorb and use other people," he can identify with the self. Although he may encounter serious problems when he tries to put this philosophy into practice and
may have to work very hard to maintain the proper image of
himself, he can still accept the philosophy as his.

On the other hand, there is no place in our society for
the woman who chooses to expand and absorb. She, by definition, is the one to be absorbed. Thus, she will have difficulty identifying with the expanding self. And if she attempts
to do so, her position in society will force her also to see her
role as other.

Sarah Margaret Fuller was as much concerned with the development of the self as were the other Transcendentalists.
Born in 1810 and growing to maturity during the nationalistic expansion and rampant individualism that characterized
the Jacksonian period, she received what at that time was a
boy's education. Overeducated and untrained in the habits of
femininity, she was unsuited to perform the traditional role of
woman. In the 1830s she wrote to a friend:

> From a very early age I have felt that I was not born to
> the common womanly lot. I knew I should never find a
> being who would keep the key to my character. . . . I
> was proud that I . . . was always to return to my self, to be
> my own priest, pupil, parent, child, husband, and wife. [22]

Here is the self of the American myth, totally self-reliant
and all-encompassing. How can such a self also accept the
American view of woman? How can such a self consent to be
"ground into paint"? Rather than acquiesce to this passive
role, Margaret Fuller insisted on her right to expansion and
self-exploration. "Very early I knew that the only object in
life was to grow" (*Memoirs*, 1: 133). Her recognition of the
conflict between individualism and woman's place led her

to write the first book on women's rights by an American woman. In *Woman in the Nineteenth Century* (1845) she asserts that human beings cannot live without expansion; women too must be allowed to grow: "It is not Woman, but the law of right, the law of growth, that . . . demands the perfection of each being. . . . What concerns me now is, that my life be a beautiful, powerful, in a word, a complete life."[23]

For a Transcendentalist, this ambition was not unusual. And it was the accepted modus vivendi of the success-seeking American individualist. But for an American woman it was unthinkable. In *Woman in the Nineteenth Century*, Margaret Fuller writes that it is inevitable that the freedom of the nation should extend to all. Women must have their turn. But, she says, women are not allowed to develop freely. Books on woman's place either fit her for heaven or "fit her to please, or, at least, not to disturb, a husband" (*Women*, pp. 24, 26, 157–158). Thus women are trained to avoid any encroachment on men's territory and to stifle their own ambitions. This obedience to men, Fuller contends, leads to passiveness, docility, and the repression of women's own natural powers (*Woman*, pp. 159, 29–30). Several problems arise, she points out, when a woman possesses creative genius. Such a woman will find it impossible to conform to the standards of passive femininity. Finding no outlet for her electricity (it is interesting that Fuller uses the same image for genius in women that Emerson applies to himself), the woman of ability often lapses into sickness (*Woman*, pp. 103–104). This explanation of the female invalidism of the nineteenth century is particularly perceptive, coming as it did during the period itself, when the general opinion, both medical and cultural, was so unenlightened. The repression of one's selfhood must have been most difficult during the expansionist period when everyone seemed to be shouting, "Expand! Grow! Do! Dare!" Young girls grew up like rats in a Skinner Box, which are given an electric shock each time they press the lever for food—although the rats in the control group are encouraged to push the lever freely. If the deprived rats develop neurotic symptoms, psychologists will note the symptoms as the result of frustration and repression. Margaret Fuller diagnosed the sickness of her day as the result of repression, and her prescription was freedom.

A woman needs room to develop her intellect, Fuller writes in *Woman in the Nineteenth Century* (*Woman*, pp. 104–105). In her journal, Fuller declared that she wanted "to show that Woman can have the free, full action of intellect" (*Memoirs*, 2: 135). Women also need self-reliance and self-respect, which are "deprecated as a fault in most women" (*Woman*, pp. 40, 175). Women should have the freedom to develop not only intellectually but physically as well, and here Fuller sees a further solution to the problem of illness. Like Walt Whitman, she advocates natural feelings about the body and recommends that fresh air, exercise, and freedom of dress are better remedies for ladies' ills than doses of opium (*Woman*, p. 164). She apparently based this opinion on personal experience, for as a young girl whose physical development was as precocious as her mental development, she was kept tightly corseted. Thomas Higginson reports in his biography that, at the ball given by her father for President John Quincy Adams when she was sixteen, Margaret was so tightly laced "that she had to hold her arms back as if they were pinioned."[24] Although Margaret Fuller may have agreed with Whitman that women should develop both physically and mentally along with men, she did not share Whitman's rationale: that women must be strong and vital so that they can produce strong and vital sons.[25] Fuller criticized those who conceded women the right to develop their abilities only to make themselves better mothers and companions of men. On the contrary, women should be allowed to develop in mind and body for themselves: "A being of infinite scope must not be treated with an exclusive view to one relation" (*Woman*, pp. 95–96). Woman also can be a center (*Woman*, pp. 29, 115–117).

Fuller's insistence on the right of women to develop for themselves is also apparent in her impatience with the stereotype perpetuated by Emerson that classified women as creatures of the affections only: "It is a vulgar error that love, *a* love, to Woman is her whole existence; she also is born for

Truth and Love in their universal energy" (*Woman*, pp. 95, 177). In the essay "Mariana" Fuller gives dramatic expression to the tragedy of women forced to see no other outlet for their energies. Mariana, who is partly based on Margaret herself, is a talented and vibrant woman. She has the misfortune to fall in love with a man whose pettiness destroys her, and she dies after writing a despondent poem about lost love. Fuller concludes:

> It marks the defect in the position of women that one like Mariana should have found reason to write thus. To a man of equal power, equal sincerity, no more!—many resources would have presented themselves. He would not have needed to seek, he would have been called by life and not permitted to be quite wrecked through the affections only.[26]

Obviously, if one sees woman as a creature of the affections, one is looking at her only in relation to man. Margaret Fuller demanded that women be regarded as people in their own right.

It is this insistence upon the independent existence of women that constitutes the initial difference between Margaret Fuller and the other Transcendentalists. Just how crucial this difference was can best be understood by taking a close look at the relationship between Fuller and Emerson. Although much has been made of the theory that Fuller was in love with Emerson, it seems to me that the relationship was less a romance than a struggle by Fuller to maintain a separate existence.[27]

Though Fuller was already an admirer of Emerson when she first met him, it was not long before the disciple became a critic.[28] Both in his life and in his work, she found him too abstract; to her, his tendency to regard life as an abstraction meant that he was lacking in humanity. Reviewing his *Essays, Second Series* in the *New York Tribune* in 1844, she complained: "Here is undoubtedly, the man of ideas; but we want the . . . heart and genius of human life to interpret it" (*Life*, p. 196).

Her essay on "American Literature" in 1846 criticized his poetry for the same failing. Noting that his "poems want the simple force of nature and passion," she continued: "While they charm the ear and interest the mind, [they] fail to wake far-off echoes in the heart."[29]

A few years earlier Fuller pointed up the same failing in Emerson's private life. His tendency to live life as a cold abstraction was most apparent in his relations with other people, she observed: "He had faith in the Universal, but not in the Individual man; he met men, not as a brother, but as a critic." At first she found Emerson's attitude difficult to contend with, but by 1842 she was resigned to his abstract insularity and could say: "Leave him in his cell affirming absolute truth . . . the calm observer of the course of things" (*Memoirs*, 2: 67–69).

As we saw in Chapter 2, Emerson conceived of friendship as a one-way relationship in which he would absorb and possess the other person. Margaret Fuller saw herself as an individual with as much right to existence as Emerson. Unlike Emerson's male friends, who could rebound from a personality-threatening relationship by asserting their own individuality, Fuller found her right to individuality denied by society and totally disregarded by Emerson. He sought to rob her of her self and to drain out of her the best that was in her for his own use. Moreover, he resented any independent actions that seemed to assert that she existed apart from him. Writing in her journal in 1842, Fuller described her relationship with Emerson and her sense of his overwhelming attempt at possession:

> After the first excitement of intimacy with him . . . came with me the questioning season. I was greatly disappointed in my relation to him. . . . I found no intelligence of my best self. . . . not only did he seem to want the living faith which enables one to discharge this holiest office of a friend, but he absolutely distrusted me in every region of my life with which he was unacquainted.
>
> (*Memoirs*, 2: 67)

On another occasion Fuller reproached Emerson directly for his tendency to look upon people as objects for his own use: "The deepest soul that approached you was, in your eyes, nothing but a magic lantern, always bringing out pretty shows of life" (*Memoirs*, 1: 288).

The validity of Fuller's accusation that Emerson saw her only in relation to himself is clear from a comment he made after learning of her death: "I have lost in her my audience," we remember he wrote in his journal in July 1850.[30] Further, as part of his general tendency to undercut her, Emerson, when he edited her *Memoirs*, wrote that although she may have impressed "ingenuous natures," her glittering language was actually a façade for the same kind of sentimentalism that pervades all women's feelings: "This is easily felt in ordinary women, and a large deduction is civilly made on the spot by whosoever replies to their remark." The content of what Fuller said was therefore valueless. According to Emerson, she was useful only because of her effect on other people: her colorful style "piqued curiosity, and stimulated thought, and communicated mental activity to all who approached her" (*Memoirs*, 1: 267, 279–281).[31] So accustomed was Emerson to viewing Fuller only in relation to himself that he could see no other reason for her to live. "She died in a happy hour for herself," he reported in a letter to Carlyle; "Her marriage would have taken her away from us all" (*LRWE*, 4: 224).

Emerson's insistence upon seeing himself as the center, and his unwillingness to admit Fuller's independence, is illustrated by his behavior when he attended one of the series of Conversations that she led in Boston in 1841. Although he was only a guest, he apparently took over the program and was criticized later for stealing the limelight from her. Referring to the incident in a letter to her, he offered simply that such behavior was "chronic and constitutional" with him (*LRWE*, 2: 384–385). Caroline W. Healey, who was present at the Conversation, complained that Emerson pursued his own train of thought, seeming "to forget that we had come together to pursue Margaret's."[32]

A reciprocal relationship under such conditions was impossible, as Fuller came to realize in 1840–1841, when she tried to establish a closer friendship with Emerson. A series of letters from this period reveals Emerson's constant attempt at possession and Fuller's struggle to maintain an independent existence. Although she eventually won her independence, she did so only by giving up her desire for a close relationship. Moreover, like F. Scott Fitzgerald, who, a century later unconscionably used his wife's private letters and journals in his fiction, Emerson made good literary use of Fuller's (and other friends') letters in the 1841 essay "Friendship" and in his poetry.[33]

On August 26, 1840, Emerson recorded in his journal that Margaret Fuller had accused him of coldness and "inhospitality of soul."[34] On September 25 he wrote to her that the problem was that they were not "inhabitants of one thought." But they might at some time be united: "I . . . will open all my doors to your sunshine and morning air" (*LRWE*, 2: 337). For Emerson, the only relationship possible was one in which *she* entered fully into *his* all-encompassing self. Fuller's insistence upon her own independence Emerson called "wilfulness," and he criticized her for her lack of "pure acquiescence" (*LRWE*, 2: 337). She replied by assuring him that she did not want to usurp his power; she only wanted to be herself: "I [am] no saint, no anything, but a great soul born to know all, before it can return to the creative fount" (*LRWE*, 2: 340–341).

Fuller's other letters during this period are lost, but in 1844, before she left New England to accept a job on Horace Greeley's *Tribune*, she wrote a long letter to Emerson that contains a perceptive analysis of their relationship. Her main point is that Emerson lacks real inspiration, partly because he remains in Concord, which lacks the depth of the greater world, but primarily because he is too self-oriented: he refuses to admit outside influences. Pompously believing that he contains all in the self, he "keeps his study windows shut." If he insists on living in such isolation, how can the Muse come to him? In a poem Fuller has Emerson answer that the Muse has no existence except in his identity:

> However voluble
> All life is soluble
> Into my thought;
> And that is nought,
> But self-discovering
> Self-recovering
> Of the One
> One Alone.

This self-assertion threatens to suffocate the Muse, who seems to represent Fuller herself. She can feel her eyes film over, her throat dry out, and her wings lose strength to fly. She resolves to find someplace where the day is not "shut from the living air."[35]

Perry Miller quotes this letter as Margaret Fuller's farewell to Emerson and New England and mistakenly describes it as her derisive reply to Emerson's failure to appreciate her love.[36] He fails to see, particularly in the "gnomic poem" (which he calls "too trivial to be repeated entire") that it is in fact Fuller's declaration of independence, an assertion of her necessity to be a person in her own right, a refusal to be absorbed and denied existence by Emerson's overwhelming sense of self. And it is, incidentally, a recognition of the narrowness of this sense of self, a criticism of the insularity that leads Emerson into a cold death-in-life existence void of other persons.[37]

It was Fuller's role as woman that helped to bring her to this realization of the error of attempting to absorb all into the self. (After all, in her relationship with Emerson, it was she who was to be absorbed.) Maintaining a strong sense of her own individuality in a society that would deny it, she was better able to see the independence of other people than were the more insular Transcendental men. This awareness gave her a perspective on American culture and ideas that most American writers lacked.

First of all, she saw what few other writers considered: the westward movement from the point of view of the women who helped to settle the new land. Her portrait of the frontier woman contrasts sharply with the happy, bright-eyed, sun-bonneted darling of the American Western idyll. Fuller's perception corresponds more closely to the picture that emerges from the journals and letters of the real women who crossed the continent. It is a panorama of hopelessness and resignation. She points out in *Summer on the Lakes* (1844) that, although men could usually get help in the fields, women worked alone inside the house and had to do everything themselves, "sick or well." Moreover, they were often unfitted for the work by eastern training, which prepared them only to be ornaments. Thus, however valiantly they struggled, the lack of training, plus the overwhelming burden of the work itself, filled women with despair.[38]

Fuller emphasizes that most women did not go west because they wanted to; they went because they had no choice:

> It has generally been the choice of the men, and the women follow, as women will, doing their best for affection's sake, but too often in heart-sickness and weariness. Besides, it frequently not being a choice of their own minds that it is best to be here, their part is the hardest.
>
> (*At Home*, p. 46)

In *Woman in the Nineteenth Century*, Fuller cites the example of a woman who had been living in a little shack on a barren mountaintop for forty years. When asked why she had come to such a lonely place, she said she didn't know: "It was the man's notion" (*Woman*, p. 174).

Throughout *Woman in the Nineteenth Century*, Fuller argues that women should be arbiters of their own destiny. A woman should not suppress her personality and her will, acting only on "the man's notion." Looking at the westward movement from the point of view of these women who traveled westward against their wills—or without even consulting their own wills—Fuller was able to see what most masculine observers could not: the whole westward movement, not from the point of view of the American individualist, but from the point of view of the other. Sharing the women's view meant looking at westward expansion as a day-to-day struggle and not as an abstract, grandiose moral drama. It also meant beginning with a question about the advisability of the endeavor. This perspective made it possible to question the motives, the means, and even the goals of the expanding nation.

Unlike the other Transcendentalists, who tended to gloss over unsavory details in their acceptance of the settlement of the West as a confirmation of America's greatness, Fuller looked at people and methods. The settlers were not Titans, she discovered when she traveled west in 1843. Their motives were often selfish and petty: "It grieved me to hear these immigrants . . . talking, not of what they should do, but of what they should get in the new scene. It was to them a prospect . . . of more ease and larger accumulation" (*At Home*, p. 14).

Manifest destiny takes on an entirely different aspect when viewed from the perspective of the other. Fuller looks at the settlement of the West from the point of view of the Indian: "The missionary vainly attempts . . . to convince the red man that a heavenly mandate takes from him his broad lands. He bows his head, but does not at heart acquiesce. He cannot. It is not true" (*At Home*, p. 95). Fuller denies that the Americans' conquest of the continent was "justified by their superior civilization and religious ideas" (*At Home*, p. 101). Having rebelled against the same kind of self-justifying propaganda in relation to women, she does not believe in manifest destiny any more than she believes in the natural superiority of the male sex. She knows that just because an idea is official opinion does not mean that it is true—however loudly it may be supported by religious and biological explanations.

What Fuller deplores most of all in the whites' treatment of the Indians is the American failure to understand the Indians' point of view. It is her ability to see the Indian as a person and to respect his way of life that demonstrates the uniqueness of her outlook. The Indians had a "clear and noble moral code" and a meaningful religion of their own, she says. Departing from the contemporary view of the Indians as either worthless savages to be destroyed or as dependent children to be protected, Fuller asserts that the Indians are capable of molding their own destiny: "Could their own intelligent men be left to act unimpeded in their own behalf, they would do far better for them than the white thinker, with all his general knowledge." Thus, rather than looking at Indians from the vantage point of a member of a superior race and civilization, she accepts them as human beings with individual thoughts and feelings and a viable culture of their own. And she rightly predicts that the perspective of history will confirm her observations. Americans may regard the Indian as a fiend today, but "at some distant day, he will no doubt be considered as having acted the Roman or Carthaginian part of heroic and patriotic self-defence" (*At Home*, pp. 94, 99, 89, 101).

It should be pointed out that Fuller's sympathetic attitude was not based on a romantic and sentimental concept of the Indian as a "noble savage." Unlike nineteenth-century romantics who refused to recognize any unpleasantness about the Indian (popular romantic painters painted Indian maidens with white skins, and writers portrayed Indians who talked and acted like European gentlemen), Fuller never attempted to whitewash the Indians. She experienced the dirt and odors of the Indian camp (*At Home*, p. 88) and such realities as the dog feast. She accepted the Indians as they were. This is what makes her attitude so unusual: she saw the Indian not as an abstraction—"noble savage" or "fiend"—but as a person like herself.

This ability to see the other as a real person is apparent in Fuller's attitude toward other minorities as well, including the lowliest of life's unfortunates.[39] Unlike Emerson, who was disgusted by the lower classes (he called them "masses of moving cheese, like ants or fleas," and "rueful abortions that squeak and gibber in the street"),[40] Fuller manifested a real concern for and involvement with all people. Horace Greeley commented that she "recognized and responded to the essential brotherhood of all human kind," and William Henry Channing noted that she had a genuine respect and concern for other people (*Memoirs*, 2: 159, 81). She wrote to her brother Arthur in 1840: "The most important rule is, in all relations with our fellow-creatures, never forget that, if they are imperfect persons, they are immortal souls, and treat them as you would wish to be treated by the light of that thought" (*Woman*, p. 348). In the 1840s the newly arrived immigrants in America were the Irish, who were scorned as dirty, drunken, lying practitioners of a suspect religion. Fuller devoted two articles in the *Tribune* to a defense of "The Irish Character." Criticizing those who denigrated the "lowly Irish," she called attention to the conditions under which they lived and the treatment they received. She asked how many of her readers ever took the trouble to know any of them as people or concerned themselves with their individual problems—even the Irish whom they saw every day in their own homes as servants (*Woman*, pp. 320–344).

In November 1844, Fuller visited Sing Sing prison. A letter to her brother Richard describes the intense sympathy she felt when she attended chapel with the prisoners, and she returned to spend Christmas day with them (*Women*, p. 374; *Memoirs*, 2: 144–149). She also visited the prisons on Blackwell's Island, where she talked with the sick and dying women in the prison hospitals (*Memoirs*, 2: 149–150).

Using her column in the *Tribune*, Fuller helped to open her readers' eyes to social injustice. In "An Appeal for an Asylum for Discharged Female Convicts," for example, she urged her readers to help in the establishment of a kind of rehabilitation center for women who had been discharged from prison (*Life*, pp. 283–286). This article provides a good example of the difference between Emerson's and Fuller's attitudes toward women. In order to make her point stronger, Fuller quotes a poem describing the ugliness and corruption of the cities. It ends with a contrasting description of the respectable home scene:

> Yet there in the parlor sits
> Some figure of noble guise,

Our angel in a stranger's form,
Or woman's pleading eyes.

Fuller exhorts these "angels" to come out of their sheltered parlors, take a look at the suffering around them, and try to do something about it. Emerson quotes this verse from the same poem at the beginning of his essay "Woman," but not to criticize the women who hide in their protected parlors. Rather, the poem confirms his point that women should *remain* in the home as comforter of man. The home should be a retreat from the cares of the world, and woman should not concern herself with political and social issues.[41]

This comparison of Emerson's and Fuller's concepts of women also suggests the principal difference between their attitudes in general. Whereas Emerson himself withdrew from social and political involvement into the self, Fuller's concern with other people led to a serious involvement in social and political issues. This commitment is particularly apparent in her European experience. In Paris (where Emerson in 1833 had found nothing to interest him but his own inkstand), Fuller visited such social institutions as the French night school for working classes; the *crèches*, or day-care centers, where working mothers could leave their children; and the School for Idiots, where an attempt was made to educate and train the mentally deficient. These progressive institutions excited her, and she hoped to see them imitated in the United States. She also visited the garrets of overworked weavers at Lyons and wrote of the hunger of the poor in Paris. At the same time, she shared enthusiastically in French intellectual life, though it is ironic that the lectures at the Sorbonne, which had only bored Emerson, were denied to Margaret Fuller because she was a woman (*At Home*, pp. 210–216, 187–188, 205, 193).

Margaret Fuller's political and social involvement culminated in her experiences in Italy. Emerson, although he was abroad during part of the same time, was unable or unwilling to acknowledge the revolutionary ferment that Fuller saw all

over Europe.[42] Preoccupied with lecturing and social invitations, Emerson took no notice of the reality of events. He
was in Paris during the revolution of May 1848 but remained
totally unaware of it until it was all over (*LRWE*, 4: 72). Fuller, however, was not only aware of the situation in Italy; she
was both an active participant and an accurate observer. Her
articles in the *Tribune* reveal a close knowledge of the situation and an ability to evaluate and predict events. While still
in England, she had met the exiled revolutionary leader Gui-
seppe Mazzini and had participated in a plot to smuggle him
into Italy in 1846.[43] In Rome she attended meetings of various
groups and parties, and, as Joseph Jay Deiss points out, she
was able to correlate all of her information into an astonish-
ingly astute evaluation of the situation (*At Home*, pp. 245,
142–243, 265–268, 320).[44]

Fuller's involvement in Italian affairs was personal as
well as political. Although American men had been frightened
by her superior intellect and independent will and seemed able
to accept her only if they could regard her as a man,[45] she
found that in Europe it was possible to be an individual *and* a
woman. In December 1847, she became pregnant by a young
nobleman-turned-patriot, Marchese Giovanni Angelo Ossoli.
Their son, Angelino, was born secretly in September 1848,
and Fuller and Ossoli were probably married the following
year.[46] Forced to leave the child in the mountains in the care
of a nurse, they returned to Rome, where he fought at the
barricades while she worked in the military hospital during
the siege of Rome. While Emerson wrote advising her that it
was "imprudent" to remain in Italy and urging her to come
back to Concord where she could settle in Mrs. Brown's little
cottage (*LRWE*, 4: 28, 61, 79), she was frantically involved in
a real-life drama, both personal and political. It is almost
amusing to read these letters from "Dear Waldo" to the Italian Margaret Fuller, whose secret pregnancy and revolutionary involvement epitomize the distance between her and the
insular Emerson.

On June 11, 1848, writing from the Apennine Mountains, where, unknown to Emerson, she was awaiting the birth of her child, she told him that she now knew that her earlier thoughts were only words (*Memoirs*, 2: 243–244). And words they must truly have seemed when, a year later, painfully separated by the siege of Rome from her still secret child, she received another letter from Emerson "amid the round of cannonade and musketry." Describing her hospital experiences with the dying and the wounded, she wondered if she would ever return to America: "It seems so far away, so difficult" (*Memoirs*, 2: 264). She was indeed a long way from the Emersonian world of abstractions and total concern with self. While Emerson was lecturing in England in 1848, Mazzini wrote Margaret Fuller an assessment of the sage that must have confirmed her own: "I feel fearful that he leads or will lead men to too much contemplation. . . . We stand in need of one who will . . . appeal to the collective influences and inspiring sources, more than to individual self-improvement."[47]

It was in Europe, away from the absorbing influences of Emerson and the constricting climate of American society, that Fuller felt herself truly able to develop as a person. She wrote to Emerson from Paris in 1846 that she had encountered much more personal opportunity in Europe: "I can enjoy a freer play of faculty." A year later she wrote to him from Rome that she had found in Europe "an atmosphere to develop me in ways I need. . . . so much strength has been wasted in abstractions, which only came because I grew not in the right soil" (*Memoirs*, 2: 184, 224–225).

With respect to the pitfall of abstractions, it is interesting to note the difference between Fuller's and Emerson's attitudes toward war. Whereas to Emerson the Civil War was a glorious abstraction, to Fuller the Roman Revolution was a painful reality. Her day-to-day contact with death and suffering gave her a perspective that Emerson lacked. Although she remained loyal to the cause, she never allowed the cause to obliterate the reality. From the battle of Rome she wrote to Emerson in June 1849 that she pitied Mazzini because, although his was a just cause, "Yet to me it would be dreadful to cause all this bloodshed" (*Memoirs*, 2: 266). After the fighting was over, she wrote to William Henry Channing of the men she had seen killed and wounded: "I forget the great ideas to sympathize with the poor mothers" (*Memoirs*, 2: 270). Unlike Whitman, who worked in a military hospital during the Civil War and attempted to reconcile his abstract faith in American progress with the reality of the suffering, Fuller could not rationalize away the horror of war. Nor did she refuse to admit the pain and despair that the experience left her with. After the siege of Rome, she wrote: "I am *tired out*,—tired of thinking and hoping,—tired of seeing men err and bleed" (*Memoirs*, 2: 302).[48]

It is this determination to see reality, which comes from a concern for persons, rather than to bask in the abstract language of an idea that gave Fuller the perspective to judge her own country more realistically than the other Transcendentalists. In a review of a book on the American Indian written before she went to Europe, Fuller called attention to the ways in which Americans had betrayed the promise of America. The "worst plague of all," she says, is the American treatment of the Indians. But other faults loom large: the overconcern with money; the sin of slavery; intolerance and bigotry (she cites the persecution of the Mormons); and the unjust war with Mexico.[49] She continued this kind of realistic criticism from Europe (see, e.g., *At Home*, pp. 254–255, 306, 326–327). Although Fuller always maintained her belief in the ideals of America, she did not make excuses for the evils she saw in her country, nor did she try to justify them by appeals to heroic ideas.

What separated Margaret Fuller from the other Transcendentalists, then, was her concern for other people. As a woman struggling to sustain a separate identity in a society that denied it, she not only saw the woman as a person but also recognized the personhood of all others. Instead of inhabiting a world of abstractions, where the only interaction took place within the mind, she saw life in terms of real people and events. Though she believed as strongly as any American in the rights of the individual, she did not subscribe to the myth of the individual, which denied the rights of others. She knew that real growth comes only from a recognition of the outside world.

PART TWO

PART TWO

THE WOMAN AS FANTASY

CHAPTER 4

CHAPTER 4

SOLITARY MAN AND SUPERFLUOUS WOMAN: JAMES FENIMORE COOPER

Marry a woman, which means a kind, gentle, affectionate, thoughtful creature, whose heart is so full of you, there is no room in it for herself.

James Fenimore Cooper,
The Ways of the Hour[1]

As we have seen, the concept of individualism, and the resulting disregard for others, not only provided the basis for American expansionism and the rise of the democratic common man; it was also sanctioned by such literary figures and intellectuals as the American Transcendentalists. In order to understand the concept of women in American fiction, it is necessary to explore the effect of this philosophy on nineteenth-century novelists. What was their attitude toward American individualism? And how was it related to their attitude toward the other and to the portrayal of women in their fiction?

James Fenimore Cooper has often been criticized for his conventional and lifeless heroines. Perhaps the most famous comment is James Russell Lowell's couplet from "A Fable for Critics" (1848):

> The women he draws from one model don't vary,
> All sappy as maples and flat as the prairie.[2]

William Dean Howells protested that Cooper's novels lacked the presence of "one genuine heroine."[3] In *Love and Death in the American Novel*, Leslie Fiedler describes Cooper's white women as sexless "wooden ingenues,"[4] and Richard Chase in *The American Novel and Its Tradition* calls them "bloodless and dull."[5]

As Kay Seymour House says in *Cooper's Americans*, Cooper's is a man's world, and women are almost completely excluded from it.[6] Cooper's heroine is superfluous to the action. She waits quietly in the wings until one of the male characters can take time off from the main business of masculine adventure and self-development to marry her. If she is swept into the action, it is as a leaf is swept along by a river. Some of Cooper's heroines are more spirited than others and may flutter about prettily in the stream, but very few of them show either inclination or ability to swim to shore. In Cooper's novels the only young women who are allowed to take action with impunity are the Indian women.

Cooper's novels do contain a few white women who are more active, but these women are never his heroines. They are older women, unsuitable for marriage—grotesques whose behavior, though it may be interesting to the reader, is not regarded as properly feminine by the author. Such characters include Betty Flanagan, the Irish camp follower in *The Spy* (1821); Esther Bush, the woman who avenges her son's death in *The Prairie* (1827); and Molly Spike, the disguised sailor in *Jack Tier* (1846–1848). These characters participate in the action in a way not permitted to Cooper's heroines, and as Cooper makes clear at the end of *Jack Tier*, the woman who behaves in such a "masculine" fashion is committing a crime against her sex. As Molly pitifully struggles to resume her feminine character after twenty years as a sailor, she tells her former husband: "It is hard for a woman to unsex herself, Stephen; to throw off her very natur', as it might be, and try to turn man" (*Works*, 18: 471).

The young white women in Cooper's novels fall into three categories. At one end of the scale are the very weak, totally dependent child-maidens. At the other end stand a few young women who are stronger and more independent, but somehow tainted; Cooper never allows one of them to be his heroine. In between one finds the majority of Cooper's women. They are not as weak as the child-maidens, but they are always dependent, and they are wholly "feminine."

The category of fragile child-maidens includes Alice Munro in *The Last of the Mohicans* (1826), Louisa Grant in *The Pioneers* (1823), Inez in *The Prairie*, Hetty Hutter in *The Deerslayer* (1841), and Grace Wallingford in *Afloat and Ashore* (1844). Perhaps the best known of these maidens are Alice and Hetty, whom D. H. Lawrence calls the White Lilies.[7] Although they are portrayed as feeble (Hetty is actually feeble-minded) and childish, with about as much sex appeal as a corpse, the author much prefers them to the stronger women in the novels, Cora and Judith, whose strength is somehow linked to tainted blood or tainted virtue. Cooper commented in a letter to Rufus Griswold in 1843 (?), "With me, Hetty Hutter is the favorite female character."[8] Major Heyward, before he even knows of Cora's black blood, singles out Alice as his choice. Obviously, he prefers her shrinking dependency to Cora's strength and vitality—a choice the reader finds difficult to understand.

The majority of young women in Cooper's novels—the second category—are dependent, emotional, and totally selfless. They include such characters as Frances Wharton in *The Spy*, Elizabeth Temple in *The Pioneers*, Ellen Wade in *The Prairie*, Alida de Barbérie in *The Water-Witch* (1830), Eve Effingham in *Homeward Bound* and *Home as Found* (1838), Mabel Dunham in *The Pathfinder* (1840), Mildred Dutton in *The Two Admirals* (1842), Lucy Hardinge in *Afloat and Ashore* and *Miles Wallingford* (1845), Anneke Mordaunt in *Satanstoe* (1845), Rose Budd in *Jack Tier*, and Mary Trapp in *The Sea Lions* (1840). Though not as feeble as Alice Munro and Hetty Hutter, these girls are always the "weaker vessel," delicately feminine, dependent "creatures." "We must protect the feeble

ones," Leatherstocking says in novel after novel. (It is significant that Cooper and Leatherstocking often refer to animals
and women as "creatures"; the only male characters they call
creatures are black slaves. Moreover, the word "feeble" is
used to describe such characters as Ellen Wade in *The Prairie*
and Mabel Dunham in *The Pathfinder*, and not just the obvious fainters like Alice Munro.) Deerslayer tells Judith that
nature intended men to protect women: "It is the duty of the
strong to take care of the weak" (*Works*, 1: 75). Even the not-
quite-genteel Mabel Dunham in *The Pathfinder* would not be
so unfeminine as to protect her own person; she would never,
as Dew-of-June's Indian mother did, tomahawk her captors
(*Works*, 3: 381). Mabel declares that she wishes to live in ignorance of arms and rely on men for her safety: "Among
Christian men, a woman's best guard is her claim to their
protection" (*Works*, 3: 12). If Mabel is spirited, she is also
"sweet" and "modest" (*Works*, 3: 3). Ellen Wade, her counter-
part in *The Prairie*, may have more substance than the pale
Inez, but she is wholly feminine, Paul Hover's "gentle and
dependent companion" (*Works*, 5: 50). When Indians appear,
Paul reaches for his gun while Ellen buries her face in the
grass, an action that Cooper says was as natural to her sex as
the young man's was to his (*Works*, 5: 37).

Certainly there must have been instances when women
relied on male protection in the wilderness. But a difference
in physical strength does not mean all women are genetically
passive. Cooper's heroines are never permitted to initiate the
action. Some are more spirited and resourceful than others,
but it is always the man who takes action. One reason for this
lack of independent female action, of course, is that Cooper's
heroines can never act with impropriety. Elizabeth Temple in
The Pioneers, for example, prefers to be burned alive in the
forest fire rather than remove her petticoat.

If a proper Cooper female is driven to act, even in a limited capacity, it is only out of a concern for others, *not for herself*, and her actions are never unseemly, her behavior never
unfeminine. When Frances Wharton in *The Spy* goes up the
mountain at night and pleads for her brother in court, she

acts only out of love for her brother, and she always behaves with "maiden modesty"—blushing, weeping, and fainting on cue, like Mildred in *The Two Admirals*, who falls "senseless on the grass" after helping to save young Wychecombe (*Works*, 11: 29). Cooper emphasizes Frances's "infantile innocency" (*Works*, 6: 9); like all of Cooper's proper heroines, she behaves more like a passionate or impetuous child than a mature adult. "Delicate and retiring herself as the fairest visions of romance had ever portrayed her sex," she cannot believe that Isabella would love unsought. When she selflessly resigns Dunwoodie to Isabella, he tells her he does not want a strong woman like Isabella; he wants a "mild, gentle, and dependent" woman like Frances (*Works*, 6: 234). Similarly, Elizabeth Temple in *The Pioneers* seems to act resolutely, but only when it is for someone else. She does not try to save herself when she is in danger, and, although she shows more spirit than her timid friend, Louisa Grant, her only action is a passive resignation—until a man appears to rescue her. Cooper emphasizes her purity, modesty, and softness (*Works*, 4: 56–57). Her earnestness is checked by "maidenly reserve"; though resolute, she is prudent (*Works*, 4: 196, 274). One knows at the end of the novel that she will obey Leatherstocking's injunction: "Trust in God, Madam, and your honorable husband" (*Works*, 4: 476).

The only one of Cooper's heroines who seems to act for herself with impunity is Alida de Barbérie in *The Water-Witch*. She disappears from her uncle's home and is believed to have run off with the pirate Skimmer of the Seas—certainly an improper and self-willed action. At the end of the book, however, we discover that Alida had been seized and carried captive on board the Skimmer's ship in order to help establish the former Skimmer's granddaughter's claims as the lost granddaughter of Alida's uncle (*Works*, 10: 438).

In a Cooper novel it is improper for a woman to act for herself because this would be a sign of concern for self, which Cooper considers unfeminine. Even a spirited woman would never be so self-oriented as to want to save her own life. Anneke Mordaunt in *Satanstoe* will not exert herself even to let

Littlepage save her life on the icy river until he reminds her that her father will miss her if she dies. She will make the effort to escape only for the sake of her father, not for herself (*Works*, 26: 312). The selflessness of Cooper's heroines is particularly apparent in their attitude toward marriage. Mr. Hardinge in *Afloat and Ashore* advises Miles Wallingford to marry an *amiable* woman. When pressed to define such a woman, he prescribes: "There must be an unusual absence of selfishness; a person must live less for herself than others; or rather must find her own happiness in the happiness of those she loves" (*Works*, 16: 384). Cooper's proper heroines love completely and with total disregard for self. Often these young women demonstrate their selflessness by giving all of their money to their husbands. Lucy Hardinge tells Miles: "All that is mine will be yours" (*Works*, 17: 409, 411). Rose Budd gives her money to Mulford to outfit his ship (*Works*, 18: 479). And Eve Effingham, Cooper's spirited, but ultimately dependent, heroine in *Homeward Bound* and *Home as Found*, resigns her inheritance in favor of Paul, refusing even to speak of money matters. He possesses her heart, her affections, and her duty, she affirms: "Of what account is money after this!" (*Works*, 14: 444–445).

Not only do these selfless maidens give all their love and money to their husbands; they give up all ideas and allegiances as well. As Edward Effingham tells the prospective bridegroom of his niece: "Your country will be her country—your God her God" (*Works*, 14: 303). Henry Wharton says in *The Spy*, "Women are but mirrors which reflect the images before them," and his sister Frances admits that on the differences between England and the colonies, she is only echoing the ideas of Major Dunwoodie (*Works*, 6: 44). The ideal Cooper female resigns herself completely to the male, giving up all pretensions of self. As Eudora passionately exclaims to the Skimmer of the Seas at the end of *The Water-Witch*, "Thy world is my world!" (*Works*, 10: 443).

The only idea that a Cooper woman will not give up for anyone is her faith in God. Real religious faith is, of course, the ultimate in selflessness, and Cooper regards religion as a peculiarly feminine province. Mary Trapp in *The Sea Lions* withholds herself from Roswell Gardiner until he sees the light and ceases his questioning of God's truth. As Herman Melville commented in his review of this novel, the heroine is the hero's reward for orthodoxy.[9] Not only does religion seem to be the one idea that the heroine is allowed to retain as her own; prayer is the only "action" that she can perform. In *The Pathfinder* Mabel Dunham's principal accomplishment is to pray with her dying father (*Works*, 3: 471). And in an emergency, the only activity that Cooper's heroines can be counted upon to undertake is prayer, which is consistent with Cooper's image of woman as passive and placid rather than active and assertive. As Jack Tier says, women are for prayer; men are for work (*Works*, 2: 55). In *The Water-Witch*, after the ship burns, the men work frantically to repair the raft while Alida and Eudora make "long and fervent petitions" to God. Alida tells Ludlow: "All that bold and skilful seamen can do, have ye done; and all that woman in such a situation can do, have we done in your behalf" (*Works*, 10: 422). All that women can do is to pray, and the selfless ladies even pray only on behalf of others.

Cooper's heroines find it so easy to give up their ideas as well as their money and affections because, like Emerson's women, they are ruled by the heart and not the head. Deerslayer observes: "Woman was created for the feelin's and is pretty much ruled by feelin'!" (*Works*, 1: 151). Lucy Hardinge comments that women love with their whole hearts and live wholly for the affections, whereas men have the world to think of (*Works*, 16: 382; 17: 418).

If the emotions of Cooper's women are strong, their intellect is not. Even the most quick-witted is limited in intelligence. In *The Pioneers* Elizabeth Temple, who has "elasticity of mind," is said to be "only" a woman and therefore limited in her intellect (*Works*, 4: 315). The supposedly intelligent Rose Budd in *Jack Tier* has had the theory of longitude and latitude explained to her several times, but, Cooper says, "womanlike," she will not remember it the next day, "for Rose was a female and had her own weaknesses as well as another" (*Works*, 18: 209). The intelligence of Cooper's heroines is also qualified by feminine proprieties. Lucy Hardinge is "an accurate thinker," but only in subjects that "became her station" (*Works*, 16: 111). Though her face might look "intent and inquiring," it is always "timid and modest." At the age of fifty she is still "ingenuous, pure of mind . . . placid" (*Works*, 17: 405, 453).

These are the majority of Cooper's heroines—spirited perhaps, but always limited, maidenly modest, dependent, and selfless. The third category of young women in Cooper's novels, the stronger, more independent characters, contains only a few examples. Moreover, these women are criticized, even punished, by the author for transgressing the bounds he has set on proper feminine behavior. Isabella in *The Spy* is brave and possesses a "courage beyond the strength of woman" (*Works*, 6: 294). Her crime is that she dared to love unsought. She confesses to Frances, the proper heroine: "I have exhibited those feelings which you have been taught to repress. After this, can I wish to live?" (*Works*, 6: 297). In a Cooper novel, she cannot live. She is killed by a stray bullet, and, as Richard Chase says, Cooper fired the shot.[10] Cooper also kills off Cora in *The Last of the Mohicans*. Cora is strong and brave, though not so indecorous as to love unsought as boldly as Isabella does (she keeps her love for Heyward to herself). Yet her black blood allows her to be more independent than Cooper's usual white heroine, and when her superior vitality attracts the love of two competing Indians, she and they must die.

Judith in *The Deerslayer* is one of the most interesting female characters Cooper created. She possesses strength and intelligence and the ability to act. (She even pushes an invading Indian into the water [*Works*, 1: 68–69].) But, although Deerslayer can almost forgive her forwardness in declaring an unsought love for him (because, as Cooper says,

her naturalness lessens the "unpleasant feature of a forwardness unbecoming to the sex" [*Works*, 1: 434]), he cannot forgive her indiscretions with the officers of the garrison. He
and Cooper, with self-righteous cruelty, turn their backs on
Judith; Deerslayer accepts the "pure" rifle, Killdeer, instead of
the "tainted" woman. Donald Davie comments that what is
wrong with Cooper's portrayal of Judith is "its inhumanity, a
cramped littleness, prurience and meanness, the complete
lack of magnanimity."[11] Certainly, one feels Cooper is unfair
to Judith, and Deerslayer's stance makes him appear pom-
pous and unfeeling.

Deerslayer seems here to be acting out the role of the
self-reliant American individualist, who must remain solitary
and uncommitted to complex human emotional involvements—particularly with an independent-spirited person like
Judith. In this respect, Deerslayer is an illiterate Emerson
denying the claims of a backwoods Margaret Fuller. When
the still solitary Deerslayer returns to the lake fifteen years
later and ties one of Judith's faded ribbons to his marvelous
rifle, Cooper neatly expresses the choice of his protagonist:
the *other* person is only an idea, a faded memory; reality is the
hard, cold symbol of maleness, aggression, and self-will.

A detailed look at Cooper's last novel will afford the
clearest picture of his attitude toward the woman who dares
to act independently. Mary Monson (Mildred Millington) in
The Ways of the Hour (1850) is independent and intelligent, and
she is the only one of Cooper's young women who acts to
save herself rather than relying on male protection. What most
sets her apart from all the other young women in Cooper's
novels is that she is self-oriented. Every other Cooper heroine who shows any signs of being able to act at all acts only
for another person, not for herself.

Falsely accused of murder, Mary Monson actively takes
part in her own defense, advising her lawyers and following
the trial proceedings carefully. She shows "remarkable ingenuity." She even takes notes in court, though her lawyer
Timms asks her to refrain, since, he says, "it gave her the appearance of knowing too much, and helped to deprive her of

the interesting character of an unprotected female." However, it is fortunate that she pays attention, because, when it is clear that her lawyers cannot save her, she takes over and in a brilliant cross-examination of the state's principal witness proves her own innocence (*Works*, 24: 365–366, 378, 422–426). She accomplishes this feat calmly and with intelligent arguments, not in the emotional, "feminine" way that Cooper finds so charming in his proper heroines.[12]

In a Cooper novel, Mary Monson's independence and strong will, her intelligence and self-assertion, are not the virtues they would be in a man. Cooper regards her as a traitor to her sex and reveals that one can see in her otherwise lovely face the "lines that indicate self-will, and a spirit not easily controlled." Women's real power, Cooper insists, comes by "keeping within the natural circle of their sex's feelings, instead of aping an independence and spirit more suited to men" (*Works*, 24: 311). Self-willed females are not real women but "creatures in the guise of a sex that they discredit and caricature" (*Works*, 24: 241).

Not only is Mary Monson a discredit to her sex, but, according to Cooper, such an aberration from the norm is actually a sign of insanity (e.g., *Works*, 24: 430). Principally, it is her self-assertion that marks Mary Monson as insane. At the end of the novel we are told that she shows a lessening tendency toward insanity as she is "gradually drawn from the exaggerated notions she had . . . of herself and her rights" (*Works*, 24: 460–461). The "remarkable ingenuity" that helped her to win her case in a murder trial helps to convict her in Cooper's case against her. Apparently, the feminine, sane thing for a woman to do would be to allow herself to be hanged.

The contrast in the novel between Mary Monson and the counter-heroine, Anna Updyke, provides us with a clear understanding of Cooper's concept of women. Anna is everything that Mary is not. Whereas Mary is self-oriented, Anna reveals a "total abnegation of self" (*Works*, 24: 228). John Milmeter, who had been attracted to Mary Monson, finds that he prefers Anna because she is so gentle and "sweetly feminine" (*Works*, 24: 311). Milmeter declares that he could not bear to be married to a woman who was too clever in "the affairs of men, out-of-door concerns, or politics, or law, or anything, indeed, that called for a masculine education and understanding" (*Works*, 24: 183). Unlike Mary, who can hold her own in any discussion of ideas, Anna shyly admits that she does not understand such things (e.g., *Works*, 24: 240, 437). Milmeter does not mind if his wife is accomplished in certain feminine areas—"small talk, and making preserves and dancing and even poetry and religion" (*Works*, 24: 183). Milmeter's uncle, Thomas Dunscomb, Cooper's wise old spokesman in the novel, advises Milmeter to marry a dependent woman:

> Marry a gentle and feminine woman. . . . Avoid what is termed a woman of independent spirit. They are usually so many devils incarnate. If they happen to unite moneyed independence with moral independence, I am not quite certain that their tyranny is not worse than that of Nero.   (*Works*, 24: 311–312)

Dunscomb is concerned about the new marriage laws that have given married women more independence. One of the "absurdities of the hour," he complains to Mary, "is a new law, giving married women the control of their property" (*Works*, 24: 275). The next step in woman's independence, he warns, will be "licentiousness" (*Works*, 24: 442). Cooper seconds Dunscomb's opinion, claiming such laws are contrary to the law of God: "The Creator intended woman for a 'help-meet,' and not for the head of the family circles; and most fatally ill-judging are the laws that would fain disturb the order of a domestic government . . . derived from divine wisdom" (*Works*, 24: 364, 431).

It is with respect to their attitudes toward marriage that the difference between Mary and Anna is most obvious. Mary, we discover, is actually Mme. de Larocheforte and is seeking to extricate herself from a marriage that she regards as debasing. Marriage, she recognizes, "crushes a woman's independence" (*Works*, 24: 436). Dunscomb reminds her that nature never intended women to be independent, however unpleasant a husband may be (*Works*, 24: 453). Mary's husband is a fortune hunter who has the offensive habit of constantly taking snuff. (It is interesting that Cooper makes Larocheforte's offense one that can seem trivial rather than something more serious, such as drunkenness or wife beating, which would lend greater credence to Mary's statements about marriage.) Dunscomb maintains that most women delight in being dependent on their husbands and points to the blushing Anna as an example (*Works*, 24: 274). For her part, Anna promises to be an obedient and submissive wife. She would never dream of keeping her own money but would go to her husband and "pour all into his lap." It is the law of nature, the church, and reason for the woman to be dependent on the man, she concludes, and the new laws that would make women independent are wrong to place "the weaker vessel uppermost" (*Works*, 24: 436–438, 179–181).

Ingenuousness, simplicity, childlike innocence—these are the qualities that Cooper emphasizes in his heroine. Mary Monson was unfeminine, even insane, because she demonstrated ingenuity instead of ingenuousness. Cooper does not believe that a woman should be too clever or have too much knowledge of the world. In *Homeward Bound*, although Eve Effingham has been educated in Europe and is one of Cooper's more interesting heroines, what first attracts Paul Powis is her "trembling simplicity and modesty, and her meek purity of mind" (*Works*, 14: 342).

With this image of women, it is not surprising that Cooper seldom portrayed mature women as serious characters, as he did mature men (e.g., Judge Temple, Edward Effingham, Leatherstocking himself, Colonel Munro). Cooper never permitted a young girl to develop traits that would make her a rational, independent individual, and it is even more difficult to portray such a limited character in a grown woman. Traits that may be charming in a young girl are ridiculous in an older woman. Thus, most of the mature women in Cooper's novels are grotesques. In *Jack Tier* Mulford tells Rose that he dislikes women who attempt to learn too much; he prefers a wife who makes "pretty blunders" (*Works*, 18: 347). But what he may regard as pretty in his blushing Rose Budd is silly ignorance in Rose's aunt, whose "very countenance expressed imbecility and mental dependence, credulity and a love of gossip" (*Works*, 18: 20). When one of Cooper's mature women does attain a dignity and stature—as in the case of Esther Bush in *The Prairie*—it is the reader who perceives it, not Cooper, who portrays Esther only as the "squatter's termagant wife."

Cooper's young women were necessary to the marriage plot that the public expected, and Cooper found their beauty, innocence, and childlike simplicity and dependence charming.[13] Without this youthful charm and marriageability, there was no reason to include such uninteresting nonpersons in a novel, unless for comic relief.

If this view of women influenced Cooper's personal life, we have no way of knowing. He asked that no biography be written of him, and his eldest daughter respected his wishes to such an extent that she had most of his journals buried with her.[14] Many letters survive, however, and they reveal a lifelong, friendly, loving relationship with his wife. When Cooper wrote to his brother Richard in 1810 that he wanted to marry Susan Augusta DeLancey, he described her as "amiable, sweet-tempered and happy in her disposition" (*Letters*, 1: 17–18). Her letters reveal her to have been a woman of spirit, and she supported and encouraged Cooper in his work. There is no evidence, however, that she sought to enlarge the role that Cooper regarded as feminine, and she apparently was, or Cooper believed her to be, totally dependent on him. "I dare not leave my wife," he wrote to Samuel B. Morse in 1832, after twenty-two years of marriage; "she quite loses her head when I am absent" (*Letters*, 2: 310).

In *The American Democrat* (1838), Cooper claimed that

women have no need of political rights because their interests are inseparable from those of their male relatives. Furthermore, civil rights for women are inadvisable because they interfere with relationships between husband and wife.[15] Cooper considered such attitudes not as a denial of selfhood but as a sign of high civilization: "After all, what nobler or more convincing proof of high civilization can be given than this habitual respect of the strong for the weak" (*Notions,* 1: 139–140).

In *Notions of the Americans* (1828), Cooper insisted that women must not be "corrupted by the baneful and unfeminine vice of selfishness" (*Notions,* 1: 40). Yet in *The American Democrat* he reasoned that selfishness is just another term for individuality: "The principle of individuality, or to use a less winning term, of selfishness, lies at the root of all human exertion" (*Democrat,* p. 128). Cooper believed that individuality is necessary for all greatness of character and for the pursuit of happiness (*Democrat,* p. 174), yet he considered it unimportant—in fact, deplorable—in women. If individuality is so crucial to human endeavor, what does it mean to deny it to women? It means that woman has no self; she is not a person in her own right. For Cooper, women have no existence except in relation to men.

Various explanations have been suggested for Cooper's view of women. W. C. Brownell contends that Cooper simply reflected the realities and conventions of his day,[16] and certainly the nineteenth-century emphasis on genteel, ladylike behavior appears in Cooper's novels. There may indeed have been women who behaved like his heroines. Yet even in his own day, Cooper was criticized for making Alice in *The Last of the Mohicans* "too shrinking," and his heroines in general were said to be "miserably deficient in the grace and ease, gentility of deportment, true delicacy, and unaffected refinement" of a true lady.[17] Moreover, although the genteel heroine was a convention, sufficient examples of fully developed women characters existed in European fiction before Cooper began to write. One has only to look at Jane Austen's heroines or even Daniel Defoe's Moll Flanders. Another explanation for Cooper's portrayal of women is Leslie Fiedler's psychological interpretation that Cooper was revenging himself against women, whom he saw as symbols of authority and society and thus as threats to men's freedom.[18] However, though one may argue that Cooper does not seem always to like his genteel heroines, his attitude toward them is not one of fearsome hostility and vengeance but rather general annoyance that he has to bother with them at all. In most of his novels, Cooper felt compelled to include a heroine and a marriage story because of the demands of the reading public, which was primarily female.[19]

Neither of these explanations adequately accounts for Cooper's failure to portray strong, independent women. Obviously, there is no simple explanation, but part of the reason, I believe, lies in his acceptance of American individualism. Cooper's most famous novels stand squarely in the American tradition of male self-exploration, which has characterized American culture and was so emphatically articulated by the American Transcendentalists. As Francis Parkman recognized in 1852, Leatherstocking—the self-reliant, solitary individualist of the wilderness—is the epitome of American history.[20] Allen Nevins calls the Leatherstocking Saga the "nearest approach yet made to an American epic."[21] It should not be surprising, then, that Cooper was hailed as the first American novelist and that the novelistic tradition to which he gave birth has dominated the American novel for more than a hundred years.

His second novel, *The Spy* (1821), established his reputation as a writer and began a tradition in the novel that has been recognized as peculiarly American: the principal setting was outside society, the wilderness, rather than the drawing room, where women figure prominently, and the principal character was a solitary male figure. *The Spy* was the first American novel to be reviewed by the prestigious *North American Review*, which acclaimed it as a specifically American novel, and a century later, it was still being praised as a "native and masculine work."[22] Although Cooper went on to write thirty more novels on a variety of subjects, American experience was oriented toward individualistic masculine achievement, and it is this aspect of Cooper's writing that has become associated with his name.

Like Emerson and Thoreau—like the American Dreamer —Cooper accepted without question the American emphasis on the individual, and his belief in American individualism finds clear expression in his fiction. First of all, there is the character of Leatherstocking, or Natty Bumppo—an almost legendary figure who possesses the superhuman powers of a Davy Crockett and surpasses even Daniel Boone as an Indian fighter.[23] Natty always wins. He survives fire and war, beats the Indians at their own game, never misses his mark, and possesses the marvelous escape techniques of his predecessor in *The Spy*, Harvey Birch, without the advantage of the double spy's personal acquaintance with George Washington. If Natty's prowess is unrealistic, as critics of Cooper have long maintained,[24] it is because he is a myth, not a man. D. H. Lawrence called Cooper's portrayal of Natty a "wish-fulfillment vision, a kind of yearning myth."[25] Whether or not Natty represents Cooper's own hidden desires, as Lawrence maintains, he clearly possesses all the characteristics of the ideal persona of generations of American males: he is strong and manly, a superperson who can do anything, and one who can do it by himself. In *The Last of the Mohicans* Natty possesses that "secret love of desperate adventure, which had increased with his daily experience, until hazard and danger had become, in some measure, necessary to the enjoyment of his existence" (*Works*, 2: 274). For readers of Cooper who may have this same secret love of adventure but who lack the ability or opportunity to live their fantasies, Natty's single-handed prowess provides vicarious wish fulfillment.

Cooper admires the behavior of his Leatherstocking hero, praising as manly his adventurous spirit and fearless warlike stance. "Manly" is a word Cooper uses frequently throughout his writing. He means much the same by it as Emerson and Thoreau do—bold self-confidence and independent action, as opposed to the feminine qualities of passivity and social orientation. Above all, he means a man who is willing, even eager, to fight. At the beginning of *The Last of the Mohicans* Cooper tells us that he admires the "manly courage" of a person who gladly meets conflict like a brave warrior. Cooper criticizes those who fear the approach of war; they should remember their manhood (*Works*, 2: 4–5). In *The Deerslayer*, when Judith asks Natty if he prefers war to the hearth and affections, he replies: "I've feelin's for the callin', which is both manful and honorable" (*Works*, 1: 564).

Cooper occasionally introduces a character who acts as a foil to Natty Bumppo, showing the absurdity of unmanly pursuits. David Gamut, the Psalmist in *The Last of the Mohicans*, is ridiculed by Natty and by Cooper for his devotion to such a peaceful, feminine calling as singing. Natty (Hawkeye in this novel) says Gamut should throw away his pitch pipe and take up a gun: "The Lord never intended that the man should place all his endeavors in his throat, to the neglect of other and better gifts! But he has fallen into the hands of some silly woman" (*Works*, 2: 133, 269). What good is Gamut, Hawkeye asks; he can't slay a buck or cut the throat of an Indian (*Works*, 2: 222). In *The Prairie* the helplessness of Dr. Battius, the naturalist, is contrasted with Natty's experience. Natty considers Battius's book learning useless and feminine (*Works*, 5: 275–286). Similarly, in *The Last of the Mohicans* Natty criticizes the writing of history, which forces a man to "misspend his days among the women, in learning the name of black marks" if he is to know of the deeds of his fathers (*Works*, 2: 27).

Although Natty Bumppo is gentle, patient, and self-effacing, he is ultimately a killer—which, according to D. H. Lawrence, all (white, male) Americans are at heart.[26]

Although Lawrence's generalization is too broad to take seriously, it is significant that, particularly in his Leatherstocking hero, Cooper applauds the quality that Americans have most admired in their folk heroes from Kit Carson to the modern television detective: the ability to fight and kill.

Like all the superheroes of American legend, Natty Bumppo is a solitary figure without family ties. He prefers the adventure of the open forest to the quieter pleasures of family life: "The Wahcondah made me to live alone. He never tied my heart to house or field . . . if he had, I should not have journeyed so far, and seen so much" (*Works*, 5: 330). In *The Pathfinder*, the one novel in which Natty faces any real danger of marriage, he explains that love for women is incompatible with his manly pursuits:

> I'm sometimes afeared it isn't wholesome for one who is much occupied in a very manly calling, like that of a guide, or a scout, or a soldier even, to form friendships for women,—young women in particular,—as they seem to me to lessen the love of enterprise, and to turn the feelings away from their gifts and natural occupations.
>
> (*Works*, 3: 199)

Like Thoreau, who maintained that the need for society was a sickness, Natty considers it a weakness to desire contact with other people. In *The Pioneers*, he remembers: "When I first came into the woods to live, I used to have weak spells when I felt lonesome . . . but it's now many a year since I felt any such longings" (*Works*, 4: 300). Although he becomes involved with a group of people in each novel, by the end of the book he leaves them. He has no identification with or commitment to any group. The perfect individualist, he lives outside white society; but neither is he part of Indian society. He enjoys a sustained relationship with only one person: Chingachgook. The Mohican is the only character whose friendship with Natty endures beyond a single novel. Yet even this relationship is an undemanding one. Natty helps

Chingachgook and Chingachgook helps Natty, but they are both free to go their own ways. Natty must deny society because his business is to develop himself.[27]

Cooper most successfully portrays this self-reliant ideal in Leatherstocking, in Harvey Birch, and in some of his seamen (e.g., Captain Truck in the Effingham novels, Moses Marble in the Miles Wallingford novels, and Oakes and Bluewater in *The Two Admirals*). Miles Wallingford is isolated during most of the two novels, though at the end he rejoins society. He recognizes, however, that in seeking companionship and esteem he compromises himself: "I know this is not the way to make a very great man; for he who cannot judge, feel, and act for himself, will always be in danger of making undue sacrifices to the wishes of others" (*Works*, 16: 361).

If Cooper shares the Emersonian belief in self-reliance, he nevertheless tempers it somewhat. As Lewis Leary notes in his introduction to *Home as Found*, Cooper preferred the term "self-confidence" to "self-reliance" because the latter "seemed to deny the instructive power of experience."[28] It is important that Natty's self-reliance is justified by a very real store of knowledge. Similarly, when Paul Powis is about to lead the attack on the Arabs in *Homeward Bound*, he possesses "perfect self-reliance, and an entire confidence in his own resources and knowledge" (*Works*, 12: 337). He is an experienced soldier and seaman. In *The Spy*, Harvey Birch relies only on himself—but he knows his business, as does the Skimmer of the Seas in *The Water-Witch* and Harry Mulford in *Jack Tier*. Each of Cooper's self-reliant heroes is competent and well-versed in his trade, whether it be in the forest or on the ocean. Moreover, theirs is an earthly self-reliance. Unlike Emerson, who sees man as god, Cooper insists that, however self-reliant a man might be, he must still turn to God for ultimate guidance. In *Home as Found*, for example, John Effingham's "governing fault" is a "self-reliance that indisposed him to throw himself on a greater power" (*Works*, 14: 399).

Given these qualifications, Cooper emphatically extols the importance of the individual in America. In *The Prairie* he praises American culture because there are no artificial, hereditary honors; the individual must rely on himself. Natty comments that in America a man is left to follow his own wishes and is "happier, ay, and more manly and more honest too" (*Works*, 5: 69–70, 410).

This belief in individualism, which is at the heart of Cooper's fiction, remained constant throughout his life. Early in his writing career, Cooper ardently embraced the American Dream, the concept that America is the land of opportunity where the individual determines his own destiny. *Notions of the Americans* (1828), which Cooper wrote while living in Europe, is one of the most idealistic and naive statements of American chauvinism ever published. When Cooper returned to the United States in 1833, however, he was saddened and disillusioned to find that America and Americans did not measure up to his image of them. Yet, though often critical of America thereafter, he never lost faith in what he considered the basic principles and values of America and its institutions. It is the failure of Americans to live up to these principles that he addresses himself to. In *A Letter to his Countrymen* (1834) and *The American Democrat* (1838) and in his later fiction (*Homeward Bound* and *Home as Found* [1838]), he attempted to educate Americans and correct their faults.

Ultimately, he feared the tendency of American society to undermine individuality. Unlike Emerson, Cooper admitted that absolute individuality was impossible because of social and family ties, but he prized the individual above all else: "The pursuit of happiness is inseparable from the claims of individuality. . . . Individuality is the aim of political liberty" (*Democrat*, pp. 174–175).

At the end of his life, Cooper was involved for many years in libel litigation and became the object of virulent criticism in the press. He maintained that he was fighting not for personal gain—though certainly he wanted to vindicate himself—but primarily to protect the rights of the individual. Through all of the attacks on him, Cooper remained an ardent believer in the destiny of his country. In his last novel, the lawyer Dunscomb speculates that America is an important part of God's plan (*Works*, 24: 10). And Cooper expressed his abiding faith in America in the introduction to his proposed *Towns of Manhattan* in the year of his death:

> The increasing and overshadowing power of the nation is of a character so vast, so exciting, so attractive, so well adapted to carry with it popular impulses, that men become proud of the name of American. . . . Every man sees and feels that a state is rapidly advancing to maturity which must reduce the pretentions of even ancient Rome to supremacy, to a secondary place in the estimation of mankind. A century will unquestionably place the United States of America prominently at the head of civilized nations.[29]

Despite his own unhappy experience and through all of his criticism of America, Cooper held to a faith in the American Dream that rivals even Whitman's for its enthusiasm and the grandeur of its vision. His aim was to establish the primacy of the American individual and to protect his rights.[30]

It is clear that Cooper's concern for the individual extended only to the native white American male. Other groups—women, blacks, Indians, Mexicans, impoverished foreign immigrants—somehow do not count in this picture of individual achievement and self-fulfillment. His Leatherstocking hero, despite his moralizing and his sense of honor, is often intolerant of those who differ from him or get in his way, whether they be "mingoes," "Frenchers," or "unmanly" men.[31]

Cooper's attitude toward the Indian provides a good example of his thinking. Although his portrayal of Chingachgook and Natty's predilection for an Indian way of life have earned him a reputation as a friend to the Indian, Cooper does not celebrate the Indian in his novels. Compliments to the Indians are condescending and reveal a smug confidence in white superiority. In *The Last of the Mohicans* Hawkeye says to Chingachgook, "You are a just man, for an Indian!" (*Works*, 2: 29). In *The Prairie* Natty comments that Indians have poor reason, but adds, "still there is a great deal of a man in the Indian" (*Works*, 5: 60). And the epitaph of Chingachgook in *The Pioneers* records: "His faults were those of an Indian, and his virtues those of a man" (*Works*, 4: 473).[32]

Despite passages that seem to lament the fate of the Indian, Cooper accepts the disappearance of the Indian as necessary. In the preface to *The Last of the Mohicans* he speaks of the "seemingly inevitable fate" of the Indian at the advance of civilization (*Works*, 2: v). His patriotic pride places him on the side of his developing country.[33] The Indian and the wilderness were just unhappily in the way of the growing Republic. However picturesque the Indian and his way of life may be in Cooper's novels, they are not important in the advance of American society. In 1831 Cooper wrote to his brother Richard from Europe that he longed for the wilderness (*Letters*, 2: 89), yet it is clear that Cooper's real sentiments more nearly resembled those of the American Cadwallader in *Notions*, who, looking down at New York State, has no regret at the loss of the woods or the Indians but feels only pleasure at the idea of progress:

> We live in the excitement of a rapid and constantly pro-
> gressive condition. The impetus of society is imparted to
> all its members, and we advance because we are not ac-
> customed to stand still.   (*Notions*, 1: 335–337)

Cooper's attitude toward people who stand in the way of or do not coincide with his definition of American individualism points up his failure to see the other as a self. He looked at other people from the point of view of the individual. Cooper is more generous toward the other than Emerson, but his total acceptance of American individualism prevents him from recognizing the claims of the other.

In all of his fiction, Cooper created only one real character: Natty Bumppo, a remarkable creation indeed. Other characters are variations of Natty: Chingachgook is a red Natty; Miles Wallingford, an ultimately socialized Natty; Harvey Birch, Natty with a peddler's pack; and there are a number of sea-going Nattys.[34] All are the same isolated, manly, independent character. Cooper created no other character who is an individual. He has some cleverly drawn character types, but no other kind of character that is a fully developed personality.

Just as Emerson was locked inside the self and refused to acknowledge the demands of the other, Cooper's acceptance of American individualism prevented him from seeing his other characters as individuals. He could imagine the existence of other people, but he saw them as *others*, not as individual selves. And he could not portray as individuals those characters whose individuality he did not recognize. In all of his thirty-two novels, Cooper has given us only one complete character. The others are shadowy nonpersons or grotesques, characters who do not really count in the life of the manly, self-reliant hero who fills the book.

Principal among the others in Cooper's novels are his female characters. The American individualist was, of course, a man, and Cooper, like his creation Natty Bumppo, saw no active role for women in the narcissistic world of the American Dreamer. He portrays women as dependent and selfless, and the woman who attempts to break out of this mold, the independent woman, is a "monster" who "usurps" the qualities of men (*Works*, 10: 114). Cooper did not regard women as real participants in American society. For him, a woman was not an individual who had the right to develop her individuality in the way that a man did. She was not even a person with restricted rights, like a European woman. She was a nonperson, a self-less creature who depended upon the male self for her very existence.

CHAPTER 5

CHAPTER 5

THE MASCULINE SEA: HERMAN MELVILLE

But of all chamber furniture in the world, best calculated to cure a bad temper, and breed a pleasant one, is the sight of a lovely wife.
Herman Melville, *White-Jacket*[1]

Herman Melville surpasses even Cooper in his failure to grant personhood to women: Melville hardly portrays women at all.[2] Most of his stories take place on shipboard, where women are present only in the minds of men as occasional hazy memories of home and fireside. When women do appear in his works, they are either little more than animated memories—traditional images of feminity as conceived by men—or overpowering nightmare figures who threaten the autonomy of the male self.

An early indication of Melville's attitude toward women appears in the essays he wrote for the *Democratic Press and Lansingburgh Advertiser* in 1839, when he was just nineteen. On May 4, one month before he went to sea for the first time, Melville imagined himself the central figure in a faceless group of admiring ladies, paying court to all of them at once. On May 18, he described the pursuit

115

of a mysterious female figure and the romantic meeting with a melancholy and awesome beauty, who *could neither speak nor hear*.[3] What is most remarkable about the attitude reflected in these early essays is not that it is an adolescent conception of women but that it is the same attitude that characterizes all of Melville's subsequent writing: woman is a beautiful abstraction, a background figure to be looked upon and revered but not interacted with as an individual. And the less she is heard from, the better.

Melville's first novels, *Typee* (1846) and *Omoo* (1847), like most of his sea stories, were based on his own experiences. They provide the reader with many descriptions of the native girls of the South Seas, but in no instance does any one of those girls emerge as a person. Whether the original of Fayaway, the narrator's special companion in *Typee*, really existed or not,[4] the character represents only a male fantasy. She is presented wholly from the point of view of the male narrator and only in relation to his needs. All we know of her is that she is beautiful and amenable. The best way to describe the women in these novels is to say that they are part of the scenery.

Melville's opinion of the woman who does not fit into this image of lovely passivity is suggested by his portrayal of Annatoo, the assertive, capable, independent Amazon wife of Samoa in *Mardi* (1849). She is not silent or docile: "Her voice was a park of artillery; her talons a charge of bayonets" (*Writings*, 3: 76). She is also "too ugly to describe" (*Writings*, 3: 99). Yet Annatoo is the only female character in *Mardi* who emerges as a person with any individuality of her own. She is too real for the narrator, however, and Melville soon arranges to have her swept overboard.

The reader next meets Yillah, and the narrative moves from realism to allegory. As a female representation, Yillah is all that Annatoo is not—beautiful, angelic, passive, gentle, and virtually silent. This fantasy figure, who must be revered and protected, represents the ideal feminine to Melville. But Yillah too soon disappears, stolen away by Queen Hautia, an evil temptress who would destroy the narrator if she could.

That Yillah and Hautia are only types is in keeping with the character of the second half of *Mardi*, which is wholly allegorical. But the *type* of woman that Melville uses for each representation is significant. The prototype of evil in this work is an emasculating witch-woman who uses all of her powers to subjugate man to her will. The prototype of good, on the other hand, is a softly yielding, angelic maiden with no will of her own and totally dependent upon man for her protection, even for her existence.

Yillah and Hautia, of course, are intended to represent more than good and bad femininity. The search for Yillah becomes the search for Truth, for the ideal, for the unknown—the same agonizing quest that later proved so tragic for both Ahab and Pierre. Thus, although *Mardi* ostensibly centers around the search for a woman, it is quite different from the European *cherchez-la-femme* tradition, in which the woman is a pivotal character. In *Mardi*, women are not important at all. Yillah is an idea, not a woman.

Redburn (1849) and *White-Jacket* (1850), although more traditional novels than *Mardi*, are no more successful in their portrayal of female characters. In *Redburn* there is mention of a mother and sisters who are worried about the young boy going to sea, and a mysterious lady passenger appears on board the merchant ship. Then the English countryside offers a glimpse of "three adorable charmers," storybook characters who speak not a word but blushingly take their places in the narrator's memory as beautiful English roses. Only Mrs. Danby, the boardinghouse keeper in Liverpool, has the solidity to cast a shadow. As the ship returns to America, Redburn concludes: "Ladies are like creeds; if you can not speak well of them, say nothing" (*Writings*, 4: 262).

Apparently in *White-Jacket*, his next novel, Melville had nothing good to say about the ladies, because women figure not at all there. Of course, no women would be present on a man-of-war, where all of the action takes place, but the conversations and memories of the men are just as void of female presence. The one significant reference to women is a rather remarkable inclusion of wives along with other objects that are pleasant to have around the house. Pretty shells, bowls, merrily bound books, and "a lovely wife" are listed as attractive "chamber furniture" to help put a man in a pleasant mood (*Writings*, 5: 46).

This conception of women as beautiful furniture fit only to decorate the home scene pervades the few references to women in *Moby-Dick*. Again women are left behind when the ship lifts anchor, but this time they appear occasionally in the memories of some of the men. As the search for the white whale intensifies, Starbuck and Ahab think of wife and child at home. But Ahab's quest proves more potent than both their memories, and the images fade. Notably, in this traditional image of woman as representative of home and fireside, the woman is always linked with a child; for Melville, the two were almost synonymous. Just how closely they were related in his mind is apparent in a curious mixed metaphor in which the gentle breezes of the air are first described as soft, fair maidens and then, on the same page, as frolicsome children.[5] For Melville, women are childlike creatures, outside the realm of real action.

Of the two women who appear in person in *Moby-Dick* before the *Pequod* sails, Captain Bildad's sister, Aunt Charity, who bustles on board with items to enhance the religion and comfort of the sailors, remains far away from the reality of the situation. Mrs. Hussey, who runs the boarding house in Nantucket, is a more interesting character, and, with Mrs. Danby in *Redburn* and Annatoo in *Mardi*, is one of the very few realistic female characters in Melville's work. None of them, however, is of marriageable age, and it is significant that, with her housewifely concern (e.g., when Ishmael threatens to break down the door), Mrs. Hussey, like the fading memories of wife and child, is clearly associated with the home.

In all of these novels the principal action takes place at sea, or at least away from home. Given Melville's association of women with the home front, what happens when he attempts to write a novel set at home? The result of such an experiment was the catastrophic *Pierre* (1852). In part, I believe, the novel's failure lies in Melville's absolute inability to portray women.

Lucy, Pierre's fiancée, arrives directly from the pages of conventional romances, which Melville detested. Whether Melville was deliberately mocking the sentimental romance or was simply using its heroine for lack of a better character, Lucy is an unsuccessful creation: she is neither amusing as a figure of ridicule nor believable as a serious character. She is helpless, passive, and wholly dependent upon Pierre. "Fair of face, blue-eyed, and golden haired" (*Writings*, 7: 33), she has no more substance than the angels with which she is compared. Pierre thinks "one husbandly embrace would break her airy zone, and she exhale upward to that heaven whence she hath hither come" (*Writings*, 7: 39, 58).

The insipid and rather characterless sweetness of Lucy does not hold the reader's interest, and one cannot help but feel secretly glad when Pierre turns from her to Isabel, who promises to be more interesting. Melville makes a great deal of the difference between the two characters, and certainly in the context of his symbolic meaning they are different. Pierre contrasts the "all-understood blue eyes of Lucy" with the "inscrutable dark glance of Isabel" (*Writings*, 7: 129). In the antithetical concepts represented by the two girls, Melville suggests the same polarity that in *Moby-Dick* he described as the lee shore and landlessness. The port is "safety, comfort, hearthstone, support, warm blankets, friends," as opposed to landlessness: "all deep, earnest thinking is but the intrepid effort of the soul to keep the open independence of her sea. . . . in landlessness alone resides the highest truth" (*Moby-Dick*, pp. 97–98). In *Pierre* Lucy represents the safe, known, everyday "inland" peace and "blessed sereneness" of "truth-blind" Saddle Meadows. When Pierre meets Isabel, however, he begins to probe and question and resolves to forsake Lucy and the "green, gentle, and most docile earth" to embark with Isabel upon the "appalling ocean" of the unknown (*Moby-Dick*, p. 236).[6] "Lucy or God?" he asks himself (*Writings*, 7: 181), and Melville expresses the choice in the image of the catnip and the amaranth—"man's earthly household peace, and the ever-encroaching appetite for God" (*Writings*, 7: 344–345).[7] Pierre, in his search for the truth associated with Isabel, sees himself as a "sky-assaulting" Titan (*Writings*, 7: 347) or a "heavenly chronometer," whose woe is brought about because he conducts himself according to God's time instead of local time (*Writings*, 7: 212).[8]

Despite this difference in symbolic meaning, there is no difference between Isabel and Lucy as fictional characters; both are cast from the same mold. Unlike the "dark ladies" in Hawthorne's fiction, who have a personality and strength of character that the "fair maidens" do not, Melville's dark lady is no different from his fair maiden. Both are conventional heroines—beautiful, awe-inspiring, and passively dependent upon the robust strength of the male protagonist.

At first Isabel tells Pierre that he makes her feel strong: "Thy catching nobleness unsexes me, my brother; and now I know that in her most exalted moment, then woman no more feels the twin-born softness of her breasts, but feels chain-armour palpitating there!" (*Writings*, 7: 160). This echo of Lady Macbeth notwithstanding, Melville fails to endow Isabel with any strength or independence. Isabel clings to Pierre, to whom she at times seems imperious and electrical but more often reflects a sweet simplicity and a melting, feminine demureness (*Writings*, 7: 151–152). Moreover, although she is older than Pierre, he notes the "artless infantileness of her face" and her "angelic childlikeness" (*Writings*, 7: 140). She begs him to take care of her, and he promises to handle her as gently as an artisan treats fragile filigree work (*Writings*, 7: 189). When they go off together, whatever strength she may have possessed disappears altogether, and she depends wholly on Pierre. She cannot even give guitar lessons and in this respect is more helpless even than Lucy, who attempts to support herself by sketching. Yet Pierre revels in her helplessness: "Thy sweet ignorance is all transporting to me! my sweet, my sweet!—dear, divine girl!" (*Writings*, 7: 334).

Significantly, Melville associates ignorance, weakness, and helplessness with divinity. Pierre's attitude toward both

Isabel and Lucy is reverential. Lucy is associated with the purity of heaven, and Isabel seems "made of that fine, unshared stuff of which God makes his seraphim" (*Writings*, 7: 191). To reverence, however, is to create a distance, to see as an image or symbol rather than as a real person. By making reverential figures of Lucy and Isabel, Melville removes them from the sphere of action. They are only reflectors of Pierre's conflicting thoughts. And Melville makes it clear that they have neither will nor personality. Lucy's one decisive action—to leave her family and go to Pierre—arises from a total abdication of personality. She can exist only in him: "How could I any way *be*, my Pierre, if not in thee?" (*Writings*, 7: 310). For her, Pierre is "all the universe" (*Writings*, 7: 311). Given Mrs. Glendinning's earlier fear of the strength of dark-eyed women (*Writings*, 7: 20), one might have expected Isabel to be more assertive, yet she is as will-less as Lucy. She is "all plastic" in Pierre's hand, she admits (*Writings*, 7: 189). His very thoughts determine her actions: "Thy hand is the caster's ladle, Pierre, which holds me entirely fluid" (*Writings*, 7: 324).

Not only are these two female characters will-less; they are not even conceived as fully adult figures. Both Lucy and Isabel are described throughout the novel as "girls," never as women. Pierre moves from spirited boyhood to tortured maturity in the course of the novel, but Lucy and Isabel seem frozen in girlhood. Despite her difficult life, Isabel remains a girl to the end. And Lucy's agonizing experience after Pierre's desertion effects no maturation but only marbleizes her in her maidenhood.[9]

There are hints early in *Pierre* that Isabel is going to be a strong, magnificent woman in the tradition of Hawthorne's Miriam, Zenobia, or Hester Prynne. But once Isabel has served her initial purpose in the novel (it is her story that disrupts Pierre's complacency and causes him to begin to question), Melville seems to lose interest in her. Pierre's conflict takes over, and Lucy and Isabel become mere shadow figures, important only for the ideas they represent. Although they figure prominently in the novel, they have no more substance than the female background figures of Melville's other novels.

The other important female character in *Pierre* is not content to remain in the background. From the beginning, Pierre's mother, Mary Glendinning, is hard at work, attempting to control and direct her son's life. Pierre has always been a very "docile" boy (*Writings*, 7: 16), and so long as life proceeds according to her wishes, Mrs. Glendinning is pleasant enough. But when Pierre goes against his mother's will, she reacts violently: "I am no lady now," she tells the Reverend Falsgrave, "but something deeper,—a woman!—an outraged and pride-poisoned woman!" (*Writings*, 7: 194). Melville's portrayal of Pierre's mother gives us some idea of what he believes a "woman" to be. He does not consider Mrs. Glendinning really feminine; she has a "reserved strength and masculineness" in her character (*Writings*, 7: 180).

In Melville's works the woman who is not weak and properly dependent is a threat to the free exercise of the male will. A woman like Mrs. Glendinning is not satisfied unless she possesses a direct "influencing and practical sorcery" over a man's soul (*Writings*, 7: 16). To Melville, the independent, assertive woman is always a kind of Hautia, a viper woman who victimizes men. "Such venom in such beauty," one character observes of Mrs. Glendinning, and she is variously described as "martial," "fierce," "strong and haughty," "proud," and "triumphant" (*Writings*, 7: 200, 20, 195, 89). Early in the novel, when Mrs. Glendinning observes that Lucy lacks the intellectual vigor that she herself possesses, Melville points out that Mrs. Glendinning's intelligence does not render her superior to Lucy. Angels do not exhibit vigor, he says; vigor means ambition, which is earthly (*Writings*, 7: 59). For Melville, angel-maidens were safer than real women, and he was unable to conceive of an attractive female character who was also strong and independent.

At the beginning of the novel, however, even Mrs. Glendinning assumes the role of a fair maiden. Both Pierre and Melville are aware of her strength, but they seem to prefer the illusion that she too is a delicate creature like Lucy. Of particular significance is the relationship between Pierre and his mother; certainly it is a peculiar one. They live in a state of perpetual courtship, with Pierre acting the jealous and ever-solicitous suitor, while his youthful mother plays the coy maiden. Melville portrays this relationship as preferable to actual courtship, because the happiness of this mock courtship never has to be destroyed by marriage. Their bliss will not be "limited in duration by that climax which is so fatal to ordinary love" (*Writings*, 7: 21).

Melville's portrayal of women in his short fiction is no different from that in his novels: women are either abstractions or nonmarriageable, or they do not appear at all. The most realistically portrayed woman in Melville's short fiction is Hunilla, the Chola widow in "The Encantadas." But Hunilla is half Indian and thus does not qualify as a heroine in a nineteenth-century novel. That Melville was able to portray her realistically only points up his inability to see potentially marriageable white women as persons.

In "The Tartarus of Maids" Melville gives us a sympathetic portrayal of the hard-worked New England mill girls. The story is unusual in that it appeared at a time when the figure of the woman factory worker was seldom seen in American fiction. However, Melville does not give these characters the individuality of the Chola widow. The story is told metaphorically; the girls are abstract images of robotlike drudgery in an inferno of machines. This work counterpoints "The Paradise of Bachelors," which portrays an ideal dinner at the Temple Bar in London, where congenial bachelors eat and drink heartily without wives and children to worry about:

> It was the very perfection of quiet absorption of good living, good drinking, good feeling, and good talk. We were a band of brothers. Comfort—fraternal, household comfort, was the grand trait of the affair. Also, you would plainly see that these easy-hearted men had no wives or children to give an anxious thought.

The pale, sickly mill maids, on the other hand, work a twelve-hour day, six days a week. Just as only bachelors can live at the Temple, only maids can work in the paper mill: "For our factory here," says the proprietor of the hellish mill, "we will not have married women."[10] Melville seems to be saying that only marriage can save these maids from the living death of the nightmare world of the mill. But by pairing "The Paradise of Bachelors" with "The Tartarus of Maids," Melville clearly implies that such salvation for the women would mean the destruction of the carefree life of the men.

In all of his work Melville prefers the woman who is an abstract, distant figure to the real flesh-and-blood person with whom men must interact. This attitude is made explicit in his short story "The Piazza" (1856). As the narrator sits on his piazza and looks up at a strange light high up on the mountainside, he imagines a beautiful fairy queen up there. When he leaves his piazza one day and climbs the mountain, he finds only a pale-cheeked, common girl behind a fly-specked window—a real girl with real sorrows. He regrets that he ever left his piazza, preferring the fairy queen who exists *only in his mind* and requires no painful involvement to the real girl with her sad story. Back on the piazza, "the scenery is magical—the illusion so complete." Looking up at the "golden window," he thinks, "How far from me the weary face behind it."[11] From a distance, woman can be a fairy queen who demands no commitment; up close, woman is a real person with human concerns.

Perhaps this attitude explains why in Melville's fiction the ideal feminine is not the wife and mother but the unreal and rather hazy figure of prenuptial maidenhood. Mrs. Glendinning and Annatoo are the most realistic of Melville's novelistic portrayals of women, but it is clear that mother and wife are too real for the author. The fair maiden, however, is an image. Since she exists only in the man's mind, she can make no demands on him. The fair maiden asks only that he reverence and protect her—a plea that does not threaten the freedom of the self but in fact reinforces its separateness.

If Melville was not able to create fully drawn female characters, he was able to portray the individual man. In his vision
of the anguished struggle of the individual man to assert the
importance and separateness of the self lies his strength and
power. Thus Ahab's defiance of the lightning is an assertion
of his own individuality:

> I own thy speechless, placeless power; but to the last gasp
> of my earthquake life will dispute its unconditional, un-
> integral mastery in me. In the midst of the personified
> impersonal, a personality stands here.
>
> *(Moby-Dick, pp. 416–417)*

In order to understand Melville's attitude toward his woman
characters, we must understand his portrayal of men. What
was his conception of the individual man, and how did it affect
his conception of other people and, ultimately, of women?

Melville did not consider himself a Transcendentalist.
He criticized Emerson's narrowness and easy optimism and
satirized his philosophy.[12] Yet he admired Emerson's probing
mind and described him as a great man. "I love all men who
dive," Melville wrote when he first heard Emerson speak in
1849.[13] In Melville's terminology, the diver is the seeker—
Taji, Ahab, Pierre—the uncommon man who tears the mask
or veil from the visible world and seeks Truth. The principal
difference between Melville and Emerson is that Emerson assumed the success of the seeker; Melville, on the other hand,
was aware of the possibility of failure and defeat. For Melville, the truth can never wholly be revealed. He writes of
Pierre: "The more and more that he wrote, and the deeper
that he dived, Pierre saw the everlasting elusiveness of Truth"
(*Writings*, 7: 339). Melville's three seekers assert their individuality and shout out their defiance, but in each case the quest
ends in death and destruction.

Although Melville did not accept the Transcendentalists'
optimism, he nevertheless insisted upon the necessity of individual assertion. "Better to sink in boundless depths, than

float on vulgar shoals," he advises in *Mardi* (*Writings*, 3: 557). Pierre sees himself as a Titan: "whoso storms the sky gives best proof he came from thither! But whatso crawls contented in the moat before that crystal fort, shows it was born within that slime, and there forever will abide" (*Writings*, 7: 347). And in this ode to Bulkington in *Moby-Dick*, Melville describes the situation of the seeker:

> [A]ll deep, earnest thinking is but the intrepid effort of the soul to keep the independence of her sea; while the wildest winds of heaven and earth conspire to cast her on the treacherous, slavish shore.
>
> But as in landlessness alone resides the highest truth, shoreless, indefinite as God—so, better is it to perish in that howling infinite, than be ingloriously dashed upon the lee, even if that were safety! For worm-like, then, oh! who would craven crawl to land! (*Moby-Dick*, pp. 97–98)

For Melville, the uncommon seeker is somehow victorious even in defeat. "Failure," he said, "is the true test of greatness."[14]

If Melville can insist upon individual endeavor even though he does not expect success, it is because, although he does not share Emerson's optimism, he does share certain aspects of Emerson's view of man. The failure that Melville foresees is due not to any flaws or limitations in the individual but to the restrictions of the outside world. Melville regards the individual as inherently omnipotent. It is the forces external to the individual—natural powers and the infringements of other people—that threaten to bring him down. Thus Pierre knows that he is great, but his greatness is hamstrung by circumstances: "He seemed gifted with loftiness, merely that it might be dragged down to the mud" (*Writings*, 7: 339). Although Melville speaks of Ahab's "fatal pride," he does not see this as a reason for Ahab's failure in the Greek sense, and he would not wish Ahab to be without it. Ahab fails because the natural powers of the universe are too much for him. And it is a magnificent failure. His pride is fatal only in that without it he would not have had the uncommon aspirations that led to his defeat.

Implicit in Melville's belief in the importance of the individual is the Emersonian belief in the great man or hero. In *Moby Dick* Melville describes such a heroic figure: audacious and daring, the great man thinks untraditionally and independently (*Moby-Dick*, p. 71). Melville admired the man whose superior qualities and powerful self-assertion thrust him above the herd of common men. In *White-Jacket* Melville wrote that one hero like Nelson or Wellington can lead a whole fleet of men just as one numeral can make an immense arithmetical sum before a lot of ciphers. "One large brain and one large heart have virtue sufficient to magnetize a whole fleet or an army" (*Writings*, 5: 112).

Like the Emersonian man, Melville's great man or seeker is a solitary figure. The search for Truth is an insulating one, says Melville in *Pierre*; it cuts off the seeker from other people (*Writings*, 7: 165–166). When Pierre learns Isabel's secret, he knows that he is alone: "Then he staggered back upon himself, and only found support in himself" (*Writings*, 7: 89). Taji rejects the human fellowship of Serenia to pursue his quest alone. And Ahab stands alone and inaccessible (*Moby-Dick*, p. 134). What Melville advocates is the utmost in self-reliance: "Those who boldly launch," he wrote in *Mardi*, "cast off all cables; and turning from the common breeze, that's fair for all, with their own breath, fill their own sails" (*Writings*, 3: 556).

All of Melville's protagonists are self-propelling, solitary men. Although in *Moby-Dick* there are indications, particularly in "The Monkey-rope" chapter, that Ishmael would like to form a closer tie with humankind, they seem to represent an impossible longing rather than a real possibility. Despite the association he establishes with Queequeg at the beginning of the book, at the end all that is left of it is Queequeg's coffin, and Ishmael is again an orphan alone on the sea.

The narrator of *Moby-Dick* is not the only "Ishmael" in Melville's work. Redburn feels himself to be "a sort of

Ishmael in the ship, without a single friend or companion"
(*Writings*, 4: 62). Pierre feels himself to be an "infant Ishmael"
in the desert (*Writings*, 7: 89). In fact, all of Melville's protagonists are Ishmaels who live apart from society and follow
the dictates of the individual will. In *The Confidence Man* the
cynical Missourian is called an Ishmael by the Cosmopolitan,
who pretends to come as an "ambassador from the human
race" (*Confidence Man*, p. 120). The fact that this ambassador
is a confidence man tells us that the Missourian is right to remain aloof from the human race—to trust no one but himself. For Melville, the ideal man is as carefully insulated from
the outside world as a whale is by his blubber:

> [H]erein we see the rare virtue of a strong individual vi-
> tality, and the rare virtue of thick walls, and the rare vir-
> tue of interior spaciousness. Oh man! admire and model
> thyself after the whale! Do thou, too, remain warm
> among ice. Do thou, too, live in this world without
> being of it. . . . Like the great dome of St. Peter's, and
> like the great whale, retain, O man! in all seasons a tem-
> perature of thine own.   (*Moby-Dick*, p. 261)

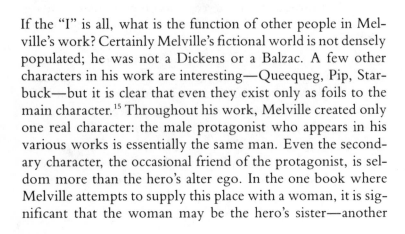

If the "I" is all, what is the function of other people in Melville's work? Certainly Melville's fictional world is not densely
populated; he was not a Dickens or a Balzac. A few other
characters in his work are interesting—Queequeg, Pip, Starbuck—but it is clear that even they exist only as foils to the
main character.[15] Throughout his work, Melville created only
one real character: the male protagonist who appears in his
various works is essentially the same man. Even the secondary character, the occasional friend of the protagonist, is seldom more than the hero's alter ego. In the one book where
Melville attempts to supply this place with a woman, it is significant that the woman may be the hero's sister—another

form of alter ego. In *Moby-Dick*, where Melville has separated the narrator from his isolated seeker, Ahab seems to represent the more extreme alter ego of Ishmael, who, by the name he assumes, reveals his own isolation.

Moreover, as Raymond Weaver pointed out, Melville's hero is always himself.[16] One should not make the mistake, as Weaver did, of reading Melville's work as autobiography, however; not all of the events that befall Melville's heroes happened to Melville himself. His male protagonists constitute a persona, a projection of Melville's conception of himself. They represent a certain personality and set of ideas and attitudes with which Melville identified. He could realistically portray only one type of character: the character whose sympathies coincided with his own.

Like the American Narcissus, Melville's protagonist exists in a vacuum. He has no permanent relationships that tie him to other people. It is significant that there are no children in Melville's books, children being the most binding of human ties. Pierre consciously severs all human bonds, and Ahab curses the circumstance that makes him dependent upon another human being:

> Oh Life! Here I am, proud as a Greek God, and yet standing debtor to this blockhead for a bone to stand on! Cursed be that mortal interdebtedness which will not do away with ledgers. I would be free as air; and I'm down on the whole world's books. (*Moby-Dick*, pp. 391–392)

Melville himself, of course, did not live in a vacuum. He maintained close ties with his large family—mother, sisters, brothers, uncles, and cousins. He was also married and by 1855 the father of four children. While Melville was writing his novels, his house was always overflowing with relatives, in-laws, and friends as visitors and permanent residents. But, although surrounded by people, he saw himself as being alone. Like Pierre in a city of thousands, he was as "solitary as at the Pole" (*Writings*, 7: 338). In a letter to Hawthorne in

1851, Melville described the man who seeks the truth as a "sovereign nature in himself." Such men are like the "unencumbered travelers in Europe; they cross the frontiers into Eternity with nothing but a carpet bag—that is to say the Ego" (*Letters*, pp. 124–125). (It is interesting that when Melville traveled to the Holy Land in 1856, he took with him only a carpet bag.)[17] In another letter to Hawthorne, he pictured himself and Hawthorne as God's solitary outposts in the wilderness, fighting off Indians and mosquitoes—the dangers and annoyances that threaten the sovereignty of the self (*Letters*, pp. 132–133).

In attempting to assert the independence of the self, Melville forfeited any real human involvement. As we shall see, his relationship with his wife was not a reciprocal one. And, although one of the recurring agonies of his life was the great need he felt for a "true friend," Melville apparently never found the friendship he sought. Perhaps one reason for his failure is that his cry for friendship was like Thoreau's: he wanted a friend who would be a reflection of himself.

The closest Melville came to finding a true friend was Hawthorne. Yet it is clear from Melville's letters that what he demanded from Hawthorne—absolute sympathy and unqualified devotion—Hawthorne could never give. In June 1851 he asked pardon for "this speaking all about myself,— for if I *say* so much on that head, be sure all the rest of the world are thinking about themselves ten times as much" (*Letters*, pp. 132–133). And in another letter the same month, he admitted:

> I talk all about myself, and this is selfishness and egotism. Granted. But how help it? I am writing to you; I know little about you, but something about myself. So I write about myself,—at least, to you. Don't trouble yourself, though, about writing; and don't trouble yourself about talking. I will do all the writing and visiting and talking myself. (*Letters*, p. 129)

A friendship that assumes the passivity of the friend in this way is hardly a real friendship. In fact, Melville liked to think of himself and Hawthorne not as two separate people but as one, or, as he said later in 1851, two parts of the same Godhead (*Letters*, p. 142).

Melville's relationship with his four children was apparently also marred by his self-absorption. His granddaughter Eleanor wrote in her biography of him that he once tormented his daughter Frances so relentlessly about a minor incident that she shrank from his sight. She also described how, when money was tight, there was often only bread and tea for supper because Melville's self-indulgence had led him to spend what money they had on *objets d'art* for himself (principally plaster busts, which his daughters particularly resented because they had to dust them). His daughter complained that he thought nothing of waking her at 2 A.M. to help read proofs of his book, and she spoke derisively of the way her father used to stride about reciting verses for the approbation of his captive wife and daughters—sadly then his only audience.[18] Perhaps most damning is the report that for birthday and Christmas gifts, Melville gave his wife and children books that only he wanted to read.[19] Melville's oldest son, Malcolm, committed suicide at the age of eighteen. Two years later, his younger son, Stanwix, left home for good. Although it is impossible to form any conclusions about the cause of these two events, there is no evidence that Melville's relationship with his sons was a close one.

The self-assertive individual must always put himself first. As Melville wrote in *Clarel* (1876):

> My kin—I blame them not at heart—
> Would have me act some routine part,
> Subserving family, and dreams
> Alien to me—illusive schemes.

For Melville, the claims of the other were always subordinated to the claims of the self.

As a writer, Melville was able to use this self-assertion to

create some of the most powerful works in American literature dealing with the struggle of the individual man. But it is
also this self-assertion that prevented him from giving sali-
ence to other characters in his works, particularly women.

What was the relationship between Melville's attitude toward
the self and toward the individualism of his contemporaries?
The denial and defiance in Melville's works do not represent a
rejection of American individualism; rather, they reflect the
same rejection of external limitations that has always characterized the American individualist. Melville's protagonist de-
fiantly rejects authority, tradition, and family ties. As Richard
Chase has pointed out, even *Moby-Dick*, which seems so emphatic in its denial, does not reject the economic and cultural
principles on which the whaling industry was based.[20] Melville accepted the premises of the American myth: individual
effort and competition. Charles Haberstroh has identified the
pressures of Melville's (male) achievement-oriented family as
the cause for his need to play the male role of dominance.[21]
However, the problem is deeper than a familial one. Rather,
the pressures of his family for what Haberstroh calls "male
aggressiveness and worldly success" were simply products of
the prevailing American culture.

Although Melville criticized certain abuses in American
political and social life (e.g., *Writings*, 3: 469–472, 512–514,
524–529) and chastised "the sophomorean pride of Americans as a new and prosperous country,"[22] he shared the Transcendentalists' belief in the superiority and greatness of the
United States. In *Mardi* he described Americans as a "great
and glorious people" and America as the "best and happiest
land under the sun" (*Writings*, 3: 528). It is a "noble land,"
"promising as the morning," a star that inspires all other
lands (*Writings*, 3: 472, 542). America, in *Redburn*, is the hope
of the world:

Not a paradise . . . but to be made so, at God's good pleasure, and in the fullness and mellowness of time. The seed is sown, and the harvest must come, and our children's children, on the world's jubilee morning, shall all go with their sickles to the reaping. . . . (*Writings*, 4: 169)

In "Hawthorne and His Mosses," Melville applied his theory of the great man and his belief in American individualism to the American writer. Sounding rather like Emerson, he urged the American writer not to imitate British or European literature but to be original: "It is better to fail in originality, than to succeed in imitation." Like the Melville protagonist, the writer should test his powers to the utmost and be guided by his native tendencies. In *Mardi* Melville had exhorted the writer to follow his own "crowned and sceptered instinct" (*Writings*, 3: 597). In "Hawthorne and His Mosses" he summarized his advice to the writer this way: "Let him write like a man, for then he will be sure to write like an American."[23] Aside from the question of what such a prescription means for the writing aspirations of American women, this statement illustrates the close affinity that Melville felt with the self-reliant, self-assertive, and, above all, manly American cultural hero.

Melville's belief in the great man and his hero-worship were, like Emerson's and the American Dreamer's, based on a democratic belief in the potential greatness of all men. As Melville explains in *Moby-Dick*:

[M]an, in the ideal, is so noble and so sparkling, such a grand and glowing creature, that over any ignominious blemish in him all his fellows should run to throw their costliest robes. The immaculate manliness . . . this august dignity . . . is not the dignity of kings and robes, but that abounding . . . democratic dignity which, on all hands, radiates without end from God; Himself! The great God absolute! The centre and circumference of

> all democracy! His omnipresence, our divine equality!
> (*Moby-Dick*, p. 104)

Not only can all men be great, but—and here Melville was closest to Emerson—all men are in fact gods. In 1846 Melville received a *New Testament and Psalms* from his Aunt Jean Melville and copied onto the front cover a statement that he underlined in part: "He [man] stands *firm to his point; he goes on his way inflexibly*; and while he exalts the lower to himself, . . . he, on the other hand, in no wise conceals his divine origin; he dares to equal himself with God; nay to declare that he is God."[24] This god-man image appears often in Melville's writings. If Melville's protagonist is defiant, self-reliant, and alone, it is because Melville sees him as a god or demigod who must assert his divinity before he perishes. Like a god, the Melville protagonist is the creator of his own universe. In *Mardi* Melville observes that no one can recall when he was not: "To ourselves, we all seem coeval with creation" (*Writings*, 3: 12). And in *White-Jacket* he declares that we all mold the world to suit ourselves: "We are precisely what we worship. Ourselves are Fate" (*Writings*, 5: 320–321). We can rely on no one: "Each man must be his own savior" (*Writings*, 5: 399).

If, in Melville's scheme of things, everything revolves around self, what of Melville's seeker, the man who "dives"? Must he not go out of himself to seek the truth? Even here, Melville looks to the self. What Melville means by the ultimate truth is to be found in the individual. The seeker dives down into the depths of his own soul, for there lies the answer to all he seeks. Water, which Melville uses so often in speaking of the truth seeker, has another quality besides its landlessness and boundless depths. It is a *reflector*:

> And still deeper the meaning of that story of Narcissus, who because he could not grasp the tormenting, mild image he saw in the fountain, plunged into it and was drowned. But that same image, we ourselves see in all

rivers and oceans. It is the image of the ungraspable phantom of life; and this is the key to it all.

(*Moby-Dick*, pp. 12–14)

What we see, what Narcissus saw, is an image of the self—for
Melville, "the key to it all." Pierre dives down to the bottom
of his soul (*Writings*, 7: 49, 284–285). Ahab pursues a white
whale that represents all of his own frustrations (*Moby-Dick*,
p. 160). Like Emerson, for whom the Universal Being was
within, Melville's quest for Truth is a quest for self.

Critics have been eager to find some kind of sexual explanation for Melville's unsuccessful portrayal of women—
sexual inadequacy, disillusionment with sex, distaste for sex,
homosexuality.[25] Whether any of these explanations is valid
or not (and there is no substantial evidence to support any
one of them), Melville's primary reason for keeping women
in the background, I believe, was his overwhelming concern
to preserve the inviolability of the self. In an interesting poem
written after his 1856–1857 trip to Europe and the Levant,
Melville expresses the annoyance that he felt because sex interfered with the development of the self. "After the Pleasure Party" describes an apparently sexual encounter with a
woman in Italy. The next morning the narrator is angered
that such interaction should be necessary; it interferes with
his higher aspirations. He concludes that both sexes should be
joined in one being. Then there would be no loss of selfhood.
It is significant that this poem, the most explicitly sexual description in Melville's work, emphasizes neither the joy and
passion of two people coming together nor a disgust with sex
or a distaste for women as sexual partners. Rather, it expresses a fear that human interaction threatens the integrity of
the self, and it suggests an intense need to keep the self intact:

> Could I remake me or set free
> This sexless bound, in sex, then plunge
> Deeper than Sappho, in a lunge
> Piercing Pan's paramount mystery! . . .

> Why has thou made us but in halves—
> Co-relatives? This makes us slaves.[26]

In order better to understand the attitude toward women expressed in Melville's work and its relation to his independent
stance, we must look at Melville's relationships with the real
women in his life. Contrary to the women in his fiction—the
passive fantasy figures who exist only as images in the male
mind—the women in Melville's life were very real. According to the American myth, which, as we have seen, Melville
had internalized, the male individualist was autonomous and
all-powerful and the female was the dependent cipher that
Melville portrayed in his fiction. For Melville, it was impossible to conform the reality to the myth—and apparently
equally impossible to accept the failure of the myth. Melville's belief in the American myth determined his attitude toward others. Discrepancies between the reality and the idea
did not lead Melville to re-examine his beliefs; rather, like the
American Narcissus, he clung to the persona that he had created for himself. A close look at his relationship with his
mother, wife, and sisters will help us to see how the myth
failed for him and will enable us to trace the origins of his
increasingly obsessive self-assertion.

Melville's mother, Maria Gansevoort Melville, provided
the basis for the character of Mary Glendinning, who, as
Raymond Weaver points out, owes more than her initials to
Melville's mother.[27] A strong, competent, and very proud
woman left in poverty by her husband's bankruptcy and subsequent death in 1832, she raised her eight children through
her own perseverance.[28] Despite her reduced circumstances,
she continued to hold her head high, and throughout her long
life she was characterized by a haughty family pride. Melville's
granddaughter, Eleanor Metcalf, says that her mother remembered Maria Melville as having a "stern, uncompromising disposition." She exacted unquestioning obedience from

her children, and Metcalf tells how, when the children were young and Maria wanted to take a nap, she would make them all sit quietly on stools around her bed so that she would know where they were.[29]

As a child, Herman was described by his father as a very "docile" boy—like Pierre (*Log*, 1: 25). Metcalf also suggests that Melville's mother was instrumental in bringing about his marriage to Elizabeth Shaw in 1847.[30] Considering the friendship between Mrs. Melville and Judge Shaw and the socially desirable position of the Shaw family, this is not unlikely. Maria Melville's influence did not end with her son's marriage. For years she lived with Melville and his wife, and when she was there, she ran the household.

Elizabeth Shaw Melville was not an assertive, capable individual like her mother-in-law. Melville's sister, Augusta, called her "kind Lizzie," and kindness seems to have been her most outstanding characteristic.[31] Melville's cousin Catherine Gansevoort wrote in 1867 that, as a parent, Lizzie was "thoroughly good but inefficient" (*Log*, 2: 691). She was also an inefficient housekeeper, although she had no other aspirations. Her granddaughter says of Elizabeth that she was "domestic in her tastes without proficiency."[32] When the Melvilles moved into Arrowhead, the farm in the Berkshires, Melville's mother and sisters came to show Lizzie how to keep house.[33]

If Lizzie's talents were not domestic, neither were they intellectual. Melville wrote to his brother-in-law, John Hoadley, in 1877, that Lizzie found his philosophy incomprehensible.[34] And Melville's grandniece reported that her mother, Maria Morewood, had said that Melville "was always challenging Elizabeth, that she did not understand it." Such challenging, she added, "was an intellectual need of Herman's."[35]

Elizabeth's letters to her mother reveal her to have been a person with limited interests and a perpetual girlishness in her tastes. For example, it gave her a great deal of pleasure as a young wife to go to a party where she "passed off for *Miss* Melville, and as such was quite a belle!" (*Log*, 1: 271). She gallantly says in 1847 and 1848 that she cares little that she has had to curtail parties and outings because of Herman's writ-ing.[36] Yet a few years later, when thanking her mother for the gift of a scarf, she adds bitterly that she will have no oppor-tunity to wear it: "I am almost sorry you did not keep it for yourself for it does not seem to me as if I should ever wear it."[37] One is tempted to conclude that Elizabeth's greatest in-terest in life was clothes. When Melville was ill and she was finally finished with childbearing, she indulged herself in fan-ciful costumes for costume picnics in the Berkshires. In later life, when her daughters were growing up, she spent a great deal of time dressmaking. In 1879 Melville wrote to his cousin that Lizzie and the girls devoted themselves to "the shrine of fashion," and a few years later Elizabeth reported that "we are dressmaking with all our might."[38]

Hardly the wife for Herman Melville, one might say. And, indeed, Lizzie has been generally faulted by Melville's biographers for her presumed shortcomings. Lewis Mum-ford regrets that she lacked Melville's "ranting high spirits" and was not his intellectual equal, as Sophia Peabody was Hawthorne's.[39] Raymond Weaver blames Lizzie for Melville's emotional crisis, citing her limitations of piety and lack of imagination (*JUS*, p. xvi). Both men agree that Melville idealized Lizzie and that after marriage, when he discov-ered her limitations, he was disappointed and disillusioned.[40] It is generally believed that Melville entered into marriage with high expectations. His cousin Anne Marie Priscilla Mel-ville describes his and Lizzie's love on their wedding day as so "ethereal" that it "bore them upward, toward a *heavenly* paradise."[41] And this description certainly is consistent with Pierre's early attitude toward marriage with Lucy.

It is significant that no one has asked what *Lizzie's* feel-ings were after her marriage. If anyone was disillusioned by marriage, it must have been she. In 1847 she married an adventurous and successful young author straight from an island paradise, but in just a few years she found herself liv-ing with a moody, dissatisfied, self-centered, debt-ridden, middle-aged hypochondriac. Forced to forgo the pleasure she took in social activities, she spent the first year of marriage copying her husband's seemingly interminable and, to her, incomprehensible manuscript (*Mardi*). For years she had to share her husband's attentions with a mother-in-law and four sisters-in-law. Furthermore, unlike Sophia Hawthorne, who was her husband's favorite companion, Elizabeth Melville was seldom included in her husband's activities: he traveled without her, he visited Hawthorne without her, he went mountain climbing without her, and he joined in Sarah Morewood's Berkshire parties without her.

It is of course impossible to know Melville's true attitude toward his wife or the kind of relationship they had. Melville burned all but one of their letters along with most other papers in his possession before he left Arrowhead in 1862. He had little to say about Elizabeth in his correspondence with others and neither Melville nor his wife kept a journal, except for the travel diaries Melville kept when he was away from home. His one surviving letter to his wife was written in 1861, when he was in Washington seeking a consulship. Although it reveals none of the passion of Hawthorne's letters to Sophia, it is certainly a friendly letter (*Letters*, pp. 209–210). It is known that Lizzie's family tried to obtain a legal separation for her in 1867 because she and they "were convinced that her husband is insane," but nothing ever came of the attempt.[42] Lizzie remained loyal to him throughout their married life, and his final collection of poetry, *Weeds and Wildings Chiefly: With a Rose or Two*, was affectionately dedicated to her, recalling the days at Arrowhead and a four-leaf clover he found on their wedding day.

The paucity of information makes it impossible to draw any significant conclusions about Elizabeth Melville's relationship to Melville's thinking and writing. However, what evidence there is does not support the claim that Melville became disillusioned by the limitations of his wife. Disillusionment implies a prior misconception, but Melville must have known Elizabeth's general character before he married her, though he may not have known her sexual capacities. Her family had long been friendly with the Melvilles, and Elizabeth had visited with Melville's sisters many times, often spending several weeks at Melville's home.[43] If Lizzie was conventionally girlish and "jejune," as Lewis Mumford maintains,[44] this was just what Melville wanted in a wife. In all of his writings, the ideal woman is weak and ignorant. Melville never expected a wife who was his equal in intelligence or emotional vigor. He regarded such women as masculine and a threat to the male ego. His comments on one of the more intellectual and certainly one of the most spirited women of his day show how he felt about such women. In an 1849 letter to a friend he mentioned the British actress Fanny Kemble, whose husband, Pierce Butler, was seeking a divorce because of her independent behavior: "She's so unfemininely masculine that had she not, on unimpeckable [sic] authority, borne children, I should be curious to learn the result of a surgical examination of her person in private. The Lord help Butler. . . . I marvel not he seeks being amputated off from his matrimonial half" (*Letters*, pp. 77–78).[45]

Melville maintained a very rigid conception of what a woman should be. In 1851 he advised his friend Sarah Morewood not to read *Moby-Dick* because it was not for women— "gentle fastidious people."[46] He was amazed when Sophia Hawthorne wrote to say that she had liked it (*Log*, 1: 443–444). Melville always regarded the *true* woman as a limited creature of feeling who lacked the intellectual powers of a man. When he read Madame de Stael's *Germany* in 1862, he was surprised to find "such penetration of understanding in a woman, who at the same time possesses so femininely emotional a nature" (*Log*, 2: 651).

Given Melville's attitude toward women, however, I believe that Lizzie was somehow disappointing to him after marriage. The disillusionment came not because she was *less* than he expected but because she was *more*. Melville conceived of a woman as an image. Fayaway, Yillah, Lucy, Isabel—none of these women exists in reality. I suspect that what Melville found disillusioning about Lizzie was that she was not only an image. So long as a woman remains only an image, she exists *only* for the man who imagines her. She has no thoughts, no concerns, no life at all except within his sphere. But the real woman, even the most self-effacing one, exists apart from man.

When Melville went to England in 1849, he wrote fondly in his journal of his Orianna—Lizzie—who waited at home for him. In fact, he was so eager to return to her and to his infant son, Malcolm, that he turned down an invitation to visit the duke of Rutland at Belvoir Castle because it would postpone his return by three weeks. "If the two images would only down for that space of time," he wrote in his journal in December.[47] The images would not "down," however, and he returned to New York—only to be sadly disappointed when the images were confronted with the reality. His son no longer said the cute things he remembered, and his wife, whom he had imagined standing on tip-toe awaiting his return, was taken up with household affairs. His journal ends with this complaint:

> Lizzie is busy with the household, her mother, her mother-in-law, Sam, Father, Uncle Peter, Allan, the sisters: she chatters on about all of them, and about what baby did last week. She will never quite realize, perhaps, what one has been through, how deep one's longing is, how strong one's need for escape is, too. She loves me, yes, but not with that gnawing intensity; she will never appreciate how lonely one has been.[48]

It seems clear from this passage that the real Lizzie did not measure up to Melville's image of her, but I wonder if anyone could have. Melville wanted total sympathy and complete devotion. He was not at all interested in what his wife had to say. He complained that she did not understand him or respond to his intense need for her, yet he expected her also to understand how much he needed to escape from her. Instead of existing wholly for him as he had imagined, she had a multitude of other interests and concerns. For Melville, the image was more satisfying than the real person.

Much has been made of the fact that in 1851, after the birth of his second child, Stanwix, Melville mistakenly wrote his own mother's name and place of birth on the birth certificate instead of his wife's. One must be careful not to attempt to see too much in this apparent Freudian slip. In view of the dominant role that Maria Melville played in Melville's household, it seems not unreasonable that her name should be placed on the line marked "mother." During this period in particular, she was the mother of the household, and Elizabeth, like Melville and his sisters, apparently accepted her own status as one of the children. In August 1851, two months before Stanwix was born, Evert Duyckinck visited Melville at Arrowhead and wrote home to his wife that he was at Melville's "daughter-full house."[49] Since at this time Melville had no daughters of his own, the daughters referred to are obviously his mother's daughters—Melville's four sisters, who were all living in Melville's house, along with his mother. The fact that Duyckinck described the house as "daughter-full" rather than "sister-full" suggests that it was Melville's mother who was the dominant figure in the house, not Melville or his wife.

What was Melville's relationship with his sisters? He apparently was fond of them, particularly Augusta. When she was dying in 1876, he "could hardly control his feelings while with her."[50] His sisters thought a great deal of him also. Augusta called him her "noble-souled brother,"[51] and they all worked incessantly copying his various manuscripts (anyone who has struggled to read Melville's handwriting knows that this must have been a labor of love).[52] Helen wrote that in 1851 she was unable to leave home (Arrowhead) all winter because she was copying Melville's manuscript (presumably *Pierre*) (*Log*, 1: 441).

The immediate proximity of Melville's sisters and mother for so many years had an important effect on the attitude toward women that is reflected in his writing. After his marriage and while he was writing his novels after *Omoo*, his mother and some or all of his sisters were living with him and his wife. That Melville felt at times overwhelmed by this infusion of female relatives is suggested by his published writings, although there is no evidence of complaint in any of his surviving private papers. In *Pierre*, written after several years of living in a "daughter-full" house, Pierre seems to be surrounded by women. His mother tries to maneuver him like a puppet, and when he breaks away from her domination, he finds himself trapped in a small apartment with Isabel and Lucy and the girl Delly, who are all totally dependent on him. Like the dependent mother and three sisters of the impoverished Charles Millthorpe, they constitute a web of strangling femaleness from which Pierre struggles to free himself. At the end, he casts them all off, declaring, "Pierre is neuter now." But it is only in death that he finds release.

"I and My Chimney," written four years after *Pierre*, shows the narrator similarly surrounded by female influence. However, whereas Pierre never openly expressed hostility toward any of the women around him (he even feels guilty about the sorrow he caused his mother), the keeper of the chimney is nothing but hostile. He sees his wife as an unprincipled usurper of masculine power:

> Not insensible of her superior energies, my wife has frequently made me propositions to take upon herself all the responsibilities of my affairs. She is desirous that, domestically, I should abdicate; . . . But, indeed, the chimney excepted, I have little authority to lay down. By my wife's ingenious application of the principle that certain things belong of right to female jurisdiction, I find myself, through my easy compliances, insensibly stripped by degrees of one masculine prerogative after another.
> (*Selected Writings*, pp. 387–388)

There is no apparent tenderness toward the women in this story, as there is in *Pierre*. Even the daughters are regarded as adversaries. The narrator is actually jealous of his wife and seems to hate her because she is more healthy and vigorous than he:

> She never has any aches; while for me with the sciatica, I am sometimes as crippled up as any old apple tree. But

> she has not so much as a toothache. . . . Her faculties are
> as alert as her limbs and her senses. . . . But the most
> wonderful thing is, my wife never thinks of her end. . . .
> Advanced in years, as she knows she must be, my wife
> seems to think that she is to teem on, and be inexhaust-
> ible forever. She doesn't believe in old age.
>
> (*Selected Writings*, pp. 384–385)

Melville wrote "I and My Chimney" in 1856, when he
was thirty-six. Yet in this and the other stories written in the
1850s, he pictures himself as an old man and may very well
have thought that he was soon going to die.[53] He lived for
another thirty-six years, but to a man like Melville, his life
must have seemed at an end: he had lost his health, his zest for
living, and his writing powers (or so it seemed). At this point
in his life it had become clear that he would not be a financial
or a critical success as a writer. His English publisher had refused to publish his books (English sales had accounted for
half of his income);[54] his books were not selling well anywhere; and the general reviewers had found little to praise in
his last works. Constantly in debt and struggling to make a
living as a writer, Melville had written feverishly during the
years 1851–1852, only to be rebuked by the reviewers for
writing incomprehensibly. In *The Confidence Man* (1857) Melville observed that the writer seeks approbation: "So precious
to man is the approbation of his kind, that to rest, though but
under an imaginary censure applied to but a work of imagination, is no easy thing" (*Confidence Man*, p. 158). However
much Melville may have pretended that he cared nothing for
what others thought of him or his work, he obviously did
care a great deal. In 1855 all of the success and esteem of his
early writing days had vanished, leaving him bitter and dis-
consolate, ready to die.

Moreover, Melville had always prided himself on his
bodily vigor. When he voyaged to England in 1849, he enjoyed showing the other passengers how he could run up and
down the rigging like a sailor, and he was pleased at his own
ability to maintain his sea legs while the other passengers

were all falling seasick (*JLC*, pp. 6–9). In the Berkshires in 1850–1851, Melville climbed mountains and went for long walks and rides on horseback. To the people about him, he seemed to be bursting with energy. But this man who in 1850 was so vital, with "life in his finger-tips," as Sophia Hawthorne said to her mother,[55] had in just a few years lost all of his energy and enthusiasm. When Nathaniel Hawthorne met him in England in 1856, Melville confided that, as Hawthorne wrote in his notebook, "the spirit of adventure is gone out of him."[56]

Like Emerson and Thoreau, Melville was a great believer in "manliness." In *Pierre* he stresses the importance of a "manly robustness" and asserts that physical strength is necessary to protect women. How irritating it must have been, then, for Melville to find himself hobbling around with sciatica at the age of thirty-six while the women around him—particularly his mother, a woman of sixty-four—remained as healthy and energetic as ever. Whether Melville's ailments were psychosomatic or not seems to me beside the point. They obviously were very real to him, and their effect on his image of himself was the same regardless of their cause.

"I and My Chimney" derives largely from Melville's life. In February 1855 he suffered his first attack of what Elizabeth Melville described as rheumatism in his back, and for a time he was quite helpless (*Log*, 2: 499). In June he had an attack of sciatica and became increasingly irritable and withdrawn. His family, confused by his morose and erratic behavior since 1853, persistently attempted to change his way of life, to force him to give up writing and come out among people more. In 1853 Melville's mother urged her brother Peter Gansevoort to help find a consulship for Melville. Writing, she believed, was "wearing him out," and he must be made to give it up: "A change of occupation is necessary for Herman. . . . he would then be compelled to more intercourse with his fellow creatures" (*Log*, 1: 469). The commanding tone of this letter and the positive way in which Maria stated her opinion that Melville's whole way of life was wrong show what a formidable person she must have been.

In a marginal note to "I and My Chimney," Melville's wife noted: "All this about his wife applied to his mother—who was very vigorous and energetic about the farm, etc." Newton Arvin, who quotes this notation, sees it as a rather pathetic attempt at self-exoneration.[57] But I suspect that Lizzie was only telling the truth; it was Melville's mother who was the manager, not she.

In "I and My Chimney" the domineering wife is also the mother of grown daughters, who support her in her attempt to work her will on the narrator. Melville's own daughters were only babies when this story was written, but his mother's daughters had been full-grown inhabitants of his house for many years. By 1855, two of Melville's sisters had married, but Augusta and her mother were still in a residence. Another sister, Frances Priscilla, had taken a room in Pittsfield but was frequently at Arrowhead. His sisters supported their mother in her attempts to change Melville's way of life. In 1857 Augusta wrote to her uncle Peter Gansevoort, expressing the same opinion her mother had offered four years earlier: Herman must give up writing (*Log*, 2: 567).

These well-meaning and apparently long-sustained attempts to change Melville are reflected in the pressures he portrays in "I and My Chimney." Melville obviously saw himself as under attack. The great chimney with its secret closet seems to represent Melville's secret self, the inner man that he somehow felt he must keep safe from the encroachment of women. The women in the story want to destroy the chimney and build something more acceptable to their tastes. A master mason, Mr. Scribe, is called in to examine the chimney, just as Dr. Oliver W. Holmes was called in to diagnose Melville's ills in June 1855. Mr. Scribe fails to find the secret closet, and apparently Melville was able to withstand the probing of Dr. Holmes.[58] The story presents a gesture of defiance:

> Some say that I have become a sort of mossy old misanthrope, while all the time the fact is, I am simply stand-

ing guard over my mossy old chimney; for it is resolved
between me and my chimney, that I and my chimney
will never surrender.   (*Selected Writings*, pp. 407–408)

Melville's defiance in this story is not on the same level as the
defiance in his other novels, of course. The defiance of Taji,
Ahab, and Pierre is portrayed as the proud challenge of a Titan before the powers of the universe. The defender of the
chimney seeks only to preserve his individuality from his
wife and daughters. But it is the same defiance—the defiance
of a man struggling to assert the primacy of the self.

Melville's attitude toward women, both in his published writing and in what is known of his private life, is consistent with
the attitude of a man who was concerned first and foremost
with the preservation and assertion of the self. An ardent believer in the American myth, he was forced to create a persona that permitted him to transcend reality. Like the American archetypal hero, Melville saw life as a stage for male
exploit. And, like Emerson, he was so concerned with this
self-assertion that he could not recognize the selfhood of the
other, least of all the female other.

If Melville was able to portray women only from a distance or as the unreal, will-less maidens of the courtship period, it was because he regarded real women—with their
own ideas and personalities—as a threat to the development
of the masculine self. The independent woman threatened to
subjugate the male will; the dependent woman suffocated the
male with burdensome responsibilities. Thus, for Melville,
women were acceptable only as background scenery or household furniture. The stage belonged to the male self, and there
was no room on center stage for a commanding or demanding female performance.

CHAPTER 6

OLD LADIES AND LITTLE GIRLS: MARK TWAIN

Wheresoever you place a woman, sir—in whatsoever position or estate—she is an ornament to that place she occupies, and a treasure to the world.

Mark Twain, speech on "Woman," 1867[1]

If, as Hemingway noted in *The Green Hills of Africa*, all of American literature has derived from *Huckleberry Finn*,[2] it is not surprising that American literature is so lacking in strong female characters. This, of course, was not Hemingway's point (although his own work reflects the same tendency), but Mark Twain's masterpiece does seem to epitomize the type of gynophobic novel that has long dominated American literature: *Huckleberry Finn* (1885) is what Leslie Fiedler called a "boy's book";[3] the main character is a self-sufficient, lone male in retreat from civilized society, as represented by women; the only real relationship that is allowed to develop is between male and male; and all female characters are peripheral figures totally lacking in individuality.

Like Cooper and Melville and the New England male Transcendentalists, Mark

Twain was unable to portray a woman as a person. His novels show us humorous old ladies and silly little girls, but there is no woman of any substance. Even the few young women of marriageable age who do appear are only little girls grown tall. For the most part, Twain is simply not interested in the female characters in his works. As his friend, William Dean Howells, commented regarding Twain's portrayal of women, "I do not think he succeeds so often with that nature as with the boy-nature or the man-nature, apparently because it does not interest him so much."[4]

Twain's first nationally published piece, "The Celebrated Jumping Frog of Calaveras County" (1865), provides a prophetic indication of what his primary interests were to be throughout his career. "Frog" is set in a miner's cabin in the hills, far away from women and society. It is a story told by men, for men, about men, and to men. Women are not even mentioned.

Twain's first book, *The Innocents Abroad* (1869), chronicles his voyage to Europe and Palestine on the *Quaker City* from June to November 1867. Although there were nineteen women on the excursion, and although Twain established a close relationship with one woman passenger that resulted in a lifelong friendship,[5] the female passengers are scarcely mentioned in the book. The only women who do appear are the foreign women whom Twain observed in the various countries he visited, and they are mentioned only occasionally and always from a distance. Twain describes the appearance of the foreign women in the same way that he describes the scenery and sanitation of other lands—as objects to assess and ironically criticize when they do not come up to American standards of excellence.[6]

Women are mentioned even less frequently in Twain's next work, *Roughing It* (1872), which is based on his adventures in Nevada and California from 1861 to 1866 and includes a section on the Sandwich Islands, which he visited in 1866 as a correspondent for the Sacramento *Union*. There was little "female scenery" in the American West in the 1860s, and Twain himself calls attention to the scarcity of women by telling how he stood in line to look through a crack in a cabin in the mining territory to see a "genuine, live woman." She turned out to be old and toothless and was frying flapjacks (*Works*, 6: vol. 2, 133–135).

The story of Twain looking at a woman through a crack in a cabin wall, whether true or apocryphal, provides a good analogy for the way in which Twain viewed women throughout his writing: from the outside, from a distance, as one would look at a picture or an abstract image. There is no suggestion that women are to be interacted with as persons.

Twain's first novel, *The Gilded Age* (1873), was written in collaboration with Charles Dudley Warner. Twain claimed responsibility for most of the Colonel Sellers–Hawkins segments, and Laura Hawkins was his creation.[7] Laura is a more interesting character than other young woman in Twain's works. However, Twain makes clear early in the book that, because of her questionable background, she does not count. As Clay, her foster brother, realizes, it is unthinkable that the other girls in the family should work for a living, no matter how poor they are, but it does not matter that Laura works. Twain allows himself a certain leeway with Laura's character that he would not have taken with a more genteel heroine.[8] He permits her to possess a forcefulness and independence of character that is lacking in most of his young women; however, it is clear that he feels that her deviation from the mold causes her destruction. The ending, which Twain and his wife and Mrs. Warner all thought so fitting,[9] conforms to the rule of nineteenth-century sentimental fiction that the morally nonconforming woman must be punished. Twain, who became famous for his realistic portrayal of the nongenteel male protagonist, held very rigid expectations for women.

Twain's definition of a proper female is made clear in *Tom Sawyer* (1876). Tom tells Huck that he is going to marry a "girl" not a "gal" (*Works*, 1: 204). His idea of a girl is Becky Thatcher, the judge's daughter, "a lovely little blue-eyed creature with yellow hair plaited into two long tails, white summer frock, and embroidered pantalettes" (*Works*, 1: 22). To Tom she is an "angel" (*Works*, 1: 22, 37). However, Tom seems attracted only to her external qualities, her appearance and her social status. To himself he admits that she is a "fool" and decides that all girls are "chicken hearted" and lacking in backbone (*Works*, 1: 172). Certainly Becky is an insipid and rather boring little girl. Twain himself can not even remember her name in *Huckleberry Finn*. She cries easily and acts shy and coy. When they are lost in the cave, it is Tom who saves them. Becky's "frail limbs" give out, and, like Cooper's shrinking heroines, she is totally dependent on Tom. Tom much prefers the more interesting male companionship of Huck Finn and Joe Harper. For him, Becky is only an image, a pretty picture whose main function is to appreciate him.

The other girl in *Tom Sawyer*, Tom's cousin Mary, is even less interesting than Becky. Twain portrays her as the embodiment of what he sees as the female civilizing influence. She works patiently to teach Tom his Sunday School Bible verses (she herself has memorized two thousand), and she makes him wash and keep his clothes tidy (*Works* 1: 29–32). Ultimately, Twain's attitude toward these girls is apparent in his portrayal of the school commencement ceremony. He is much more interested in the boys' prank with the cat and the schoolmaster's toupee than he is in the girls' tedious compositions (*Works*, 1: 177, 184). Yet, although this type of feminine behavior bored Twain, it was the only kind that he permitted in proper female characters. The proper Twain female is an abstraction, a distant image of gentility—sweet, innocent, gentle, modest, selfless, preferably pretty, dependent, and a staunch preserver of society.

If Twain's little girls are uninteresting and characterless, his old ladies are more appealing only because they at least provide Twain with someone to make fun of. In *Tom Sawyer* Aunt Polly is kind and good-hearted, but she is rather slow-witted. She has all of the character traits of the little girls, except that she is no longer pretty. She is an amusing stock figure, whose simplicity and gullibility make her the easy butt of Tom's and Twain's good-natured humor.

Aunt Polly appears again in *Huckleberry Finn* (1885) along with her sister, Aunt Sally. Both women are kind but easily duped, and they are so lacking in individuality that they could change places without the reader knowing the difference. The other old ladies—Miss Watson, the Widow Douglas—are vaguely defined civilizers who worry about manners, clothes, and religion. The younger female characters in *Huckleberry Finn* are even less fully developed than the old ladies. Huck meets three briefly sketched girls as he travels down the river: Sophia and Charlotte Grangerford and Mary Jane Wilks. Mary Jane Wilks is the only one with whom Huck interacts. Yet, even though Huck concludes that she has a lot of "grit," she is little more than an image of a "good girl." Again, the girls in the novel are static, uninteresting characters. It is the male adventurer who interests Twain.

The Prince and the Pauper (1882) and *A Connecticut Yankee in King Arthur's Court* (1889) feature no more memorable female characters than *Tom Sawyer* or *Huckleberry Finn*. Lady Elizabeth and Lady Jane in *The Prince and the Pauper* are only storybook characters, and Sandy in *A Connecticut Yankee* is a shallow simpleton. Hank Morgan complains that she chattered endlessly and "never had any ideas, any more than a frog has" (*Works*, 5: 98). In "Huck Finn and Tom Sawyer Among the Indians" (1884), Twain's abortive attempt to write a sequel to *Huckleberry Finn*, the young Peggy Mills is the same stereotypical maiden that Twain portrays throughout his work—sweet, pretty, innocent, and ingenuous to the point of stupidity.[10]

Only in *Pudd'nhead Wilson* (1894) is Twain able to create a believable female character. The initial description of Roxana, the young slave woman, presents a character worthy to stand beside the strongest heroines of history and myth:

> She was of majestic form and stature, her attitudes were imposing and statuesque, and her gestures and movements distinguished by a noble and stately grace. Her complexion was very fair, with the rosy glow of vigorous health in her cheeks, her face was full of character and expression, her eyes were brown and liquid, and she had a heavy suit of fine soft hair which was also brown.

> . . . Her face was shapely, intelligent, and comely—even
> beautiful. She had an easy, independent carriage.
>
> (*Works*, 3: 11)

Neither a silly little girl nor a laughable old lady, Roxy is a strong, passionate young woman. She reacts with believable terror and passion to the realization that her baby could be sold down the river, and her decision, first, to kill herself and the baby and, then, to switch babies is portrayed as the moving story of a person with real fears and emotions. Roxy is capable of acting independently, and even her son is forced to admire "her strong character and aggressive and commanding ways" (*Works*, 3: 79).

What is most significant about Twain's portrayal of Roxy, however, is that, apparently, it is her race that enables him to endow her with strength of character and individuality. Twain's awareness of her social status frees him from the restrictions that he held so sacred to the image of the genteel woman. Like Laura Hawkins, she does not count as a lady. Only she and Laura are permitted to possess a sexual identity; the other Twain maidens never seem to reach puberty.[11]

Even so, the remarkable portrait of Roxy is buried under a mountain of dialect and comic situations that all but obscure her character, and a casual reader who misses the above description of her may never even realize what Roxy looks like. (It is significant that the illustrator of Twain's works drew her as the stereotype of the fat black mammy.) Moreover, the plot itself also undercuts Roxy's possibilities as a protagonist. Ignoring the criticism of slavery and society represented by Roxy's tragic situation, the plot moves in the opposite direction. Judge Driscoll, the representative of the white aristocracy, becomes the victim, and the villain of the piece turns out to be a black man masquerading as white.[12]

Mark Twain's own favorite among the female characters in his work was Joan in *Joan of Arc* (1896). In a 1904 essay he called her "the most extraordinary person the human race has ever produced."[13] Earlier he confessed in a letter that the book "was written for love."[14] Joan is the only female character in Twain's work that he really seemed to care about. Just how much he cared is evident from a letter that his daughter Susy wrote to her sister from Florence, where Twain was working on *Joan*:

> The character of Joan is pure and perfect to a miraculous degree. Hearing the m.s. read aloud is an uplifting and revealing hour to us all. Many of Joan's words and saying are historically correct and Papa cries when he reads them. In fact he almost always fills up when reading any speech of hers.[15]

Critics have been puzzled by Twain's serious treatment of Joan of Arc. Maxwell Geismar notes that St. Joan represents everything that Twain despised: religion, patriotism, nationalism, purity, self-sacrifice, and sentimentality.[16] James Cox insists that *Joan of Arc* is a denial of Twain's identity because Joan is "the embodiment of all the conventions which Mark Twain had humorously subverted during his career."[17] However, as the previous discussion of Twain's works should make clear, *Joan of Arc* is not inconsistent with Twain's attitudes. Twain did indeed ridicule all of these conventions—*but not in women*. Joan is Twain's principal female character, the only one that he treated in any detail. The despised qualities that Geismar lists are exactly the qualities that Twain required in women.

In *Joan of Arc* Twain takes his ideal of the genteel maiden and develops her as fully as he can within the restrictions of the image. George Bernard Shaw called the resulting character Twain's "beautiful and most ladylike Victorian."[18] Twain describes Joan as "wholly noble, pure, truthful, brave, compassionate, generous, pious, unselfish, modest, blameless as the very flowers in the fields—a nature fine and beautiful" (*Works*, 2: 200). These characteristics may not apply to Huck Finn and Tom Sawyer, and certainly not to Hank Morgan and Philip Traum, but they do apply in varying degrees to Becky Thatcher and Mary, Peggy Mills, Sophia Grangerford, and Mary Jane Wilks, even to Aunt Polly. In Joan of Arc they are only extended and concentrated. She is more selfless, more modest, purer, and more pious than any other one female character. She is the epitome of Twain's genteel maidens. In his essay "St. Joan of Arc" Twain insists that the artists who have painted her as a strapping peasant woman are wrong: "Always she was a *girl*; and dear and worshipful as is meet for that estate" (*Essays*, p. 332). To Twain she was obviously a child, not a woman, and like his other girls, he portrayed her as prepubescent and asexual. He describes her as "the most innocent, the most lovely, the most adorable child the ages have produced."[19] Not only is she a child-maiden, but Twain suggests that she is more spirit than flesh. Thus, like all of Twain's female characters, except Laura and Roxy, Joan is an abstract image of what Twain saw as the ideal.

Twain's portrayal of his female characters can be more fully understood if we look at his attitude toward some of the real women in his life. It was not only in his fiction that Twain created *images* of women; he viewed his mother, his wife, and his friend Mrs. Fairbanks not as they were but as he wanted them to be. Once we recognize how thoroughly Twain insisted on casting even real women in this role, we will be able to understand the reason for his portrayal of his fictional women as abstract images. It is necessary to explore in detail the way in which Twain's attitude toward these individuals converted them into abstractions who existed for him and through him. The only way to accomplish this task is to determine in each instance, as closely as possible, the difference between the real woman and Twain's image of her. The image that he created followed the pattern of his fictional creations: he portrayed his women as conventional representatives of society and Sunday school, whose concern with propriety and morals provided him with something to react against. His relationship with his wife demonstrates this pattern most obviously, but there are indications of the same tendency in the impressions he gives of his mother.

It is difficult to separate Twain's image of his mother from the distorted version of it in Van Wyck Brooks's *The Ordeal of Mark Twain* (1920). Twain told a story (which he later contradicted) of how, when his father died in 1847, his mother extracted a promise from the twelve-year-old Samuel that he would be a "good" boy.[20] Brooks concludes from this meager evidence and from Mrs. Clemens's one-time association with Presbyterianism, that she was an iron-bound Calvinist who repressed her son's individuality and creativity.[21] Brooks's thesis has been sufficiently refuted by others.[22] However, Twain himself provided the germ for Brooks's portrait of his mother, which seemed to Brooks to be supported by Twain's portrayal of Tom Sawyer's Aunt Polly, whom Brooks regards as "a symbol of all the taboos."[23] Twain told his biographer, Albert Bigelow Paine, of another promise to his mother in 1853, when he left home at the age of seventeen: his mother asked him not to drink and gamble while he was away.[24] And he seemed always to speak of mothers and other female guardians as the watchdogs of morality and convention—to be outwitted wherever possible.[25]

The real Jane Lampton Clemens was not at all the conventional, pious moralist implicit in Twain's portrait of her. Paine describes her as "gay, buoyant, celebrated for her beauty and grace; able to dance all night and all day too."[26] Rachel M. Varble points out in her biography of Jane Clemens that one aspect of her nature outshone all others: "She wanted every living creature to have fun."[27] People who knew her in Hannibal characterized her as witty and good-humored, "a woman of the sunniest temperament, lively, affable, a general favorite."[28] She often amused her children with her clever imitations of other people,[29] and Twain himself obviously patterned his own dry sense of humor after his mother's. As he commented to Paine: "She had a sort of ability which is rare in man and hardly existent in woman—the ability to say a humorous thing with the perfect air of not knowing it to be humorous."[30] Far from repressing Twain's individuality and rebelliousness, his mother, because of her own sense of humor and easygoing nature, actually encouraged him. In 1854, when he returned from New York, his mother made some remark about his carelessness, and his answer made her laugh. Annoyed, his more serious sister Pamela rebuked her mother for laughing at Samuel, recalling that she had always encouraged him by laughing at him. It was her fault, said Pamela, if he was the way he was; her laughter was a way of applauding his behavior.[31]

Jane Clemens was not the kind of person to repress or to be repressed. Her behavior was always unorthodox. She liked to cobble shoes for relaxation, and this hobby, in addition to her odd conversation, her careless housekeeping, and the feathers on her hat, caused comment among her more conventional neighbors. She smoked a pipe, used slang, offered cordial to her tea-drinking callers, and, except for a period of Presbyterianism around 1843 after her son Benjamin died, attended church erratically, sampling various churches (including the Jewish synagogue) or not going to church at all.[32]

Obviously, Jane Clemens was not the conventional stereotype of Twain's fiction. When she could, she even objected to his attempt to cast her in this role. Twain dedicated his first book, *The Innocents Abroad*, to "my aged mother," soberly declaring that she was his "most patient reader and most charitable critic," but Jane Clemens took issue with this cozy portrait: "I've not been his patient reader, ever, nor an easy critic, either. Sometimes I've roasted him. And I'm a far piece from aged."[33]

At the age of thirty-one, Mark Twain found a new mother in Mrs. Mary M. Fairbanks, whom he met on the *Quaker City* excursion. "Mother" Fairbanks, as Twain called her, was a cultured and educated woman seven years his senior. She possessed a gentility and elegance of taste and manner that Mrs. Clemens lacked. Twain made her into his personal reformer. At the same time, however, he was prepared to take only the advice he wanted. In his writing he accepted only certain suggestions having to do with matters of taste.[34] Regarding his personal behavior, he liked to have her scold him, and he promised to reform, but he never gave up anything unless he wanted to.[35] He enjoyed teasing Mrs. Fairbanks, shocking her with tales of his behavior that he felt would earn her disapproval. In 1868 he wrote to his fiancée, "I have got Mother Fairbanks in a stew again—I named that lecture just for her benefit. And I sent her an absurd synopsis of it that I knew would provoke her wrath—I intimated that I was idling somewhat. I like to tease her because I like her so" (*Fairbanks*, p. 47).[36]

Mrs. Fairbanks was not the stuffy, convention-bound prude that Twain's letters represent her to be. Had she been so, she would never have allowed herself to enter into a friendship with Mark Twain, who at the time of the *Quaker City* expedition was a hard-drinking, carelessly dressed westerner who deliberately flouted convention.[37] She had received a very liberal education, and she was sufficiently independent to be traveling without her husband and children as a correspondent for the Cleveland *Herald*. It was Twain who cast her in the role of reformer. Over and over again in his letters to her, he urged her to reform him. On December 2, 1867, he begged: "Give me another sermon!" He encouraged her on September 24, 1868, "Don't be afraid to write sermons—I am perfectly willing not only to receive them but to try to profit by them." On January 7, 1869, he told her not to be afraid to give advice: "Suggest—I listen; advise—I heed; command—I obey." And in April 1869 he wrote: "Your Motherly 'officiousness' is always welcome, & always *required* of you" (*Fairbanks*, pp. 5, 37–38, 65–66, 91–94).

Twain followed the same pattern in his relationship with his wife. He married Olivia Langdon on February 2, 1870, when he was thirty-four and she was ten years younger. The most important fact about their relationship was that Twain fell in love with her *image* long before he met her.[38] According to Albert Bigelow Paine, Twain became fascinated with an ivory miniature of Livy that her brother, Charles Langdon, had on the *Quaker City* voyage in 1867.[39] It was several

months before he saw the original and eight more months before he saw her again, but presumably he carried her image in
his mind all that time.[40] Whether or not the story of the miniature is true, Twain did not really need the picture; he already
had an image in his mind of the woman he wanted to marry.[41]
Like Tom Sawyer, he was not looking for a "gal" but a "girl"
—the genteel, respectable, pure, ladylike maiden that he later
drew in his fiction.[42] On December 12, 1867, before he had
met Livy, he wrote to Mrs. Fairbanks that if he could afford
to marry, he would try to "swindle" some girl into marrying
him: "But I wouldn't expect to be 'worthy' of her. I wouldn't
have a girl that *I* was worthy of. *She* wouldn't do. She
wouldn't be respectable enough" (*Fairbanks*, p. 8).

With this preconceived idea of what his wife should be,
Twain proceeded to mold Olivia Langdon according to the
image he desired for a wife; in a sense, he created her. In his
early letters to her, he made very clear what he wanted. He
summarized the traits of his ideal woman that he saw represented in her: "You are all good & true, & generous & forgiv-
ing & unselfish—all things that are a glory to womanhood."
He also prescribed that his ideal woman would stay safely at
home, untouched by the world outside her parlor, and he
praised Coventry Patmore's poem of domesticity, "The Angel in the House," which, as we have seen, Emerson also admired for its picture of the innocent woman sheltered by the
fireside.[43] Moreover, Twain made Livy an object of reverence. When he first saw her, he said, she seemed a "*Spirit*
from the upper air," "something to *worship*, reverently & at a
distance—& *not* a creature of common human clay, to be pro-
faned by the love of such as I" (*Love Letters*, p. 43).

Livy would have had to have been very obtuse not to
have understood that Twain wanted her to be a pure and innocent model of decorum and domesticity and an object of
worship. At first Livy objected to being elevated to such
heights, but she really had no choice. She was in love with
him, it was her first experience with love, and he was ten
years older than she. If he said her purity and delicacy were
her most precious possessions and the chief ornament of any

woman, she would have been a fool to deny these qualities. Aside from the fact that she was probably very flattered by his picture of her, Twain made the image so important to him and identified it so positively with all that he admired in women that for Livy to have actively disputed it would have been to reject his love and to deny her place as a true woman.

An important part of the image Twain created of Livy was to make her a reformer, just as he had done with Mrs. Fairbanks. In his very first letter to her, on September 7, 1868, he wrote that he needed her "pure judgments" to guide him, and he urged her to reform him. Maintaining that he needed her and Mother Fairbanks to "scold and upbraid" him, he assured her that he would do anything she wanted (*Love Letters*, pp. 18–20). Livy apparently complied, and he wrote to Mrs. Fairbanks three months later that in her letters Livy lectured him "like smoke, too." "But," he said, "I like it" (*Fairbanks*, p. 55). He should have liked it; it was what he wanted.

As with Mrs. Fairbanks, Twain asked for reform in his personal behavior and in his writing. Regarding his behavior, he wrote to Mrs. Fairbanks a month before his marriage that Livy had "civilized" him—stopped his drinking, cut down on his smoking, reduced his slang and boisterousness, and made him keep his hands out of his pockets (*Fairbanks*, pp. 112–117). With respect to his writing, he said he wanted Livy to read everything he wrote, to advise him on style, to "erase improprieties," and to censor what was bad (*Love Letters*, p. 67). In May 1869 he wrote to Livy from Ottawa: "You should mark it *all* out, if you wanted to, for if Livy didn't like it nobody else should have a *chance* to like it" (*Love Letters*, pp. 90–92). Thus, from the very beginning, Twain was urging—demanding—that Livy be both reformer and censor. That Livy accepted this aspect of her role is even more understandable than her acceptance of the rest of the image. Twain made it appear as if he could not function without her.

Cast in this role by Twain himself, Livy cannot be said to have imposed *her* will upon him. Twain's tendency to create an unreal image of the women in his life had very real consequences for his wife. Unable to withstand Twain's absorption of her, and motivated to please by culture and inclination, Livy ultimately gave up her personality. An analysis of how she lost her individuality is essential if we are to understand Twain's relationship to American individualism and its denial of female authenticity.

A gentle, quiet person, Livy did her best to live up to the role that Twain assigned to her. Her powers were very limited, however. Twain made an effort to accommodate himself to Livy's tastes at first, but, although he cut down on his smoking, stopped drinking, and even participated in an evening Bible reading for a while,[44] within a few months after his marriage—at most a year—he had resumed all of his former habits. Far from criticizing him, Livy apparently accepted him as he was. Katy Leary, who worked in the Clemens household for thirty years, reports that Livy confided that when she was married, she made up her mind that her husband would always be able to act and speak freely, without her criticism.[45] And it is significant that in 1874, just four years after their marriage, Twain was able to write from London to this daughter of a temperance home asking her to have whiskey on hand for him when he came back (*Love Letters*, p. 190). Nor in his writing did Twain follow Livy's advice. The manuscript of *Huckleberry Finn* shows little serious editing by Livy, less than was done by Richard Watson Gilder when the book was published in *Century Magazine*.[46] Paul J. Carter's study of the manuscript for *Following the Equator* shows that Livy's suggestions dealt mostly with accuracy and readability and that Twain freely rejected any he did not like.[47]

Van Wyck Brooks maintains that Twain made Livy's gods his gods. In fact, the reverse was true. Livy not only acquiesced to the role Twain had designed for her; she came to accept all the vices that originally she had sought to change in her husband—his smoking and drinking, even his swearing. The best indication of who followed whom is found in the question of religious thinking.[48] When Twain first met Livy, she was religious to the extent that in her letters to him she often enclosed copies of her minister's sermons. Twain professed no belief in any religion, but he indicated a willingness to try to change. Within two years after their marriage, however, it was Livy who had changed. She wrote to him in December 1871 that she no longer had faith, that she felt cold toward God (*Love Letters*, pp. 166–169). This attitude continued throughout her life. When their daughter Susy died suddenly in 1896 and both Livy and Twain were inconsolable with grief, Twain told Livy to rely on the Christian faith for comfort if it would help. Livy replied that she could not; she had no faith.[49]

In *Eve's Diary*, which Twain wrote around the time of Livy's death in 1904 and which is thought to be a portrait of his wife, Eve says of Adam: "I wish to learn to like everything he is interested in."[50] And this is what Livy did. She spent hours reading Twain's manuscripts and painstakingly making comments and corrections, and in later years she patiently listened to the tirades of rage and bitterness that no one else heard, while keeping her own depression to herself in order to provide him with the solace he needed. In 1894, for example, when Twain was forced to declare bankruptcy and the family had been living in Europe for three years to economize, Livy wrote to her sister that she was homesick for America and heartsick about the bankruptcy: "Most of the time I want to lie down and cry. Everything seems to me so impossible. I do not make things go very well, and I feel that my life is an absolute and irretrievable failure."[51] Yet she apparently never let Twain know of her own longings. He wrote to a friend a few months later, when it was clear that the Paige typesetter machine (in which he had invested a total of $200,000) was a failure: "Nothing daunts Mrs. Clemens or makes the world look black to her—which is the reason I haven't drowned myself."[52]

After their daughter Susy died, Twain became enraged at fate, and Livy this time could not hide her own grief. Yet she listened to Twain's bitter tirades and did her best to keep him sane until her own illness in 1902. Their daughter Clara tells of how Twain would rage on the injustices of life, "thunderous outbursts of bitterness shading into rugged grief." Then suddenly he would cease, pat Livy on the head, and say, "Don't mind anything I say, Livy. Whatever happens, you know I love you."[53]

Justin Kaplan feels that Livy's illness may have been motivated by the need to escape Twain's rages.[54] Maxwell Geismar criticizes Kaplan's suspicious treatment of Livy's final illness, because, he says, Kaplan does not consider the love between them and thus distorts the central relationship.[55] It is true that Kaplan overlooks the devotion of Twain and Livy to each other, but it does seem as though Livy's final illness may have been partially brought about by the constant strain she had been under. Her love for Twain must have made his unhappiness even harder to bear. Twain himself felt he was a cause of her illness. He wrote to Livy in her sickroom: "It so grieves me to remember that I am the cause of your being where you are. . . . I drove you to sorrow and heartbreak just to hear myself talk."[56] William Dean Howells said that around 1900 Twain's ranting about the "damned human race" was intolerable, and he speculated that Livy's retreat to the sickroom must have provided her with some compensation.[57] Around 1902, two years before her death, Livy wrote a letter that reveals the extent of her concern for Twain and also the effect his rages must have had upon her:

> Does it help the world always to rail at it? . . . Why always dwell on the evil until those who live beside you are crushed to the earth & you seem almost like a monomaniac. Oh! I love you so & wish you would listen & take heed. (*Love Letters*, p. 333)

Howells commented on the extraordinary tact Livy exercised with Twain, who, Howells said, was often deliberately the most outrageous of men.[58] Livy must have been constantly on the alert for signals from Twain to indicate how she should act, and she had to give up her own individuality to do so. Livy organized her life around her husband's pleasures and subordinated her own wishes to his. Katy Leary says that Livy was happy when Twain was pleased and tells how Twain would often say to Livy that he wanted something, a dinner party, for example, and she would plan it for him. He always came first with her: "Whatever he wanted to do—no matter what it was, she always wanted him to do it."[59] In 1890, when they had to cancel a trip to Europe because of trouble with the Paige typesetter, Livy wrote to Twain: "Don't let the thought of Europe worry you *one bit* because we will give that all up. . . . I want to see you happy much more than I want anything else even the childrens [sic] lessons. Oh Darling it goes to my very heart to see you worried" (*Love Letters*, pp. 255–256).

Livy existed *for Twain* and, as the preceding letter indicates, she willingly adapted herself to all aspects of the life he had chosen. Her individuality was totally submerged in his. Even if she was unhappy about what he was doing, she apparently did not let him know, so long as he was happy doing it. Twain enjoyed the constant company of his friends and admirers, for example, and although the demands on Livy that this continual entertaining required interfered with any life of her own that she might have had, she felt that she must accept them for him. From the huge mansion in Hartford that Twain built and that was always filled with guests, she wrote in the 1880s:

> The house has been full of company. . . . I cannot help sighing for the peace and quiet of the farm. . . . Sometimes it seems as if the simple sight of people would drive me *mad*. . . . if I would simply accept the fact that this is my work and let other things go, I know I should not be so fretted; but I want so much to do other things, to study and do things with the children, but I cannot.[60]

This letter reveals a sense of the *person* buried under the image of "Mark Twain's wife." That Livy was a person in her own right is never considered by Twain scholars, who, whether they accept Twain's image of her or not, nevertheless do not see Livy as a person separate from Mark Twain. Even those critics who have defended her from Brooks's charges have seen her only in relation to Twain. James Cox, for example, whose discussion of Livy is one of the most perceptive and who recognizes that Twain invented her, defends Livy by pointing out her usefulness *to Twain*: it was his marriage to Livy that freed Twain to write about the past.[61]

It is not surprising, perhaps, that Twain critics should see Livy only in relation to Twain, since they are after all writing about Mark Twain and not Olivia Langdon. Moreover, according to the customs of our society, it is not usual to investigate the individuality of the wife of a famous man (unless she is notorious for her sexual adventures). What is important here is that these critics seem to reflect Twain's own projection of Livy. Twain himself saw Livy not as a separate person but as an extension of Mark Twain. He constructed an image of her and molded her to fit his image; he designed a place for her in his life and relied upon her to fill it.

It should not be assumed that Twain was unkind in regarding Livy as part of himself. Twain and Livy were very much in love throughout their life together, as their letters and the comments of their contemporaries show. Also significant is the portrayal of their relationship in Twain's *Diaries of Adam and Eve*, where Adam has inscribed on Eve's grave: "Wheresoever she was *there* was Eden" (*Diaries*, p. 63). Most touching is the description Katy Leary gives of the meetings during Livy's final illness: "She'd put her arms around his neck the first thing, and he'd hold her soft, and give her one of them tender kisses. Oh it was lovely! It was a great love."[62] There was nothing cold or cruel in Twain's absorption of his wife's personality; it was simply a part of the way he viewed women.

Twain was able to absorb Livy into himself because he did not see women as complete individuals in the same way that he saw himself and other men. Her pet name for him was "Youth," because of his high spirits and sometimes outrageous behavior. But it was really he who regarded Livy as a child. In his letters he called her "my precious child," and he always insisted that she was a girl and not wholly a woman (*Love Letters*, pp. 154–155, 186–187).[63] His emphasis on her purity, and on the purity of women in general, implies a desire to keep her in a state of childlike innocence—or ignorance—like his Joan of Arc. He saw her as a limited person, and he wanted her to remain that way. Soon after their marriage, he described her to his childhood friend Will Bowen as the "*best* girl, & the sweetest, & the gentlest, & the daintiest, & the most modest & unpretentious, & the wisest in all things she should be wise in & *the most ignorant in all matters it would not grace her to know.*"[64] Here is Twain's ideal woman: gentle and sweet, but ignorant as a child.

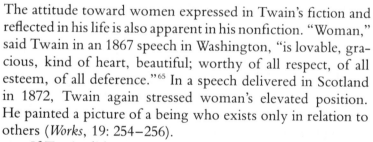

The attitude toward women expressed in Twain's fiction and reflected in his life is also apparent in his nonfiction. "Woman," said Twain in an 1867 speech in Washington, "is lovable, gracious, kind of heart, beautiful; worthy of all respect, of all esteem, of all deference."[65] In a speech delivered in Scotland in 1872, Twain again stressed woman's elevated position. He painted a picture of a being who exists only in relation to others (*Works*, 19: 254–256).

If Twain did not regard woman as independent of man, what were his feelings about women's rights and female suffrage? In an 1873 essay on the temperance crusade, Twain conceded that women's involvement in the election process might be of value, if only because women were morally superior to men. Moreover, he shared the opinion of many Americans during a period of mass immigration that an educated, intelligent, native-born woman might as well vote if "every ignorant whiskey-drinking foreign-born savage in the land" had that privilege (*Essays*, pp. 666–668). In theory, Twain believed that it was "just" that women should vote, and he advocated equality of the sexes.[66] But he did not think that it was "right." The idea of women entering the political arena repulsed him. He was distressed by the thought of seeing these "earthly angels" at the polls or out electioneering.[67] Such ideas conflicted with his image of female purity.

Twain's concern with female purity brings us to the question of why his fiction is so lacking in references to sex and sexually active women. His attitude toward sex clarifies for us the relationship between his conception of women and his concern with the self of the American myth.

As we have seen, the image of women in Twain's life and writing implies a rigid insistence on sexual purity—to the extent that his fiction avoids the subject altogether by dealing primarily with little girls or old ladies. This prudishness cannot be ascribed solely to the reticence of Twain's era. Twain's prudery exceeds even that of his contemporaries Howells and James.[68] And it seems odd that a man who could be so forthright in dealing with sham and hypocrisy in other areas should have been publicly so silent on this subject. It is not that Twain was not interested in sex himself. His letters and other evidence attest to the enjoyment of a full physical relationship with his wife.[69] Nor can Twain's silence on sexual matters be blamed on his wife's censorship. As research has shown, it was clearly Twain who made those deletions in his manuscripts.[70]

Notebooks kept during the years prior to his marriage contain no references to sex or to any relationships with women; in fact, they make no mention of any women with whom he might have established a relationship. It is as if sex and sexually available women did not exist. Dixon Wecter maintains that Twain was a virgin when he married at thirty-four, and the evidence tends to support his claim.[71] Alexander Jones, however, argues that such a conclusion is unwarranted, and he cites other evidence supporting his contention that

Twain had ample opportunity for sexual relationships and very probably did have sexual experience before marriage.[72]

I cannot see that it makes any difference whether Twain was sexually active before his marriage or not. If he was, he took great pains to conceal all evidence of it. Such an intense concern for the concealment of sexual activity, it seems to me, amounts to the same thing as not having any sexual experience at all: both patterns point to a stringently moralistic attitude toward sex and an overriding fear of censure. An exploration of these two attitudes will, I believe, lead to a better understanding of Twain's sexual timidity in print.

Twain's prudishness is particularly apparent in his French notebooks. In 1879, while living in France with his family, he railed against French immorality and called France a "nation of the filthy-minded." According to Twain, the whole of French society—books, daily papers, even matchboxes— "reeked" of nastiness. Nor was it only the French who offended Twain's moral sense. He was disgusted with books like Henry Fielding's *Tom Jones* (*Notebooks*, 2: 294) and was incensed by the sexuality of paintings like Titian's *Venus*.

In dealing with his daughters, Twain was strict, conventional, and very concerned about appearances. They never went anywhere without a chaperone.[73] In Germany in 1891, when Clara was seventeen and Livy was away, Twain kept Clara locked in her hotel room for several days because she had been receiving attentions from a German officer. It was not until Livy returned and told Twain how ridiculously he was acting that the irate father let Clara out of her tower.[74] Twain was disturbed by any behavior that he deemed "unladylike." Once in Italy, when he saw some officers staring at Clara in a tea room, he cut the artificial fruit off her hat because he thought it looked coquettish.[75] He also scolded Clara about her free behavior at a ball when she was studying music in Berlin in 1893, and he wrote her a long letter that gives a clear idea of his values: "We want you to be a lady—a lady above reproach—a lady always, modest, and never loud, never hoydenish—a lady recognizable as such at a glance."[76]

Yet, despite Twain's prudishness in print and in his personal life, he wrote very explicitly on sex in works not intended for publication. In perhaps the best known of these, *1601, or Conversation as it Was by the Social Fireside in the Time of the Tudors* (1876), Queen Elizabeth, Sir Walter Raleigh, and other Elizabethans talk frankly and bawdily in carefully researched contemporary language. The work uses the most common Anglo-Saxon four-letter words and deals with such subjects as sex and other bodily functions. Twain himself found it highly amusing and wrote in his notebook that though he seldom laughed at his own work, he could not think of *1601* without laughing (*Notebooks*, 2: 303). Other men of his day also found it amusing, and it was privately printed and circulated among friends. In 1879 Twain was a member of The Stomach Club in Paris, a men's social club at which members spoke on various men-only subjects. Twain's speech on masturbation, "Some Remarks on the Science of Onanism," delivered in June 1879, is filled with puns and cleverly rephrased proverbs. Also, Twain copied into his notebooks, particularly in 1879, a number of pornographic jokes (see *Notebooks*, 2: 342–350). Around 1902 Twain wrote a humorous letter for a group of male friends with whom he was to go on a fishing, drinking, and card-playing cruise. The letter refers to the group as the "Mammoth Cods," and the joke turns on the question of whether the pseudonymous writer of the letter is eligible or even willing to join an organization whose requirement for membership is an unusually large penis. Finally, in a rather sad poem on the impotence of old age, "A Weaver's Beam," Twain coined one of the more clever puns in the English language: "The Penis mightier than the sword."[77]

What is one to make of these explicit discussions of sex, which contrast so strongly with Twain's fiction and his personal disgust with immorality? The answer seems to lie partly in Twain's attitude toward women. Twain considered it not improper to write such essays as "The Mammoth Cod" because they were intended only for men. What he always objected to was the corrupting influence of literature and art on women, particularly young women. That was his main objection to Titian's *Venus*: "Young girls can be defiled by looking at V[enus]" (*Notebooks*, 2: 319). That was his reason for censoring Livy's reading: works like *Don Quixote* and Shakespeare were not "proper books for virgins" (*Love Letters*, p. 76). That was his principal objection to the "nastiness" he saw in French society: it corrupted the minds of young girls (*Notebooks*, 2: 324). In one sense, Twain's attitude reflects the nineteenth-century double standard. He wanted a wife who was a pure, respectable lady whom he himself was not "worthy" of.

Why was female purity so important to Twain? In order to answer this question, it is necessary to recognize that Twain distinguished between proper women and improper women. The woman he is concerned about is the genteel lady (like his wife and daughters), the "girl" who is eligible for marriage or the wife. He is concerned to preserve her as an image of innocence and respectability, pure in mind and body. The lower-class or impure "gal," whom Twain does not regard as a marriage partner, is associated with sex and other ungenteel aspects of femaleness. Although she may sometimes be more interesting because her character is not so limited, Twain condemns her. The contrast in Twain's mind between the ideal woman and the woman of lower status is spelled out in two dreams that he recorded. In one dream, which Twain described in January 1897 in his notebook, a Negro wench accosts him and makes disgusting propositions to him. He is repelled by her (*Works*, 22: 351–352). The other dream, which he described in an essay called "My Platonic Sweetheart," is a recurring one. Throughout his life, he says, he has had a dream in which he meets an innocent young girl (always the same sweet, earnest girl of fifteen). Then, before there can be any kind of consummation or conclusion to the relationship, she disappears, and Twain is left feeling cold and empty (*Works*, 8: 287–304). Whether Twain really dreamed these dreams or simply created the situations, they are significant as an indication of the polarity he felt between the ideal image of female purity and the woman who does not fit the image. The latter is aggressive and repulsive to him; yet the ideal woman is only an image to be worshipped at a distance.

There is more to Twain's insistence on sexual purity than the Victorian double standard. The woman who repels him is not only sexually aware, she is independent, aggressive, and selfish—the opposite of all the qualities he associated with ideal womanhood. It is significant that the only two women in his novels who have any sexual identity are aggressive and "masculine" in the sense that they dominate or try to dominate the men in their lives. Roxy is strong and shrewd, with "aggressive and commanding ways" (*Works*, 3: 79). Laura Hawkins is selfish and manipulative. In Twain's mind the two seem to go together; female impurity is somehow related to independence—or what he considers unfeminine behavior. A pure woman, a lady, is properly dependent and selfless; she does not interfere with what Twain sees as man's rightful role.

This association is particularly clear in Twain's comments about French immorality. The French, he says, have been ruled by concubines for a thousand years in all walks of life, which helps to account for the littleness and nastiness of French society:

> In countries where wives hold first place in the husbands' hearts, the men govern the country—they govern it, receiving wise & unselfish counsel from the wives. The wives do not *govern* the country, for they do not govern its men. But concubines do govern the men, & in the very nature of things they govern them with selfish ends in view. A nation governed in all its big & little details by foul & selfish & trivial-minded prostitutes is not likely to have much largeness or dignity of character.
>
> (*Notebooks*, 2: 323)

The wives are selfless and dependent upon the men; the concubines are selfish and dominating. It seems evident that Twain's insistence on purity in women, his creation of an ideal image, was more than an obsession with morality; it was also a concern to keep women from asserting an independence that would interfere with the autonomy of the male self.[78]

This, then, is the main reason why Twain was so careful to exclude all references to sex from his fiction: he was governed by a prudishness predicated on the fear that sexually active women were a threat to the male self. There was another reason as well, one that also derived from a concern for self: he was very much concerned with his own reputation. Although he portrayed himself as a rebel and enemy of society, he was very much a creature of convention. Despite his rough appearance and primitivism of his materials, he was basically very middle-class in his values. He deliberately sought out a genteel, bourgeois wife, he sought advice on matters of taste and etiquette, and he adhered to a strict moral code in his personal life and in the upbringing of his daughters. He was not Huck Finn, the rebel who lived outside society; he was what Leslie Fiedler called the "Good Bad Boy," a Tom Sawyer who only made a show of being bad to shock Aunt Polly.[79] Twain might flout certain aspects of convention in line with his Tom Sawyer image, but he would do nothing that would cast him outside of society. Thus, he could drink, swear, and dress eccentrically, but he would never openly transgress a rule as basic to his society as the sex taboo either in his personal life or in his public utterances.

Twain complained in his notebooks that a writer would be criticized for describing in print what an artist could display on canvas (*Notebooks*, 2: 312, 319). Despite the façade he presented of not caring, public opinion was very important to him. He withdrew his support from the Russian revolutionary Maxim Gorky in 1906 when it was discovered that the woman who accompanied Gorky to the United States was not his wife. He scolded his daughter Clara, warning her not to offend against propriety because she would have herself "and us talked about."[80] And in Hartford in 1872 he sided with the majority of the Nook Farm residents who refused to believe that the esteemed Henry Ward Beecher was guilty of adultery. He even forbade Livy to visit or have anything to do with Beecher's sister, Isabella, because Isabella, a feminist and friend of free-love advocate Victoria Woodhull, had publicly declared her belief in her brother's guilt.[81]

Twain used his wife, Mrs. Fairbanks, and William Dean Howells to censor his writings because he wanted to protect his reputation. As he told journalist F. M. White: "I don't always know just where to draw the line in matters of taste. Mrs. Clemens kept a lot of things from getting into print that might have given me a reputation I wouldn't care to have."[82] That this concern with public opinion was Twain's own and not imposed upon him by his wife is clear from an autobiographical passage in *Mark Twain in Eruption*. Twain relates a conversation with the British author Elinor Glyn in 1908, four years after his wife's death. Glyn was trying to obtain his public support for her unconventional novel, *Three Weeks*, in which two lovers disobey society's laws. Twain agreed with her and made strong statements himself during their private conversation, but when she asked if she could publish some of his statements in order to help her cause, he refused. He could not support her publicly: "I said we were servants of convention. . . . I said it would damn me before my time and I didn't wish to be useful to the world on such expensive conditions."[83]

Twain's failure to deal with sex in his fiction, then, was determined primarily by his concern to preserve the purity of the female image—and thus her selfless dependence—and his concern to preserve his own reputation. Both of these factors derive from his principal concern: the self.

It is this concern for self and its effect upon his relationship with others that provide the key to Twain's attitude toward and portrayal of women. Twain was the American individualist *par excellence* both in his life and in his writing. In some ways, Twain was probably the most obviously self-oriented of American writers. He enjoyed making himself conspicious and was always happiest when he was the center of attention. In his autobiography he tells how, as a child in Hannibal, he pretended to be hypnotized in a visiting hypnotist's show, even allowing himself to be stuck with pins so that he might continue night after night as the star of the show (*Eruption*, pp. 118–128).

Throughout his life, Twain liked to be on center stage. His daughter Susy wrote in her biography of her father around 1885: "He told us the other day that he couldn't bear to hear any one talk but himself, but that he could listen to himself for hours without getting tired" (*Autob.*, Paine, 2: 83). Clara tells how family and guests listened at dinner while Twain led the conversation by himself.[84] Like Emerson, Twain enjoyed playing host to the "stream of visitors" and admirers he entertained in his Hartford house.[85] He apparently obtained the same ego gratification from his lecturing, which he described as "gymnastics, chest-expander, medicine, mind-healer, blues destroyer, all in one."[86]

Twain delighted in recognition and attention. When he went to England in 1872, he had intended to write a book satirizing the English. But he liked England and found the English so appreciative of his work—he was applauded and praised on all levels of society as he had not been in the United States—that he was converted to an Anglophile and never wrote his book.[87] When he was living in Hartford in the 1880s, he walked down the streets as though he were on a stage. People stopped to look at him, pointed him out or asked who he was, and listened to his every word.[88] Twain thrived on this kind of attention. His daughter Clara tells how in Germany in 1899 he was recognized in a crowd by a mounted policeman, who ordered the guard to let him pass, and he walked through like a royal personage. "My! But that makes me feel d____ good!" Clara quotes him as saying.[89] When he lived in New York in the 1890s and again after Livy died, he was constantly in the public eye. He spoke at banquets and dinners, and reporters telephoned him almost daily for his opinions on all matters. He enjoyed and played up to the title given to him in 1893: "The belle of New York."[90]

Twain once said that he wanted to be "the most conspicuous person on the planet."[91] If he wanted to be conspicuous, it was not just to be noticed but to be admired. When he attended a dinner at Oxford, where he had received an honorary degree in 1907, he wore a black evening suit. Everyone else was in crimson gowns, and Twain felt uncomfortable—not because he looked different but because he looked drab compared to the others:

> Was it my conspicuousness that distressed me? Not at all. It was merely that I was not beautifully conspicuous but uglily conspicuous. . . . If I had been . . . shining like the sun, I should have been entirely at ease, utterly happy, perfectly satisfied with myself. (*Eruption*, pp. 322–323)

In his later life, Twain took to wearing an all-white suit, which with his white hair created a dramatic effect, particularly in winter, when other men wore dark colors.[92] Justin Kaplan theorizes that Twain wore white because of a fetish for being clean, which was associated with guilt feelings.[93] It seems to me, though, that Twain's purpose was much simpler than that: he had found a way to be "beautifully conspicuous."[94]

Twain himself was aware of how important to him was the applause of others. When he told William Dean Howells he was writing his autobiography, Howells "applauded, and was full of praises and endorsement." Twain commented that this reaction was "wise in him and judicious. If he had manifested a different spirit I would have thrown him out of the window" (*Autob.*, Paine, 2: 246–247). In the short story "The £1,000,000 Bank Note" Twain describes a situation very much like his own:

> You can imagine how it was with a young fellow who had never been taken notice of before, and now all of a sudden couldn't stir abroad without constantly overhearing the remark flying from lip to lip, "There he goes; that's him!" . . . Why, I just swam in glory all day long.
> (*Works*, 15: 119)

Twain often portrayed characters who win admiration and applause, but the character with whom he identified most is the glory-seeking Tom Sawyer. Like Twain, Tom always plays to an audience. Tom wants to win the Sunday school prize, not for the prize itself, but for the glory of it. When he takes the blame for Becky in school, he is "inspired by the splendor of his own act." He is constantly fantasizing about the effect his actions will have on other people. He imagines himself dead and delights in how sorry "they" will be. The "proudest moment in his life" is when he attends his own funeral—a dramatic gesture deliberately planned to elicit the maximum effect. But in order to accomplish this coup, Tom must selfishly allow those who love him to believe him dead (*Works*, 1: 31, 64, 104, 24, 144).[95]

As Tom's actions with respect to the funeral indicate, this craving for attention derives from an excessive concern with self, which necessitates a disregard for the feelings of others. Twain loved his wife, but, as we have seen, he saw her primarily in relation to himself. His self-considerations were greater even than his concern for her, just as Tom's need to derive satisfaction from his death hoax was greater than his concern for his aunt.[96]

Twain's tendency to view other people in relation to his own needs is spelled out in a letter written to his life-long friend Joe Twichell in 1905, the year after Livy died. Livy was no longer available to absorb his moods. Susy was dead. His daughter Clara had suffered a nervous breakdown after her mother's death, and his daughter Jean was an epileptic. Twain needed someone to administer to his needs:

> I have written you to-day, not to do you a service, but to do myself one. There was bile in me. I had to empty it or lose my day tomorrow. . . . I *have* to work my bile off whenever it gets to where I can't stand it but I can work it off on you economically, because I don't have to make it suit me. It may not suit you, but that isn't any matter.[97]

Twain's relationship to other people differed from that of

Emerson and Thoreau in the sense that, whereas they believed in the total sufficiency of the self and were unable to establish a reciprocal relationship with other people, Twain did relate to other people, as, for example, in his love for Livy. However, his intense self-orientation prevented him from regarding other people as separate individuals.

If Twain saw his family and friends primarily in relation to himself, it was because, for him, the self was of primary importance. Twain was aware of this self-orientation and generalized it into a philosophy of mankind. *What is Man?* (1890–1899) became a bitter indictment: "Man never does a single thing which has any FIRST AND FOREMOST *object but one—to secure peace of mind, spiritual comfort, for HIM-SELF*" (*Essays*, pp. 343–344; Twain's italics). Although Twain wrote *What is Man?* at a period in his life when he was particularly depressed, this philosophy cannot be attributed simply to his depressed state or regarded only as a phenomenon of his later years. Twenty-five years before, when Twain was reading Lecky's *History of European Morals*, he wrote in the margin, "all our acts, reasoned or unreasoned, are selfish," and agreed with Lecky that the only reason for virtuous actions is that they bring us the most happiness.[98]

Twain gave the self such importance because, like Emerson, he saw the self as all-inclusive. Bernard DeVoto prints as a preface to *Mark Twain in Eruption* a passage that Twain wrote in 1907:

> Every man is in his own person the whole human race, with not a detail lacking. . . . I have studied the human race with diligence and strong interest all these years in my own person; in myself I find in big or little proportion every quality and every defect that is findable in the mass of the race.　　　　　(*Eruption*, n.p.)

For Twain, the self is the world, and the world is absorbed into the self. Twain created a persona that represented the self as he saw it. He called this persona Mark Twain, and his principal occupation was to preserve and develop it. One of the major concerns of Twain's life was the creation of his own autobiography, which he envisioned as a model for all autobiographies. It would be read for two thousand years, he said, and would contain enough volumes to fill a library (*Autob.*, Paine, 2: 245–246).

As we have seen throughout this work, such an inflated view of the self is consistent with the narcissism of American individualism. All of Twain's fiction emphasizes the importance of the individual: he writes of the solitary protagonist; he seldom portrays interpersonal relationships; and he often contrasts the strength and/or wisdom of the individual with the folly of the community. In *Tom Sawyer* the other characters are primarily stock figures who provide the backdrop for Tom's adventures. In *Huckleberry Finn* Huck travels down the river on a raft, testing and rejecting life in the different communities on shore. His relationship with Jim—the only felt relationship between two people in all of Twain's fiction—is presented more as a vehicle of growth for Huck than as a relationship for its own sake. At the end, Twain makes it clear that Jim really is not important. Huck goes along with Tom's plan, which provides humor for the reader and an adventure for Tom at the expense of Jim's humanity. In the end Huck decides to leave the community behind and "light out for the territory"—in the manner of the prototypical American hero.

The superior individual who stands head and shoulders above the crowd is a common theme in Twain's work. Hank Morgan's possession of nineteenth-century technological knowledge in Arthurian England makes him seem almost superhuman. Joan of Arc is set apart by her superior knowledge and uncanny military ability. And Pudd'nhead Wilson is so far above the crowd that he is regarded as a fool. In *Huckleberry Finn* Colonel Sherburne stands up to the mob that has come to lynch him and contemptuously dismisses the average man as a coward: "The idea of you thinking you had pluck enough to lynch a *man!*" (*Works*, 9: 202). The ultimate in Twain's superior individuals is Philip Traum, or Satan, whose superior knowledge and contempt for man in *The Mysterious Stranger* derive from his extraplanetary origins.

Twain's interest in the individual is also apparent in his nonfiction. He admired the strength and power of a man like Ulysses S. Grant,[99] and he considered the only great era in French history to be the one under Napoleon (*Notebooks*, 2: 325). Twain particularly praised the practical, self-reliant individual. Of Napoleon III he said, "I do admire his nerve, his calm self-reliance, his shrewd good sense," and he called him the "genius of Energy, Persistence, Enterprise" (*Works*, 2: vol. 1, 144, 123). Twain's appreciation of these qualities helps to explain his admiration of the American businessman, particularly the self-made man who could build a huge fortune from nothing. Twain numbered among his personal friends Andrew Carnegie and Standard Oil magnate Henry Huttleston Rogers. He admired Rogers's cleverness and financial know-how. He wrote to Livy in 1894, when Rogers was helping him to salvage what he could from his bankruptcy: "He is the only man I care for in the world; the only man I would give a *damn* about" (*Letters*, 2: 612). In *Mark Twain in Eruption* he spoke of Andrew Carnegie's "great achievements." His only criticism of Carnegie seems to have been that Carnegie took a juvenile delight in trivial flattery (*Eruption*, pp. 36–51).

Twain's emphasis on the individual is significant as an indication of the extent to which he was in tune with American thought. Born in 1835, he lived in an America characterized by territorial and economic expansion and by a faith in unlimited opportunities for the development and expansion of the individual. Twain's first book, *The Innocents Abroad* (1863), reveals a complacent belief in the political and economic superiority of American institutions. The narrator compares the American way with other cultures, arrogantly concluding in each instance that no one can compete with American technology, freedom, and opportunity. In 1873, however, in *The Gilded Age*, Twain criticized the political corruption in Washington and the money orientation of Americans. He wrote to his brother Orion in 1875 of the national "rottenness" and the "moral ulcers" in American society.[100] Yet, no matter how harshly he attacked certain aspects of American society, Twain always believed in the superiority of American institutions and ideas. In April 1887, in a speech before the Union Veterans Association of Maryland, he offered only praise for America:

> [T]his freest of free commonwealths the sun in his course shines upon; this one sole country nameable in history or tradition where a man *is* a man and manhood the only royalty; this people ruled by the justest and wholesomest laws and government yet devised by the wisdom of men; this mightiest of the civilized empires of the earth, in numbers, in prosperity, in progress and in promise; . . . our land, our country, our giant empire. (*Life*, p. 218)

Twain regarded himself as a self-made man in the American tradition. At least, this is how he described himself in the capsule biography he wrote to be signed by his nephew, Samuel Moffatt, for the 1899–1919 edition of his complete works. He also described himself as "characteristically American in every fiber" (*Works*, 16: pp. 387–389). Despite his criticism of American materialism, Twain throughout his life remained a dedicated participant in the American Dream.

Van Wyck Brooks portrays Twain as an unwilling adherent of these ideas.[101] But the childhood rebellion that Brooks points to as evidence of Twain's artistic nature (which, Brooks maintains, was suppressed by society) is consistent with the self-assertion of the American individualist. As a child, Twain's rebellion (like Tom Sawyer's and Huck Finn's) was directed against institutions like the church and school—anything that imposed limits on the self. It is part of the American myth for the individual to revolt. Emerson, Thoreau, Whitman—all rebelled against what they saw as a curtailment of the individual.

In his own life, Twain followed the star of success just as avidly as any other aspirant to the American Dream. He sought constantly and deliberately to improve himself. In his autobiography Twain cites as very influential in his life the advice given him by statesman Anson Burlingame in 1866: "Avoid inferiors. Seek your comradeships among your superiors in intellect and character; always *climb*" (*Autob.*, Paine, 2: 125). Twain was attracted to his wife because she represented to him respectability and success. And one cannot ignore the fact that she was to inherit a quarter of a million dollars. Twain always insisted that he would be the breadwinner, but when he married, he accepted from his father-in-law with no apparent difficulty the gift of a $43,000 house fully furnished and staffed with servants and a part interest in the Buffalo *Express*. When he left Buffalo, he sold the house and the interest and used the profit to establish himself in the prestigious Nook Farm community in Hartford, where he built a magnificent mansion. Twain's desire to build the biggest and showiest house around cannot be blamed on his wife; in her letters Livy constantly stated her own preference for a simple life. Furthermore, after his wife was dead, Twain built another magnificent house in Connecticut, modeled after an Italian villa. Twain liked the material evidence of success. William Dean Howells observed that Twain "luxuriated in the lavish use" of money and had a "love of magnificence."[102] As Livy once commented, "Mr. Clemens seems to glory in his sense of possession."[103] Livy herself was one of these possessions, which, to Twain, represented success and the achievement of the American Dream.

Like any Horatio Alger hero, Twain's primary goal was monetary success and the esteem that went with it. Howells said that money was Twain's dream.[104] Twain desired to become a riverboat pilot because that position represented the apex of his social aspirations at that time. He wrote in *Life on the Mississippi* (1883): "I had comforting daydreams of a future when I should be a great and honored pilot with plenty of money" (*Works*, 7: 37). When the Civil War forced Twain to give up piloting, he sought his fortune in gold and silver mining.[105] He stopped mining only when he found that newspaper work offered a greater opportunity for success. Ultimately, he obtained his greatest success through literature, and in fact he always thought of his writing as a means to financial and social success. He deliberately used the method of subscription publishing for his first books because he felt it would be more profitable (see, e.g., *Letters*, 1: 141–142). Throughout his life, he succumbed to one get-rich-quick scheme or investment after another. Twain could write so sympathetically of Colonel Sellers, the financial visionary of his fiction, because, as his wife and friends observed, there was a part of him that *was* Colonel Sellers.[106] In Twain's fiction, the acquisition of money is the basis for *The Gilded Age* and *The American Claimant*. At the end of *Tom Sawyer* the boys find $12,000, which is invested for them in the best capitalist tradition. And in *A Connecticut Yankee* Hank Morgan uses his superior nineteenth-century technology to reap financial profits, social prestige, and political power in Arthur's England.

Twain's later fiction shows a continuing obsession with money. But in the later works, which reflect Twain's problems with his dwindling fortunes and eventual bankruptcy, money is a source of destruction and corruption. In *Pudd'n-head Wilson* Tom's need for money drives him to murder. The priest in *The Mysterious Stranger* is destroyed by the purse he finds. And in "The $30,000 Bequest" Aleck and Sally destroy themselves in anticipation of an inheritance that never comes. "The Man That Corrupted Hadleyburg" demonstrates that no one is exempt from the corrupting influence of money. Yet, despite his bitter indictment of money, Twain had struggled to regain his fortune, sought every means he could to amplify it, and once again enjoyed displaying the material evidence of his success. His last years, after the deaths of his wife and daughter, were spent as the "pet" of successful American businessmen. He enjoyed dinners and New York society. He took cruises on his friend's yacht, voyaged to Bermuda, and built himself a new mansion. It is also significant that in 1889, soon after writing the nightmare ending to *A Connecticut Yankee*, which might be interpreted as symbolizing his disillusion with the American idea of progress, Twain wrote a letter to Walt Whitman on the occasion of Whitman's seventieth birthday that is itself a very Whitmanesque ode to progress:

> What great births you have witnessed! The steam-press, the steamship, the steel-ship, the railroad, the perfected cotton-gin, the telegraph, the telephone, the phonograph, the photograph, the photogravure, the electrotype, the gaslight, the electric light, the sewing machine, and the amazing, infinitely varied and innumerable products of coal-tar, those latest and strangest marvels of a marvelous age. . . . Yes, you have indeed seen much; but tarry yet awhile, for the greatest is yet to come! You shall see marvels upon marvels added to these whose nativity you have witnessed; and conspicuous above them you shall see their formidable Result—Man at almost his full stature at last!—and still growing, visibly growing, while you look.[107]

During most of his life, then, Twain maintained a belief in American individualism that was reflected in his own pursuit of the American Dream of success and in his tendency to view the self as all-important. His all-encompassing "I" left no room for other people and ideas except as they were a part of him. His self was the world. And woman, as an abstract symbol of purity and selflessness, existed only as part of that world. Twain acknowledged the existence of women and interacted with them in a way that the self-sufficient Emerson did not, but he did not regard woman as an independent person. Thus he was unable to portray in his fiction a woman with a personality of her own. For Twain, woman existed only as imaged by and in relation to the male self.

Even at his bitterest, Twain held to his original view of woman as the pure, innocent ideal of preadolescence. *Joan of Arc*, which he wrote after his bankruptcy ,and the failure of the typesetter, is the ultimate expression of this ideal. And Mary Baker Eddy, whom he vilified in *Christian Science* (1907), is the ultimate example of the woman who did not fit the image. What most incensed Twain about Eddy was that she sought money and power *for herself.* The drive that governed his own life and that he admired in other men, he abhorred in women. The difference between Joan and Mary Baker Eddy is that Joan, although she acts independently, remains pure and modest and never acts for herself. Eddy soiled her hands in the making of money and, according to Twain, acted only for herself. This was what Twain could not tolerate in women. The woman who is not selfless cannot be contained within another self.

During his last years Twain clung rather sadly to his ideal of girlish purity. With his wife and daughters no longer around him, he sought friendships (apparently platonic) with very young girls, whom he called his "Angel Fish." In one sense they represented surrogate daughters and helped to compensate for the loss of his daughter Susy. But they also provided him with the kind of relationship that his self-assertion required. They were like playthings, these little girls, who amused him and brought him pleasure. They represented no threat to the self. He insisted that they must remain young and unspoiled—the symbol of pretty innocence and girlish selflessness that had always characterized his view of women.[108]

PART THREE

PART THREE

THE WOMAN AS PERSON

CHAPTER 7

THE CLAIMS OF THE OTHER: NATHANIEL HAWTHORNE

*[That] struck me as the intensity of masculine
egotism. It centered everything in itself, and deprived woman of her very soul, her inexpressible
and unfathomable all, to make it a mere incident
in the great sum of man.*

Nathaniel Hawthorne,
The Blithedale Romance[1]

The reader of Nathaniel Hawthorne's fiction
cannot help but be struck by the vividness of
the portrayals of certain of his female characters. To be sure, Hawthorne's fiction contains
its share of conventional heroines, but in
three of his novels Hawthorne was able to go
beyond this stereotyped image of American
femininity to produce real flesh-and-blood
women. Hester Prynne, Zenobia, Miriam—
all are center-of-stage characters who cannot be downstaged by assertive male superpersons. It is true that Hawthorne's strong
women are never allowed to pursue what
might seem to be the implications of their
characters; they do not become heroic lead-
ers or independent public figures. Although
this hesitation is owing in part to Hawthorne's
belief in a conventional image of feminine
behavior, it is also important to remember

that there are no male heroes in Hawthorne's fiction either. Hawthorne did not countenance individual self-assertion in anyone—man or woman.

In many respects, Hawthorne's view of women differed little from that of his contemporaries. He wrote to Sophia before they were married, "I deem a true woman holier than an angel."[2] In his later life he greatly admired Coventry Patmore's poem, "The Angel in the House," which presents an exalted picture of married love, with the gentle, loving wife adored for her adoration of her husband.[3] Hawthorne apparently believed that it was possible for women to possess talent and even genius, but he was concerned that the public exercise of talent would destroy what he regarded as the essence of a woman's femininity. In an 1830 essay on Anne Hutchinson, Hawthorne admonished: "Woman, when she feels the impulse of genius like a command of Heaven within her, should beware that she is relinquishing a part of the loveliness of her sex and obey the inward voice with sorrowing reluctance."[4] Twenty-six years later Hawthorne still felt the same way. In a letter to Sophia in 1856 he wrote that he was glad that she was not a public woman:

> With a brighter and deeper intellect than any other woman, thou hast never . . . prostituted thy self to the public. . . . It does seem to me to deprive women of all delicacy; it has pretty much such an effect on them as it would to walk abroad through streets, physically naked.
> (*Love Letters*, 1: foreword; 2:248)

Most of Hawthorne's written comments about public women refer to women writers. With respect to them, he was not only concerned about the loss of feminine delicacy; he was also motivated by a fear of competition in the marketplace. In the essay on Anne Hutchinson, after noting that more and more women were writing, Hawthorne complained that soon women would push men from the field (*Writings*, 17:1–2). In later years, as his books struggled to compete in popularity with the sentimental romances of popular women writers, this fear intensified into hatred. "*All* women, as author's [sic], are feeble and tiresome," he wrote to his publisher, James T. Fields, in 1852; "I wish they were forbidden to write, on pain of having their faces deeply scarified with an oyster shell."[5] A few years later he complained to Fields's partner, William Ticknor, from England: "America is now wholly given over to a d—d mob of scribbling women, and I shall have no chance of success while the public is occupied with their trash."[6]

In his next letter to Ticknor, however, Hawthorne qualified his attitude toward women writers:

> In my last, I recollect, I bestowed some vituperation on female authors. I have since been reading "Ruth Hall"; and I must say I enjoyed it a good deal. The woman writes as if the devil was in her; and that is the only condition under which a woman ever writes anything worth reading. Generally women write like emasculated men, and are only distinguished from male authors by greater feebleness and folly; but when they throw off the restraints of decency, and come before the public stark naked, as it were—then their books are sure to possess character and value.   (*Letters*, 1:78)

This comment helps to clarify Hawthorne's attitude toward women writers. Apparently he felt that women who wrote in the straitjacket of conventional femininity were simply bad writers. Although he did not like to see a woman lose that restraint—and he would have been distressed to have his wife thus exposed to the public—he believed that it was only with the loss of conventional inhibitions that a woman could develop her talents. And he admired the woman whose writing he respected.

It was Hawthorne's concern for feminine delicacy that complicated his position on women's rights. Though sensitive to and in sympathy with the plight of women in nineteenth-century society, he did not like reformers of any kind. He was also troubled by the fear that the independent woman would lose her femininity, that "ethereal essence, wherein she has her truest life" (*Works*, 1:165–166). Yet his fiction is filled with references that reveal a sympathetic understanding of the problems that women faced. Hester's reflections in *The Scarlet Letter* (1850) on the injustices of woman's position—though they take her farther than Hawthorne is willing to follow—are not unsympathetically written. That Hawthorne agrees with Hester on the need for a more equitable treatment of women is apparent in his portrayal of the situation of Hester herself. He obviously believes that Hester was cruelly wronged by Chillingworth and comments on the injustice of the deformed old man's having persuaded a young girl into a loveless marriage at a time when "her heart knew no better" (*Works*, 1:74, 176–177). In Hester Prynne, Hawthorne created a woman of strength, intelligence, and resourcefulness, whose very existence gives the lie to those who would argue the natural inferiority of women. Hawthorne respects and admires Hester and the strength that enables her to withstand the scorn of the community and the failure of her lover.

Hester is a more admirable character than either of the men in the novel, both of whom are totally self-oriented. Of the three, only Hester is able to rise above the circumstances in which she finds herself. Chillingworth becomes a malicious fiend and Dimmesdale, a weak hypocrite. If Hawthorne draws back at the suggestion of restructuring society, if he fears the loss of feminine delicacy, he nevertheless sympathizes with the situation that would put a woman such as Hester Prynne at the mercy of arbitrary laws and masculine injustice. Though Hawthorne does not believe that Hester should attempt to change society, he sympathizes with her belief that one day, "in Heaven's own time, a new truth would be revealed, in order to establish the whole relationship between man and woman on a surer ground of mutual happiness" (*Works*, 1:263, 165–166).

If Hawthorne does not make Hester into a prophet and the leader of a sexual-social revolution, it is because, although he himself is very much aware of the problems that she perceives, he does not believe that she can accomplish any changes. Hawthorne was not a reformer, and he could not conceive of good coming through the imposition of abstract ideas. Those critics who see the ending of *The Scarlet Letter* as a cruel, misogynistic hamstringing of Hester's powers are reading into the novel a typically American concept of positive action.[7] For Hawthorne, Hester's choice to remain with her child and then, after Pearl has grown up and gone her own way, to devote the remainder of her life to selflessly helping the people of her community as a kind of volunteer nurse and social worker is more indicative of strength of character than would be the solitary pursuit of an ideal, however worthy. That the ending of *The Scarlet Letter* cannot be read as an attempt to circumscribe female action is clear from the conclusion of Hawthorne's second novel, *The House of the Seven Gables* (1851), in which a male character gives up his Emersonian devotion to ideals and his ambition to change the world for what Hawthorne considers more important, that is, a close association with humankind.

What seems to disturb Hawthorne most of all in his observations on the position of women is the misuse that men have made of their dominance. Chillingworth uses the youthful Hester for his own comfort (*Works*, 1:176–177). Judge Pyncheon is said to have killed his wife early in their marriage by requiring her to serve him "in token of fealty to her liege-lord and master" (*Works*, 2:123). And Colonel Pyncheon wore out three wives by the "remorseless weight and hardness of his character in the conjugal relation" (*Works*, 2:123). In *The Blithedale Romance* (1852), after the self-oriented Hollingsworth characterizes woman as nothing but a reflection of man, Coverdale comments that Hollingsworth has only expressed what "millions of despots like him" really feel. This kind of thinking, says Coverdale in Hawthornian accents, deprives woman of her "very soul" to make her "a mere incident in the great sum of man" (*Works*, 3:123). The cause of so many of the wrongs of women, Coverdale asserts, is the egotism of men. When Zenobia drowns herself, he reflects:

> It was a woful thought, that a woman of Zenobia's diversified capacity should have fancied herself irretrievably

> defeated on the broad battle-field of life . . . merely be-
> cause Love had gone against her. It is nonsense, and a
> miserable wrong,—the result, like so many others, of
> masculine egotism. (*Works*, 3:241)

One of the problems Hawthorne notes is the lack of opportunities for women. Hester must turn to needlework because, "then as now," it is almost the only work available to
women (*Works*, 1:81). Hepzibah must become a petty shop-
keeper for the same reason (*Works*, 2:38). And in the preface
to *The Blithedale Romance* Hawthorne characterizes Zenobia
as a type of "the high-spirited Woman, bruising herself against
the narrow limitations of her sex" (*Works*, 3:2).

Hawthorne regrets this circumscription. Although he
was concerned that women should not lose their femininity, he
apparently believed that it was possible for woman to expand
her horizons. In the story of Queen Christina Hawthorne
proposed: "It is very possible for a woman to have a strong
mind, and to be fitted for the active business of life, without
losing any of her natural delicacy" (*Works*, 6:283–284). His
French and Italian Notebooks contain a description of Louise
Lander, a New England sculptor in Rome: "a young woman,
living in almost perfect independence, . . . with no household
ties, no rule or law but that within her; yet acting with quiet-
ness and simplicity, and keeping, after all, within a homely
line of right" (*Works*, 14:78). And in *The Marble Faun* (1860)
he uses Hilda as an example of such a woman. The freedom
of female artists in Rome makes it apparent to Hawthorne
that women can be released from traditional restrictions:

> The customs of artist-life bestow such liberty upon the
> sex, which is elsewhere restricted within so much nar-
> rower limits; and it is perhaps an indication that, when-
> ever we admit woman to a wider scope of pursuits and
> professions, we must also remove the shackles of our
> present conventional rules, which would then become
> an insufferable restraint on either maid or wife. The sys-

tem seems to work unexceptionally in Rome.

(Works, 4:54–55)

Despite his nineteenth-century concern for femininity, then, Hawthorne was able to regard women as independent persons and could therefore accept the independent actions of women. Moreover, it is apparent from his journals and letters that he truly admired a number of public women. He apparently maintained a friendly relationship with Fanny Kemble, who was one of the most public and publicized women in America at the time.[8] Before his marriage to Sophia, he had been friendly with her sister Elizabeth, certainly a public woman. When in later years he became annoyed with Elizabeth, it was because of her private actions, not her public ones.[9] But it was in Europe, where Hawthorne himself was a more public figure, that he frequently met public women. In April 1856 he wrote in his notebook that he liked Miss Glyn, the actress. She retained her natural goodness and simplicity, he found, and was a "good, simple, and intelligent lady" (*English Notebooks*, pp. 312–317). In the same month, he described Mrs. S. C. Hall as "a literary lady, unspoilt by a literary career" (*English Notebooks*, p. 319). He liked Mrs. Jameson, with whom he was friendly in Rome, and he respected her works (*Works*, 14:200). When he met Elizabeth Barrett Browning in July 1856, he immediately liked her "very much": "She is of that quickly appreciative and responsive order of women, with whom I can talk more freely than with any men; and she has, besides, her own originality wherewith to help on the conversation" (*English Notebooks*, pp. 381–382).

It is significant that the people whom Hawthorne liked—whether man or woman, writer or nonwriter—were modest and unaffected people. As he said of Harriet Hosmer, the young New England sculptor whom he met in Rome in 1858: "She seemed to be her actual self, and nothing affected or made up; so that, for my part, I gave her full leave to wear what may suit her best, and to behave as her inner woman prompts" (*Works*, 14:158). Hawthorne disliked pretension and exaggerated self-importance. He was particularly impatient with people who concealed the truth about themselves by pretending to be what they were not. As he advised at the end of *The Scarlet Letter* and emphasized throughout his fiction: "Be true! Show freely to the world, if not your worst, yet some trait whereby the worst may be inferred!" (*Works*, 1:260).

This attitude, I believe, helps to explain the stinging comments that Hawthorne made in his Italian Notebook about Margaret Fuller on April 3, 1858. While in the United States, he had enjoyed a cordial relationship with her. He and Sophia privately called her Queen Margaret, apparently because of her majestic ways (*NHW*, 1:256–257). But they had private names for other people as well, including Emerson, whom they called Plato.[10] In his American Notebooks, Hawthorne tells of friendly conversations with her, particularly one in Sleepy Hollow Cemetery in 1842, and on at least one occasion comments that he had read an article of hers in *The Dial* "which was good." She loaned him books and regarded him as a brother. The Hawthornes invited her to visit them in Concord, which she did many times, apparently even spending a night at the Old Manse.[11]

Sophia Hawthorne very kindly omitted the passage on Margaret Fuller from her edition of the French and Italian Notebooks, but Julian Hawthorne printed it in his 1884 biography of Hawthorne, and it is now also included in the Centenary Edition (*NHW* 1:259–262; *Works*, 14:155–157).[12] The quotation begins with Hawthorne's record of what he had heard about Margaret Fuller from Joseph Mozier, an American merchant turned sculptor living in Italy. Julian introduces the quotation by saying that in Rome Hawthorne "came across some facts regarding her marriage," but the passage notes only that Mozier told Hawthorne that Margaret Fuller's husband was not very intelligent and that she had lost all of her literary powers in Italy. I suspect that Mozier also told Hawthorne something respecting the belatedness of Fuller's marriage; but if Hawthorne made a record of that fact, it has not survived. What Hawthorne quoted Mozier as saying with regard to Fuller's husband and her literary powers is hardly sufficient to warrant Hawthorne's conclusion that there was "a total collapse in poor Margaret, morally and intellectually," that she must have had a "defective and evil nature," and that she "fell as the weakest of her sisters might."

Mozier was in a good position to know, or at least to suspect, the facts about Fuller's marriage. He and his wife had taken care of her when she became ill while visiting Florence in the fall of 1847. She did not see them again until the fall of 1849, when she returned to Florence after the siege of Rome with her husband and child. The reaction of the American colony to Margaret Fuller's appearance in Florence with a hitherto unsuspected husband and child over a year old is suggested by Elizabeth Barrett Browning, who observed in December 1849 that Margaret's "American friends stood in mute astonishment." That Margaret was not actually married until after her arrival in Florence can be inferred from a letter that her husband's sister wrote to Margaret's sister. It is possible that the late marriage was known to Mozier and his wife, with whom Fuller was friendly while she was in Florence.[13]

Although not a church-going Christian, Hawthorne was very concerned about propriety and held high moral standards. In an 1838 notebook entry, he expressed great surprise that a friend of his should not feel that one "deviation from chastity" in a woman did not disqualify her as a candidate for marriage (*Works*, 8:145–146). In England he is said to have refused to visit George Eliot because she was not married to the man she lived with.[14] His distaste for nude paintings and sculpture is reiterated throughout his European notebooks (e.g., *English Notebooks*, pp. 556, 561; *Works*, 14:177). And his attitude toward sexual transgressions is apparent in notebook entries like the passage in which he expresses shock that his English friend Francis Bennoch could tell him of the "dissolute life" of another man in such a "careless and unhorrified way" (*English Notebooks*, p. 283). Because of these attitudes, I believe that if Hawthorne had learned that, without a doubt, Margaret Fuller had had an illicit affair with an indigent nobleman and that she had borne an illegitimate child, he could very well have reacted in the way that he did. Hawthorne could not tolerate sham, and to him it would have been a sham for a woman to act as though she were, as he said of Margaret, "the greatest, wisest, best woman of her age," when all the time she was as weak as the "weakest of her sisters."

Hawthorne's criticism of Margaret Fuller was directed not at her actions, however much he may have deplored them, nor at her role as a public woman, but at her pretense to be what she was not. For Hawthorne, with his strict moral sense, the greatest woman of her age would not have been sexually indiscreet. But, once he has brought her down to size, he can sympathize with her as a woman and as a human being. Hawthorne ends his judgment of Margaret Fuller with the admission: "On the whole, I do not know but I like her the better for it; because she proved herself a very woman after all" (*NHW*, 1:261–262).

Although this statement might be interpreted specifically as a comment on the failings of women, it seems to me that, in view of Hawthorne's opinion of humankind, it is ultimately a comment on human fallibility in general. Throughout his fiction, Hawthorne probed the impossibility of human perfection, insisting that human beings, in all their frailty and error, were mere creatures of clay. In this passage in the Italian Notebooks, Hawthorne has apparently found out something about Margaret Fuller that reveals to him that she too, in spite of all of her grandiose claims, is only human.

Hawthorne's criticism of the female self cannot be separated from his criticism of the male self. He severely judged any individual who attempted to elevate himself/herself above common humanity. It is the universality of Hawthorne's message that critics of Hawthorne have failed to perceive when they have attempted to use his portrayal of individual women as an indication only of his views on women. Thus Michael Bell notes that Hawthorne objects to pride in Anne Hutchinson and that he censures Catharine in "The Gentle Boy" because she leaves her child to give herself up to an idea.[15] But Hawthorne also criticizes pride in his male characters, and he censures anyone who devotes himself to 'an idea at the expense of human ties. The old Quaker (man) is guilty of the same fanaticism as Catharine is; he left his dying child to pursue an idea. And when Hawthorne faults Anne Hutchinson for her pride and reproaches her for love of power, he is not condemning such qualities simply because they are found in a woman; he is rejecting the qualities themselves. The men in Hawthorne's fiction who are guilty of pride, who put power or individual concerns before natural ties and love of humankind—men such as Dimmesdale, Judge Pyncheon, Ethan Brand, Richard Digby, and Hollingsworth—these men are censured for the same faults that Hawthorne criticizes in women. Hawthorne may have felt that such transgressions were more serious in a woman, since woman, in her role as mother, represented for him the epitome of the tie with humanity. Like most of his contemporaries, Hawthorne regarded love and tenderness as feminine characteristics. Hence, Hester is saved from isolation by Pearl, and Hawthorne sometimes uses a female character to represent human love, such as Phoebe or Mary Goffe. But the whole thrust of Hawthorne's fiction is that no human creature, male or female, should put individual concerns above human relationships.

In Hawthorne's fiction, these feminine characteristics are more valuable than the masculine traits of aggression and self-centered individualism, whether they are manifested by a man or by a woman. Thus, in Hawthorne's retelling of the story of "The Duston Family," in which a mother kills and scalps—apparently for the bounty—the Indians (including seven Indian children) who are holding her captive, it is not Mrs. Duston, with her masculine prowess, who is the hero of the tale, but Mr. Duston, the "tender-hearted" father who jeopardizes his own chance of survival by remaining with his own seven children in their slow retreat from the Indians (*Writings*, 17:229–238).

Hawthorne's attitude toward women cannot be understood without looking at his relationship with the important women in his life: his mother, his sisters, and his wife. A very private person, Hawthorne never discussed his feelings with other people, and little is known about his relationship with his mother and sisters. But it is clear that his feelings were deep and that for him each woman was significant in her own right. Hawthorne's mother was reclusive in her habits, yet his letters to her from college and when he was separated from her prior to college reveal an earnest trust and a forthrightness that can exist only in a relationship of mutual respect. When she was dying in 1849, Hawthorne described it as "the darkest hour I ever lived" (*Works*, 8:429).[16] The death of his younger sister Louisa in a boat accident three years later again deeply affected him (*NHW*, 1:457). Hawthorne's older sister Elizabeth and his mother were women of independent judgment and "strong feelings" (*Works*, 8:429), and Hawthorne once commented that Elizabeth was the only person whose criticism he feared (*NHW*, 1:5). For many years Hawthorne's sisters were his principal companions: he explored the Maine woods with them as a child, and as a young man he enjoyed card games with Louisa and intellectual discussions with Elizabeth. His letters to them are frank and open. For Hawthorne, his mother and sisters were not merely incarnations of conventional femininity; he obviously regarded them as significant individuals.

Perhaps the best way to understand Hawthorne's attitude toward women is to look at his relationship with his wife. More is known of this relationship, and we must analyze it in detail in order to have a clear understanding of Hawthorne's fictional portrayal of women. It was not until after his marriage that Hawthorne wrote the novels that contain his marvelous female creations. A close look at his relationship with Sophia will help to explain how he conceived of women and why he portrayed them as he did.

Sophia Peabody Hawthorne was a real presence in Hawthorne's life. She was not the shadowy figure that Lidian Emerson was for her husband. Lidian is hardly mentioned in her husband's copious journals; what kind of person she was and how Emerson felt about her does not figure in the journals at all. On the other hand, Sophia is always present in Hawthorne's notebooks, as she was apparently in his life. Marriage, for Lidian, meant total subordination of her personality and made her into a chronically ill nonperson. For Sophia, marriage meant liberation from the overprotectiveness of her family, with whom she had lived as a semi-invalid, and made her into a strong individual and a person in her own right. Just how important a role Sophia played in Hawthorne's life is suggested by the way in which her children saw her. Whereas Edward Emerson made little mention of his mother in his detailed notes to the many volumes of his father's essays and journals, Julian Hawthorne considered his father's marriage to Sophia Peabody "probably the most fortunate event of his life" and stated that it would be impossible to describe his career without considering it (*NHW*, 1:39–40). Significantly, Julian's biography of his father is entitled *Nathaniel Hawthorne and His Wife*.

For Hawthorne, his relationship with Sophia was more important than ideas or individual triumphs. "We have found all in each other—all that life has to give—and a pre-taste of eternity," he wrote to her in 1839 (*Love Letters*, 1:92). He yearned for "the solitude of a united two . . . and freedom to think, and dream, and feel" (*Love Letters*, 1:214). For Emerson, who subordinated his relationships with persons to what he regarded as the really important things in life, such statements would have made no sense at all. He could not find "all" in another person; the all was in himself. Moreover, solitude for Emerson was the solitude of an all-encompassing one; though thinking and dreaming might be acceptable activities, the isolated self would have no cause to feel. For Hawthorne, on the other hand, true reality did not exist without this kind of close personal relationship. In 1840 he told Sophia:

> We are but shadows—we are not endowed with real life, and all that seems most real about us is but the thinnest

substance of a dream—till the heart be touched. That
touch creates us—then we begin to be—thereby we are
beings of reality and inheritors of eternity.

(Love Letters, 1:225)

This was not simply the exaggeration of a lovesick suitor.
Hawthorne was still saying the same thing after fourteen
years of marriage. In 1856, when Sophia was spending the
winter in Lisbon, he wrote to her from London:

> Oh my wife, I do want thee so intolerably. Nothing else
> is real, except the bond between thee and me. The people
> around me are but shadows,—till thou takest me in thy
> arms, and convertest me into substance. Till thou comest
> back, I do but walk in a dream. (*Love Letters*, 2:256)

Hawthorne saw Sophia as an independent person. Although she was a devoted, almost worshipful wife, he never
attempted to make her only a reflection of himself. As Julian
Hawthorne commented, Hawthorne "was not, as so many
men are, a merely passive and complacent absorber of all this
devotion. What she gave, he returned" (*NHW*, 1:41). Soon
after their marriage, Sophia wrote to her mother: "Do not
fear that I shall be subject to my Adam. . . . He loves power
as little as any mortal I ever knew."[17] Before their marriage,
Hawthorne had vowed to her: "I would leave you as free as
you leave me. . . . I would not tame you for the whole universe" (*Love Letters*, 1:3, 127). Apparently, both Hawthorne
and Sophia thought of their marriage as a relationship between equal individuals. In response to her question regarding religious belief, he assured her before their marriage that
married people did not have to agree in everything. So long
as they felt a general sympathy, they need not be each "reflected in the alternate mirror" (*Love Letters*, 1:159). During the early years of their marriage Sophia affirmed to her
mother that a true marriage is a partnership: "In perfect, high
union there is no question of supremacy. Souls are equal in
love and intelligent high communion" (*NHW*, 1:256–257).

It is important to recognize, however, that although Hawthorne thought of his wife as an independent being and not as a part of himself, that although his relationship with her took precedence over abstract ideas and personal ambitions, he still maintained a conventional nineteenth-century image of the woman's role. In this respect, his attitude was European rather than American. It was the American male individualist who insisted upon the priority of the claims of the self. Although the nineteenth-century European male may not have shared this belief in the primacy of the self and therefore would be better able to grant an independent existence to others, European men certainly had not relinquished traditional ideas of femininity and a woman's place.

Sophia apparently shared Hawthorne's traditional view of women. She was shocked at the idea of women speaking in public, and she agreed with her contemporaries that a woman's place was in the home: "Home, I think, is the greatest arena for women, and there, I am sure, she can wield a power which no king or conqueror can cope with" (*NHW*, 1:256–257). Sophia seemed content to remain in this arena. She wrote in her journal in 1843: "For the world's eye I care nothing. . . . Behold a true wife's world! It is her husband only." [18]

Because of his own preferences, Hawthorne seems to have reinforced Sophia's tendencies toward conventional femininity. The mistake that his biographers have made in supposing that this was all there was to Sophia is a mistake that Hawthorne himself did not make, however. Early in their relationship, he called her his Dove, and he liked to think of her as a gentle innocent. He wrote to her before they were married that her letters were sacred to him, that he did not like to read them around other people, and that he always washed his hands before reading them (*Love Letters*, 1:34). For the most part, Sophia lived up to this image. But Hawthorne knew that there was another side to her. In their early letters he often referred to her as two people—his "meekest little Dove" and "that naughty Sophie Hawthorne." The Dove is always gentle and good; but Sophie Hawthorne is assertive and more independent. "Belovedest, I love thee," he wrote to her in June 1840:

> But then that naughty Sophie Hawthorne—it would be out of the question to treat her with tenderness. Nothing shall she get from me . . . save a kiss upon her nose; and I should not wonder if she were to return the favor with a buffet upon my ear. Mine own Dove, how unhappy art thou to be linked with such a mate! . . .—and me unhappy, too, to be forced to keep such a turbulent little rebel in my inmost heart. (*Love Letters*, 1:202;
> see also pp. 110–111, 117, 135, 143, 161)

In his fictional portrayals of women, Hawthorne found himself in the same predicament. The gentle, good, passive, angelic, and virginal Priscilla or Hilda appears as the embodiment of what Hawthorne believed the conventional heroine should be. But in his "inmost heart" Hawthorne knew that this was not a true picture of womanhood. And so the "turbulent rebel" also appears—the independent, rebellious, strong-willed Hester, Zenobia, or Miriam.

If Sophia had really been only the humorless, stiff-necked prig that Hilda is or the weak-willed "gentle parasite" that Coverdale calls Priscilla, she would not have possessed the substance to attract and sustain Hawthorne's interest. She would have been like the "colorless and insipid" American ladies whom Hawthorne complained about at his boarding-house in Liverpool (*English Notebooks*, p. 573). Although Hawthorne loyally portrayed the vacuous conventional heroine in his fiction, he did not seek out such a woman as a wife. Sophia was an independent and unusually accomplished woman who had mastered several languages, including Greek and Hebrew, and was gaining a local reputation as an artist when she married Hawthorne. Moreover, Hawthorne was conscious of a depth and strength in Sophia that his dovelike maidens do not possess. In 1849, when, for political reasons, he was removed from his post at the Salem Custom House, he wrote to his friend George Hilliard that Sophia would "bear it like a woman—that is to say, better than a man" (*Writings*, 17:430). The story is that Sophia showed Hawthorne the money she had saved from painting lampshades and fire screens and told him to go ahead and write, that she could manage.[19] With this example of a woman's strength, Hawthorne wrote *The Scarlet Letter*.

If Sophia was not the weak-willed girl Hawthorne portrays in his dove-maidens, neither was she the moralistic prude these maidens often are. Much has been made of the moralistic influence that Sophia is supposed to have exercised on Hawthorne. Randall Stewart castigates Sophia for the Victorian changes in Hawthorne's notebooks, presumed to be the result of her editing, and Frederick Crews, characterizing her as a pious moralist whose taste Hawthorne was afraid to offend, claims that Sophia, as a principal influence on Hawthorne, "domesticated" his interests and encouraged him to repress his own instincts.[20] Sophia was not the sexless and censorious Pollyanna that these portrayals make her out to be. If she is indeed responsible for the changes in Hawthorne's notebooks, one cannot therefore conclude that she made them simply to conform to her own taste. It is more likely, given her belief in Hawthorne and her concern that the world share her high opinion of him, that she made changes in the notebooks in order to preserve what she took to be Hawthorne's good name and reputation. If she erred in attempting to present Hawthorne as a genteel nineteenth-century gentleman, it does not mean that this was the Hawthorne she herself preferred; it only means that this portrait was her conception of what the nineteenth-century reading public wanted in a literary man. Moreover, she very probably made changes in the belief that she was acting as Hawthorne would have desired. Certainly Hawthorne had made it clear during his lifetime that he did not believe in the public airing of dirty linen, and he himself always maintained a strong sense of what was proper and morally correct. The extent of Hawthorne's belief in propriety is suggested by an incident from 1855 mentioned in his English Notebooks: he met some friends in St. Paul's Cathedral but did not stay to go through the cathedral with them because one of them was wearing a hat, and he was "ashamed of being seen in company with a man who would wear his hat in a Cathedral" (*English Notebooks*, p. 224). In an 1868 letter to James T. Fields, who helped her to edit the American Notebooks and who, say the editors of the Centenary Edition of the American Notebooks, was responsible for many of the decisions made, Sophia wrote that she wanted to be loyal to what Hawthorne would approve: "I had rather starve than do what he might think an impropriety."[21]

That the censoring of Hawthorne's notebooks does not simply reflect Sophia's own attitudes is apparent from the evidence that survives of her opinions. For example, although the editor of the notebooks systematically erased any mention of Hawthorne's drinking intoxicating liquor, however moderately, Sophia herself was sympathetic even to immoderate drinkers. In an 1853 letter to her mother, she commented on reports that Franklin Pierce was a heavy drinker, saying that she would not fault him for it. Her own early use of morphine, she added, had given her "infinite sympathy and charity" for people who drink too much (*NHW*, 1:483). Moreover, Sophia herself was not a teetotaler. When Hawthorne was working at Brook Farm in 1841, he wrote to Sophia that he knew she would like "a great quantity" of the wine if they made it (*Love Letters*, 2:54). After she was married, Sophia wrote in her journal in 1843 that wine helped her when she was depressed or could not get to sleep: "My husband rose & got me some of Mr. Bridge's ancient wine & a cracker at about twelve. These were of admirable effect & in a few minutes I was comforted & almost asleep."[22]

The folly of equating the censoring of the Notebooks with Sophia's opinions is most apparent in the antisexual, antiphysical character of so many of the corrections. Sophia apparently agreed with Hawthorne that private sexual opinions and experiences did not belong in the public arena, and she correctly guessed that the nineteenth-century reading public would be offended by certain incidents and expressions. But this does not mean that she herself was prudish or that she exercised an inhibiting influence on Hawthorne's sexual appetites. Rather, their correspondence tells of a passionate, physical relationship. Three years before their marriage, Hawthorne desired her warmth close to his bosom; he longed to share the same pillow and to wake with her in his arms (*Love Letters*, 1:foreword). One cannot imagine the virginal Hilda receiving such letters with favor, yet there is no indication that Sophia felt any qualms about the blatant sexual desire that Hawthorne expressed. Certainly the letters kept coming. In 1841 he wrote: "I love thee—I love thee. . . . Never before did my bosom so yearn for the want of thee—so thrill at the thought of thee. . . . kiss me—or I die!" (*Love Letters*, 2:69). And in January 1842, six months before their marriage, he wrote:

> We have left expression—at least such expression as can be achieved with pen and ink—far behind us. Even the spoken word has long been inadquate. Looks—pressures of the lips and hands—the touch of bosom to bosom—these are a better language; but bye-and-bye, our spirit will demand some more adequate expression even than these.[23]

After their marriage, in an era that regarded sex as an unfortunate necessity and female sexuality as a curse, the Hawthornes apparently enjoyed a passionate sexual relationship. In August 1842 Hawthorne wrote that after seeing their house guests to bed, "then came my dear little wife to her husband's bosom" (*Works*, 7:334–335). In 1844 he asked Sophia, who was visiting her family in Boston, "dost thou yearn for me? does thy breast heave and thy heart quake with love for thy husband?" (*Love Letters*, 2:147). Four years later he wrote: "There is no thinking how much I love and desire thee" (*Love Letters*, 1:foreword; 2:191). And in 1856, when he was fifty-two years old, his heart was still burning "with a hot fire" for Sophia (*Love Letters*, 2:256–257).

For Hawthorne, Sophia was both the spiritual innocent and the physical woman. On March 15, 1843, he called her "a *woman* and an angel," underscoring the word "woman" (*Love Letters*, 2:112). In an 1839 letter, written three years before they were married, he expressed the duality of his feelings for her:

> How strangely we should have felt, had we been compelled to meet and part without the pressure of one another's lips! It would have seemed all a vision then; now we have the symbol of its reality. You looked like a vision, beautifullest wife, with the width of the room between us—so spiritual that my human heart wanted to be assured that you had an earthly vesture on, and your warm kisses gave me that assurance.
>
> (*Love Letters*, 1: foreword, 67)

The picture of Sophia that has come down to us is not accurate, but it is probably the one that Hawthorne would want us to have. It is interesting to consider that, although Sophia apparently only censored Hawthorne's letters to her, he completely destroyed almost all of hers to him. In June 1853, before they left for England, he recorded in his notebook that he had burned "great heaps" of old letters and papers, among which were all of Sophia's maiden letters.[24] That Hawthorne's own letters were not also burned at the time suggests that it was Sophia's image that had to be protected. I suspect that her letters revealed an unreserve that Hawthorne did not believe should ever be witnessed by anyone but her husband.

Hawthorne's recognition of and respect for Sophia as an independent person and his simultaneous preference for gentle femininity in a wife help to explain why in his fiction he balanced his independent women characters with gentle dovemaidens. His ability to see women as separate beings enabled him to create women who were not abstractions. Hester, Zenobia, Miriam are not mere shadows of the male self. The strength and depth, the richness and passion that Hawthorne in his "inmost heart" knew could exist in a woman are magnificently developed in his strong women characters. But Hawthorne's conscious preference for maidenly virtues in a wife made it impossible for him to conceive of such a woman as a heroine because the traditional heroine was, after all, a potential wife. Although he admired and respected the independent woman, he did not encourage these qualities in his wife, particularly in her public role. Thus, two of his novels introduce an innocent young girl who is draped in white and, dovelike, maintains the gentle maidenly decorum of a virtuous heroine.

In *The Scarlet Letter* there is no such heroine because there is no danger that anyone will mistake Hester for a conventional heroine. Her story begins long after the marriage that usually ends the traditional heroine's story. She is a married woman, a mother, and an adultress before the action even starts. In *The House of the Seven Gables* Hawthorne attempts to combine the two aspects of womanhood in one character, Phoebe, who, he says, is both spirit and substance (*Works*, 2:168). If Phoebe is not as successful as a creation, it is because Hawthorne was unable to portray Phoebe, a potential wife, with the same objective spirit that he could apply to Hester. Thus, although Phoebe has more substance than Priscilla or Hilda, and although her homely reality makes her more likable and more believable, she is seen primarily as a means to someone else's happiness. In his portrayal of Phoebe, Hawthorne was guided too much by what Sophia meant *to him*. He had called Sophia "Phoebe" and said that she brought sunshine and reality into his life and into his own House of the Seven Gables, which he called the Castle Dismal. (See *Love Letters*, 1:162–163; 2:76, 113, 158; *Works*, 8:214.)

Hawthorne is best able to portray strong women characters when he does not place them at all in relation to a man. They are not the conventional marriage-candidate heroines who exist only to be found by men. Hester can be no one's fiancée, and there are hints that Zenobia and Miriam—

always referred to as women, not as girls—have already been married or are in some way experienced. This status effectively disqualifies them for the role of traditional heroine. Since Hawthorne does not see such a woman in relation to a man, he can see her as an independent person, an individual. In fact, he himself sometimes identifies with these women— something he could never do with his dove-maidens, who are always the other. Hawthorne's emotional involvement in the story of Hester Prynne is suggested by the strong emotions he felt when he read the last scene of *The Scarlet Letter* to Sophia, just after writing it: "tried to read it, rather, for my voice swelled and heaved, as if I were tossed up and down in an ocean as it subsides after a storm" (*English Notebooks*, p. 225).

Hawthorne's tendency to identify with these strong women is apparent in the way in which he sometimes speaks through them. Zenobia in *The Blithedale Romance* obviously speaks for Hawthorne in her judgment of Hollingsworth. "It is all self!" she exclaims, and she charges Hollingsworth with having wasted his human affections for a project that is only a mask of self-deception (*Works*, 3:218). We also know from Hawthorne's notebook entries that Miriam in *The Marble Faun* echoes Hawthorne's own opinion on nude sculpture (*Works*, 4:123–125, 134–135). How much of the philosophizing of these women can be taken as Hawthorne's own speculation cannot be determined, but they ask questions that Hawthorne himself seems to ponder, even if he is not prepared to agree with their conclusions. Thus Hester and Zenobia confront the whole question of the position of women, and Zenobia's ideas are reflected in the final opinions of Coverdale. Similarly, Miriam's opinions on the concept of the Fortunate Fall are later echoed by Kenyon, though they are dismissed by Hilda.

That Hawthorne may in fact have held *both* opinions on some of these controversial issues is suggested by his tendency to split up his opinions among his characters. For example, in 1858 he wrote in his notebooks that the stained glass windows in an Italian church were "bright in themselves, but dim with tenderness and reverence, because God Himself was shining through them." And then he added, "I hate what I have said" (*Works*, 14:286). In *The Marble Faun* Kenyon repeats these words almost exactly—except for the last sentence. In the novel Donatello is the doubter.

Hawthorne's view of life reflects a recognition of a duality that many of his contemporaries did not share. He saw good and evil, sunshine and shadow. And his attitude toward women is one aspect of this recognition of duality. In many of his tales, the basic mistake of the Hawthorne protagonist is his failure to recognize this duality in life. In "Rappaccini's Daughter," when Giovanni discovers that Beatrice is physically embued with poison, he cannot see her spiritual goodness until it is too late. Young Goodman Brown, once he becomes aware of evil, can no longer believe in good. He fails to see that his wife, Faith, is an angel *on earth*.

It is apparent, then, that in his attitude toward women and in his portrayal of women in his fiction, Hawthorne differed markedly from his contemporaries among American writers. Why was Hawthorne able to conceive of women as persons when most nineteenth-century American male writers did not? In order to answer this question, it is necessary to recognize that Hawthorne also differed from his contemporaries in his attitude toward the dominant American culture. Hawthorne did not share his countrymen's enthusiastic belief in American individualism. Although a contemporary and sometime neighbor of Emerson's, Hawthorne dissented emphatically from the Transcendentalists' attitude toward the individual and the other. It is this difference in cultural attitudes, I believe, that explains Hawthorne's ability to portray women of substance in his fiction.

The first work of Hawthorne's that Emerson read was "Foot-prints on the Sea-Shore," which Elizabeth Peabody showed to him in June 1838. Emerson commented that there was "no inside to it."[25] Why Emerson found this sketch so lacking in substance is not hard to determine. In "Foot-prints on the Sea-Shore" Hawthorne writes about a day alone near the sea. Emerson would recognize the concept of solitude in nature suggested by this situation. But, given his emphasis upon solitude as a retreat from man and his belief in the relative unimportance of human ties, how could Emerson accept the message of Hawthorne's little sketch—that the best thing about solitude is the warmth and sense of human kinship one feels after rejoining people? After the day is over, says Hawthorne, "I shall walk among men kindly and as a brother, with affection and sympathy." Hawthorne's point is that, although solitude is valuable in helping to give one a sense of individuality, it is even more important as a reminder that "there are men and women in the world" (*Works*, 9:451–462). For Hawthorne, there are always footprints on the seashore.

Herein lies the essential difference between Hawthorne and Emerson. Whereas Emerson, in making his claims for the self, denied the substantial existence of other people, Hawthorne was always conscious of other people and his kinship with them. Although Hawthorne was a more reserved person than Emerson and did not encourage a great many friendships, the relationships that he did enjoy with people were very important to him. He had a warm relationship with his wife and a strong feeling for his mother, his sisters, and his three children. Hawthorne also sustained warm relationships with a few very close friends, particularly those he had known before his marriage, such as Horatio Bridge and Franklin Pierce. That his relations with people were of primary importance to him is most evident in the way in which he defended Pierce when Pierce was politically unpopular. Hawthorne wrote the campaign biography for his friend in 1852, and during the Civil War he persisted, against the advice of his friends and publisher, in dedicating *Our Old Home* to Pierce, whose friendship had meant so much to him during his daughter Una's illness in Rome. (Significantly,

Emerson could not understand Hawthorne's concern for persons, and, unable to prevent Hawthorne from dedicating the book to Pierce, tore the dedicatory pages from his copy.)[26]

Not only did Hawthorne have deep feelings for his family and close friends, he was also profoundly interested in people in general. The mystery of human existence fascinated him. Human beings, in all their many guises, were very real to him. Hawthorne's interest in people is particularly evident in his notebooks, which, in contrast to Emerson's journals, are filled with sketches of real people, from detailed descriptions of strangers he met in taverns, stagecoaches, and railroad stations, to intimate portrayals of his friends and family, even his children. In Emerson's journal the focus is on words and ideas—what people said and what Emerson thought and read. The people themselves figure hardly at all; even Emerson's family is scarcely mentioned. Of course, part of the reason for the many sketches of people in Hawthorne's notebooks is that he was, after all, a fiction writer looking for material. In fact, many of the evocations in his notebooks reappear in some form in his fiction. However, this does not explain why Hawthorne was interested in people in the first place. Moreover, it is obvious from the descriptions that Hawthorne did not regard people simply as material. He was interested in the people for themselves.

It is impossible to convey here a sense of the vast numbers of individuals who appear throughout Hawthorne's notebooks. His feelings about these people are made clear, however, in this passage from the English Notebooks describing a poor Irish family that he had met while waiting for a ferry:

> There is not much more that can be caught in the description of this scene; but it made me understand, better than before, how poor people felt, wandering about in such destitute circumstances. . . . somehow or other, I got into the interior of this poor family, and understand, through sympathy, more of them than I can tell.
>
> (*English Notebooks*, pp. 34–35)

It is this ability to get "into the interior" of the other person that comes through in all of Hawthorne's fiction—a willingness to sympathize, a respect for each person as a fellow human being, and an ability to see from many different points of view. Julian Hawthorne wrote of his father: "Hawthorne, both by nature and by training, was of a disposition to throw himself imaginatively into the shoes (as the phrase is) of whatever person happened to be his companion" (*NHW*, 1:88). The flowers on the wild rosebush outside the prison door in *The Scarlet Letter* remind the prisoner that "the deep heart of Nature could pity and be kind to him" (*Works*, 1:48). Throughout his fiction, Hawthorne expresses this kind of sympathy for his fellow human creatures. As Sophia Hawthorne wrote to her mother in 1850, Hawthorne "sees and sympathizes with all human suffering."[27]

This intense feeling for humankind helps to explain the complexity of Hawthorne's vision. There are no easy answers to the questions that critics have raised about Hawthorne's characters because Hawthorne did not see people in terms of black and white. Even the most villainous characters in Hawthorne's major fiction are usually treated with understanding and compassion. Thus, although Hawthorne deplores the "depth of malice" in Roger Chillingworth in *The Scarlet Letter*, he describes Dimmesdale's persecutor as an "unfortunate old man" who is more wretched than his victim (*Works*, 1: 139, 141). Not only can Hawthorne sympathize with the evildoers in his fiction; he can also criticize his good characters. For example, Hilda in *The Marble Faun* is too harsh and unbending, even selfish, in her concern to preserve her own unspotted innocence rather than help her erring friend (*Works*, 4:385–386, 207–209).

Since Hawthorne does not see people in terms of black and white, there are no "heroes" in his fiction, no superpersons in the tradition of the American myth. Instead, there are only men and women with the strengths and weaknesses of real human beings. In *The House of the Seven Gables* Hawthorne comments that there is always something ludicrous and mean mixed together with the tragedy and pathos in anyone's life: "Life is made up of marble and mud."[28] No human being can have the perfection of marble; he or she is also made out of mud or clay. Hawthorne did not believe in human perfection.[29] As Aylmer discovers in "The Birthmark" when he attempts to remove his wife's only blemish, once "that sole token of earthly imperfection" is removed, Georgiana can no longer live on earth. Aylmer himself has never attained the heights he aimed at. However spiritual man thinks he is, says Hawthorne, he is mere man after all—"the spirit burthened with clay" (*Works*, 10:36–56).

With such a view of man, it is impossible to see him as a heroic figure. Hawthorne always reveals this duality about the young men in his novels, so that, even if the character conceives of himself as heroic, the reader knows that he is not. Arthur Dimmesdale can hardly be called the traditional hero. In the first place, he is weaker than the woman in the novel. But the most significant factor in Hawthorne's characterization of Dimmesdale is the revelation that Dimmesdale, despite his guilt and shame, is not what he pretends to be even to himself. When Dimmesdale learns that the ship will not sail for four days, he is glad that he will be able to preach the election sermon. Hawthorne, however, points up that although Dimmesdale may tell himself that he wants to preach the sermon as a public duty, he is really motivated by ambition and pride (*Works*, 1:215–216).

Holgrave, in *The House of the Seven Gables*, has the strength and integrity that Dimmesdale lacks. Yet Hawthorne does not allow him to assume heroic proportions:

> At almost every step in life, we meet with young men of just about Holgrave's age, for whom we anticipate wonderful things, but of whom, even after much and careful inquiry, we never happen to hear another word. The effervescence of youth and passion, and the fresh gloss of the intellect and imagination, endow them with a false brilliancy, which makes fools of themselves and other people. Like certain chintzes, calicoes, and ginghams, they show finely in their first newness, but cannot stand

> the sun and rain, and assume a very sober aspect after
> washing-day.   (*Works*, 2:181)

Coverdale, the narrator of *The Blithedale Romance*, is aware of the imperfections of man, and by the end of the novel he himself has faded in the way that Hawthorne predicted of Holgrave. Coverdale's own feelings about heroism are stated early: "The greatest obstacle to being heroic is the doubt whether one may not be going to prove one's self a fool" (*Works*, 3:10). Kenyon, in *The Marble Faun*, is a well-meaning young man, but hardly a hero. When Miriam wants to unburden herself to him, he pretends to be all sympathy, but he is really suspicious and horrified at the thought of what she might tell him. Like Dimmesdale, he does not admit his real reasons even to himself (*Works*, 4:128–130).

Because Hawthorne does not believe in heroism and human perfection, he is not sympathetic to the claims of the inflated self. He himself was a modest person who disliked affectation and was embarrassed by praise. His English Notebooks are filled with references to the discomfort caused by well-meaning admirers, whose laudatory remarks he compared to "butter and treacle" and whose homage made him feel like a "strange bug under glass" (*English Notebooks*, pp. 255–256, 292, 210–211, 238). Nor was he guilty of false modesty; Hawthorne simply did not see himself as a Titan. Unlike Emerson, who dreamed that the world was his apple, Hawthorne dreamed that the world had passed him by. In December 1854 he wrote in his notebook of a dream that had recurred for twenty to thirty years: that he had made no progress in life at all, that his life was "hopelessly a failure" (*English Notebooks*, p. 98). Thus, although Hawthorne lived for a time in Transcendentalist territory, he never shared the Emersonian belief in the self. In 1846, after living for three years in Concord, Hawthorne wrote in the preface to *Mosses from an Old Manse* that, though he admired Emerson as a poet of "austere tenderness," he "sought nothing from him as a philosopher" (*Works*, 15:30–31).[30]

The person who exalts himself can do so only if he looks at the world wholly from inside himself. One of Hawthorne's most important qualities as a man and as a writer was his ability to stand outside himself. In "The Seven Vagabonds," an early story published in *The Token* in 1832, Hawthorne's narrator reflects: "If there be a faculty which I possess more perfectly than most other men, it is that of throwing myself mentally into situations foreign to my own" (*Works*, 9:352). This faculty was Hawthorne's special talent. In the Custom House essay he advised that it was morally and intellectually healthy for a man to be with people unlike himself, "who care little for his pursuits, and whose sphere and abilities he must go outside himself to appreciate" (*Works*, 1:24). Because of this ability to get outside himself, Hawthorne could see himself from a broader perspective. When a person sees himself from the outside, his own claims cannot help but be diminished. Just as important, Hawthorne discovered when he left literary Concord for the Salem Custom House, "It is a good lesson . . . for a man . . . to step aside out of the narrow circle in which his claims are recognized, and to find how utterly devoid of significance, beyond that circle, is all that he achieves, and all he aims at" (*Works*, 1:26–27).

As a writer, then, Hawthorne was always conscious of other people, other modes of thought, and other points of view. In addition to this awareness, Hawthorne had a very strong sense of the complexity of life in general. To a man with Hawthorne's sense of infinitude, the Transcendentalists' assertion that the individual contains all must have seemed absurd. Hawthorne saw man as a finite creature, and his awareness of the infinite variety, the vastness of life, only accentuated for him man's limitations. In July 1844 Hawthorne conducted an experiment in which he sat down in the woods and attempted to record everything in the scene around him. The impossibility of the task demonstrated for him his own limitations and the limitations of man in general (*Works*, 8:245–250).

In his fiction Hawthorne emphasizes the insignificance

of the individual and illustrates the folly of exaggerating one's own importance. When Wakefield leaves home, for example, he is worried that someone might have seen him. "Poor Wakefield!" Hawthorne chides; "Little knowest thou thine own insignificance in this great world. . . . among a thousand such atoms of mortality" (*Works*, 9:133–135). In "The Ambitious Guest" Hawthorne shows the ephemeral nature of life and the folly of man's ambition. A young man stops for the night with a simple mountain family and tells them of his ambition to be famous. All are killed in a sudden avalanche, and no one ever knows that the young man was even there: "Wo, for the high-souled youth, with his dream of Earthly Immortality" (*Works*, 9:333).

Although the dominant themes in Hawthorne's fiction are familiar to most readers, they take on a new significance when viewed in relation to Hawthorne's attitude toward American individualism. A particularly important factor is his conception of the past. In Hawthorne's fiction, the past is a reality. Hawthorne never believed in the Transcendentalist assertion that one can escape the past simply by declaring oneself free of it. "The past is gone!" says Hester Prynne when she takes off the scarlet letter. But soon comes little Pearl, the living embodiment of the scarlet letter, and Hester must wear the letter again (*Works*, 1:202–211). The events of *The House of the Seven Gables*, Hawthorne comments, illustrate how important a part the past plays in our lives, "how much of old material goes to make up the freshest novelty of human life" (*Works*, 2:6). The narrator of "Alice Doane's Appeal" makes a deliberate effort to make his auditors recognize their connection with the past, and the past figures also in such stories as "Main Street," the Province House tales, and "Fort Ticonderoga" and "Old News." The presence of the past in Hawthorne's view of life forces the individual to see himself in perspective. The individual occupies only one short segment of time in a long continuum. As Hawthorne observes in *The Marble Faun*, individual life is nothing when compared with the vastness of the past apparent in Rome (*Works*, 4:410–411).[31]

This view of man's limited role in the universe led Hawthorne to be particularly critical of the self-oriented individual. Roderick Elliston in "Egotism; or the Bosom Serpent" is too involved in himself: "Could I, for one instant, forget myself, the serpent might not abide within me. It is my diseased self-contemplation that has engendered and nourished him!" (*Works*, 10:268–283). Richard Digby, "The Man of Adamant," devotes himself so exclusively to the self that he ultimately turns to stone, confirming Hawthorne's admonition: "Indeed, it is a great folly for men to trust to their own strength" (*Works*, 11:161–169). And when Arthur Dimmesdale sees the letter A in the sky, as if all of nature reflects his own state of mind, Hawthorne ascribes it to his diseased egotism:

> It could only be the symptom of a highly disordered mental state, when a man, rendered morbidly self-contemplative by long, intense, and secret pain, had extended his egotism over the whole expanse of nature, until the firmament itself should appear no more than a fitting page for his soul's history and fate. (*Works*, 1:155)

In Hawthorne's fiction the only salvation for the individual who mistakenly withdraws into himself is for him to make contact with other people. Roderick's "bosom serpent" leaves him when he can forget himself in his love for Rosina. But Richard Digby loses his chance for salvation when he refuses the help of Mary Goffe. For Dimmesdale, salvation lies in his acknowledgment of the ties between him and Hester Prynne and Pearl. When he takes Pearl's hand on the scaffold at midnight, he feels himself a part of life:

> There came what seemed a tumultous rush of new life, other life than his own, pouring like a torrent into his heart, and hurrying through all his veins, as if the mother and the child were communicating their vital warmth to his half-torpid system. The three formed an electric chain. (*Works*, 1:153)

This concept of a human chain is one of the most important in Hawthorne's work. Hawthorne uses it to symbolize the individual's connection with mankind, his involvement in human sympathy. In *The House of the Seven Gables* Hawthorne associates it with Phoebe, who brings Holgrave into contact with "the whole sympathetic chain of human nature" (*Works*, 2:141). In "Ethan Brand," when Brand ceases to care for mankind, Hawthorne remarks that he has "lost his hold of the magnetic chain of humanity" (*Works*, 11:98–99). And in "Lady Eleanor's Mantle," Jervayse Helwyse warns the scornful Eleanor not to "withdraw . . . from the chain of human sympathies" (*Works*, 9:280). In Hawthorne's fiction exclusion from the chain of humanity is the worst fate that can befall anyone.

If the worst fate, according to Hawthorne, is to lose one's place in the chain of human sympathies, the worst crime is to violate those human ties by using another human being for the furtherance of one's own selfish purpose. Ethan Brand travels the world in search of the Unpardonable Sin and finds that he himself is guilty of it. He has sacrificed human brotherhood to his own "mighty claims" (*Works*, 11:90, 98–99). Dr. Rappacini has made the same mistake. His patients are "interesting to him only as objects for some new experiment," and he sacrifices the life of his only daughter in order to advance his scientific knowledge (*Works*, 10:91–128). Roger Chillingworth probes into Dimmesdale's heart with such a passionate single-mindedness that the once kindly old physician becomes an ugly fiend who shrivels up when Dimmesdale escapes from him by publicly confessing his guilt. Hawthorne apparently agrees with Dimmesdale when he tells Hester that Chillingworth's sin is worse than theirs: "He has violated, in cold blood, the sanctity of a human heart" (*Works*, 1:195).

Hawthorne's belief in the sanctity of the individual is reflected in his attitude toward hypnotism, the basis of which is the subjugation of the will of one person to the will of another. When Hawthorne was courting Sophia, he urged her not to allow herself to be hypnotized because "the sacredness of an individual is violated by it" (*Love Letters*, 2:62–63,

103–104). The young Matthew Maule, who took possession of Alice Pyncheon's soul in *The House of the Seven Gables*, lacks the forebearance of his descendant, Holgrave, who refrains from hypnotizing Phoebe because he has "reverence for another's individuality" (*Works*, 2:212).

Hawthorne believed that the most important good for the individual is his involvement with humanity, by which he meant a sharing of the joy and suffering of mankind, a feeling of love and sympathy for other human beings. Gervayse Hastings, in "The Christmas Banquet" (1844), is the most miserable man alive because he has never been able to feel anything, "neither joys nor griefs." His life is a cold abstraction, and he himself is as unreal as a vapor (*Works*, 10:284–305). In *The Scarlet Letter* Pearl, the elf-child, is outside of life. Sharing the vacant circle imposed on her mother by society, Pearl lacks feelings of human sympathy. Despite her charm, there is a marble coldness about her, says Hawthorne, and she needs a grief to "humanize and make her capable of sympathy" (*Works*, 1:184). It is not until the end of the novel, when she shares the intensity of her parents' feeling as Dimmesdale confesses his guilt, that Pearl's own sympathies are awakened and we know that she will become fully human (*Works*, 1:256).

One of the most important questions raised in *The Marble Faun* is the necessity of becoming involved in life. Both Hilda and Kenyon fear involvement. Miriam tells Hilda, "As an angel, you are not amiss; but, as a human creature, and a woman among earthly men and women, you need a sin to soften you!" (*Works*, 4:207–209). Hawthorne would not necessarily agree that Hilda needed a sin, but he apparently felt that she lacked involvement in human experience. She is like a grown-up Pearl, whose sympathies have never been awakened. Although Hilda is an excellent copyist, she is a more perceptive artist after her experience with suffering; she can then recognize what is true in art and what is only a shallow semblance of reality. She can also fall in love (*Works*, 4:338, 375).[32]

In *The Marble Faun* the character in whom Hawthorne

works out his theory of the necessity of involvement most obviously is Donatello, the living faun. Before the murder he is a carefree boy, incapable of the deeper sensibilities. But, cautions Hawthorne, what is attractive in a young boy would be repulsive in an old man. Hawthorne projects what Donatello would be like if he had not become involved; he would have been a sensual old man, "heavy, unsympathizing, insulated in surly selfishness" (*Works*, 4:235). After the suffering caused by the murder, Donatello becomes more fully human. "Out of his bitter agony," he acquires a depth of feeling and intelligence.[33]

Hawthorne's values, then, are the reverse of Emerson's. Hawthorne's official rejection of the easy optimism of the Transcendentalists is his 1843 allegory, "The Celestial Railroad." The modern pilgrim finds at the end that his genial guide, Mr. Smooth-it-away, who has shown him the way to get through life without trouble or pain, is in fact a fiend, and the whole venture is a delusion.

Whereas Emerson gives priority to the concerns of the individual and insists on the unreality of pain, Hawthorne believes that human relationships, with all their joy *and* sorrow, are most important. Throughout his work, Hawthorne puts involvement with other people above abstract ideas and individual ambition. This philosophy is clearly developed in *The House of the Seven Gables*. Both Clifford Pyncheon, with his love of the beautiful, and Judge Jaffrey Pyncheon, who cares only for practical concerns, are self-oriented. And Holgrave, the daguerreotypist with wild plans to change the world, lacks human sympathy. It is his love for Phoebe that saves Holgrave from an empty life. This love Hawthorne describes as the miracle "without which every human existence is a blank" (*Works*, 2:307).

In Hawthorne's work the Emersonian individualist is not a hero. Hollingsworth in *The Blithedale Romance* is so dedicated to his idea that he can give no time to people, and he can maintain friendships only with people who mirror his ideas. His fixation causes him to trample on human relations. He is willing to sacrifice the whole Blithedale project for his own aims, and he is interested in Zenobia only so long as he thinks she will be able to provide money for his project (*Works*, 3:55, 57, 70, 132, 135). Symbolically, it is Hollingsworth who thrusts the boat hook through the heart of the drowned Zenobia. Although Hollingsworth's native tendencies are good ones, he had become so dedicated to his idea that "there was nothing to spare for . . . individual attachments, unless they could minister, in some way, to the terrible egotism which he mistook for an angel of God" (*Works*, 3:55).

In Hawthorne's view of life, it is human love that takes precedence over wealth and power, intellectual aspirations, or religious fervor. Ilbrahim, "The Gentle Boy," has the true religion—love—that both the Quakers and the Puritans in the story lack (*Works*, 9:104). Moreover, Hawthorne did not believe that love was only for simple people like Ilbrahim; the heart is also an important factor in his conception of Genius. In "A Select Party" (1844) the Master Genius of all time has "a great human heart as the household fire of a grand intellect" (*Works*, 10:65–66).[34] Emerson, Hawthorne observed, with all of his wisdom was unable to understand the heart of many an ordinary man (*Works*, 10:31). In "The Great Stone Face," published in the *National Era* in 1850, the Great Man is Ernest, whose heart has "deeper sympathies than other hearts"; his teacher is the Great Stone Face, which expresses the "glow of a vast, warm heart, that embraced all mankind" (*Works*, 11:33, 27).

Concern with human sympathy and other people, rejection of unalloyed optimism, insistence that the individual does not have unlimited rights and powers—all of these characteristics are, of course, un-American in the sense that they deny the foundations of the American myth. Hawthorne was not unpatriotic. He expressed warm feelings for his country and its institutions, and his visit to England later inspired comparisons in his notebooks that were favorable to his own country. (See, e.g., *English Notebooks*, pp. 108, 225, 456, 462, 519.) But Hawthorne did not see Americans and America as the culmination of centuries of progress. In fact, Hawthorne felt that something of value had been lost in the transition to the New World.[35] The people of the Old World have a healthy vigor and warmth that is lacking in America. In his notebooks Hawthorne commented that American life is "drier and less genial"; there is a coldness and "meagreness" about it that excludes the richness and beauty of the Old World (*English Notebooks*, p. 606; *Works*, 14:230).[36]

Hawthorne did not regard America as an improvement on all preceding civilizations. Moreover, he never subscribed to the American theory of the necessity of progress. Although he apparently hoped that American institutions would help the poor immigrant to find a new and better life in America (*Writings*, 17:218), his view of life differed from the predominant American outlook. He refused to accept the optimism of the age, and he rejected the idea that whatever is new is better than the old. He insisted on the reality of the past and denied that one could completely escape the past for a new and better future.

Hawthorne was also un-American in his attitude toward wealth and success. He himself entertained little of the ambition for worldly success that characterizes the American Dreamer. In a letter from college to his sister Louisa in 1825 he expressed the feeling that was apparent throughout his life: "I have thought much upon the subject and have finally come to the conclusion that I shall never make a distinguished figure in the world and all I hope or wish is to plod along with the multitude."[37] In his children's biography of Benjamin Franklin, Hawthorne criticized Poor Richard's sayings for being all about making money and for thus teaching men "but a very small portion of their duties" (*Works*, 6:274). In Hawthorne's fiction the pursuit of wealth does not make a man great, wise, or even happy, as is apparent in such characters as Gervayse Hastings in "The Christmas Banquet," Gather Gold in "The Great Stone Face," and Judge Pyncheon in *The House of the Seven Gables*. In the latter novel Hawthorne compares man's pursuit of money with the antics of an organ grinder's monkey, whom he calls the "Mammon of copper coin" (*Works*, 2:164).

All of the characteristics of the American myth—individualism, emphasis on the self at the expense of the other, optimistic pursuit of individual achievement, and expansive faith in American progress (all of the qualities so basic to Emersonian thought)—are missing from Hawthorne's view of life. Hawthorne, whose work is wholly American in its use of American materials and American history, remained outside the mainstream of American culture.

Why was Hawthorne able to resist the individualism of his culture when other nineteenth-century American writers did not? It seems evident from what is known of Hawthorne's life that he was less vulnerable to his culture primarily because of his sense of *detachment* from it. Despite his warm sympathy for individuals and his love for his country, Hawthorne did not throw himself into the flow of his culture but always remained aloof—an observer, not a participant in society. It was this detachment, I believe, more than any other single cause, that prevented Hawthorne from internalizing the individualism of his culture.

What, then, are the reasons for his detachment? Freudian critics have concluded that Hawthorne suffered from oedipal guilt, which caused feelings of isolation and alienation.[38] However, this theory depends upon a biographical interpretation of Hawthorne's fictional themes, which may or may not be valid. If we limit ourselves to what is actually known of Hawthorne's life without attempting to impose theory upon fact, the explanation for his detachment becomes more understandable.

In 1808, when Hawthorne was four years old, his father died, and his mother withdrew totally from society. The Freudian would focus on the early death of Hawthorne's father, but his mother's withdrawal from society is even more significant. Hawthorne's son Julian wrote in his biography of his father that this closure had an important effect on Hawthorne and his two sisters: "They had no opportunity to know what social intercourse meant; . . . they grew to regard themselves as *something apart from the general world*" (*NHW*, 1:5; my italics). It is important to recognize that it was not only the little boy in the so-called oedipal stage who grew up to become an isolated adult; the two girls remained just as isolated. Neither ever married, and his older sister Elizabeth was almost a recluse. To rely on the oedipal explanation for Hawthorne's feelings of isolation totally disregards his two sisters and assumes that it is only the male psyche that counts. That all three children were affected in the same way suggests that the cause was family-related rather than the result of Hawthorne's individual psychological development.

However, another factor in Hawthorne's childhood affected him more than anyone else. His early isolation was intensified when, at the age of nine, he suffered an injury to his foot that was not fully cured for three years. For the first fourteen months and for an unspecified time thereafter, Hawthorne was unable to go to school and could not leave the house without being carried. Whether or not he deliberately prolonged the duration of his lameness (he implied in later life that he made the most of it in order not to have to go to school [*NHW*, 1:95]), the effect was the same: further isolation from the "general world." While confined to the house, Hawthorne spent most of his time lying on the floor reading. "It was during this long lameness," his sister Elizabeth wrote in 1865, "that he acquired his habit of constant reading" (*NHW*, 1:100).

The final significant fact of Hawthorne's childhood is one that again affected all three children. In 1816, when Hawthorne was twelve and his lameness was finally cured, his mother moved with the children to Raymond, Maine, near Lake Sebago. Hawthorne returned to Salem for schooling for a while, but until 1819 he spent most of his time in Maine. Few boys his age lived nearby, and he seldom went to school. Instead, he ran wild in the woods and fields alone or with his sisters and spent much time in desultory reading. His companions were adults, his sisters, or books. Between the ages of nine and twelve he read such works as Shakespeare, *Pil-*

grim's Progress, Spenser's *Faerie Queene*, and *The Castle of Indolence*. In his early teens he read all of Scott, *The Arabian Nights*, *Tom Jones*, Rousseau's *Heloise*, *Roderick Random*, and *The Mysteries of Udolpho*. For the most part, Hawthorne's childhood years were spent apart from society in close association with his family. While other boys were imbibing American culture in school and with their peers, Hawthorne was reading of other cultures, other times.

The other significant period of Hawthorne's life with respect to his attitude toward his culture followed his graduation from Bowdoin College in 1825. Having just sufficient means to support himself so that he could write, he settled down in his mother's house in Salem, where he lived for twelve years with his mother and two sisters. He and his sisters did not enter into the society of Salem, and Hawthorne spent most of his time reading and writing in what he later called his "lonely chamber" (*Love Letters*, 1:224). He took long solitary walks and went on a trip for two or three weeks once a year. He negotiated with publishers and corresponded with his college friends, but he did not have a regular involvement with society. He remembered in later years that for months at a time he did not speak with anyone but members of his own family (*NHW*, 1:97). His only social activity seems to have been occasional whist games with his sister Louisa and two neighbors. It was not until 1837, when *Twice-told Tales* was published, that the world began to seek him out.

This mode of life may seem odd to the modern American critic who assumes that there must be something pathological about a young man of twenty-one who chooses to live with his family. However, given the events of Hawthorne's childhood, his limited finances, and his desire to write, the choice does not seem unreasonable. His isolation from society during his childhood had well prepared him for the long solitary years during which he struggled to make a name for himself as a writer. He did not have the means to set himself up in a house independently. (He was only able to do so in 1842, when he married, because he had begun to earn some money from the works he had completed while living at home; yet, even then, he and Sophia were hard pressed financially.) If he had wished a more active participation in society, he would have had to earn his living in another way—something he did not want to do.[39] That Hawthorne's family accepted his choice and apparently did not urge him to thrust himself into the competitive race for wealth and worldly position in nineteenth-century America suggests that Hawthorne's un-American attitude toward society was a familial one. Unlike Melville's family, for example, which constantly urged him to play the assertive male role of the American success myth,[40] Hawthorne's immediate family (though not his practical uncles) supported, or at least did not criticize, his nonparticipation in society. His sister Elizabeth's comment on the three-year isolation caused by Hawthorne's childhood lameness indicates no concern to fit Hawthorne to the mold of the American hero: "Undoubtedly he would have wanted many of the qualities which distinguished him in after life, if his genius had not been thus shielded in childhood" (*NHW*, 1:100).

Ultimately, whether Hawthorne's isolation was caused by oedipal guilt or, as I believe, by family attitudes and a pattern established in childhood, the result was the same: a lifelong feeling of detachment from American culture. Most significant in establishing this attitude was the period after Hawthorne's graduation from college, when he lived for twelve years in comparative isolation. The childhood years, during which Hawthorne was constantly reading and in the "companionship of older persons," as his son-in-law later said,[41] rather than at school or with his peers, made possible what Hawthorne called his "long seclusion" (*NHW*, 1:98). And it was the years of seclusion between the ages of twenty-one and thirty-three that ultimately determined his relationship to his culture. If after graduation from college Hawthorne had been forced to earn a living or had been involved in an active social life, he would very probably have lost much of his detachment from his culture. Other children who have experienced solitary childhoods owing to illness or other circumstances have not maintained the detachment that Hawthorne did. His childhood engendered in him a taste for solitude and developed the resources necessary to sustain it. But the many solitary years of his young manhood were the deciding factor. At a time when other young men were taking their places in the expanding world of nineteenth-century America, Hawthorne was comfortably ensconced in his chamber.

Never a hermit or out of touch with reality, he remained interested in what was going on in the world and sometimes had heated political discussions with his sister Elizabeth. But he was not a part of the world. He watched it from his chamber window or as a spectator in a crowd. (It is interesting that although Hawthorne did not enjoy social activities, he liked any public excitement that attracted crowds—a parade, fireworks, a fire.)[42] Like the narrator at the top of the steeple in "Sights from a Steeple," he was "a watchman, all-heeding and unheeded" (*Works*, 9:192).

In 1840 Hawthorne wrote of the room in which he had spent so many solitary years: "If ever I should have a biographer, he ought to make great mention of this chamber in my memoirs, because so much of my lonely youth was wasted here, and here my mind and character were formed" (*Love Letters*, 1:223). It should not be surprising that Hawthorne could maintain the detachment necessary to resist the individualism of his culture. When his work began to receive attention and he began to come out into the world, he was thirty-three years old. By then his "mind and character" were indeed formed. He had established the principles by which he would be guided. They were formed by constant reading and by a close relationship with his family, not by an active participation in his own culture—and thus they did not include the American emphasis on the individual.

Hawthorne, then, did not subscribe to the individualism that characterized nineteenth-century America. Always sympathetic to the claims of the other in his life and his fiction, he was consequently able to portray woman—the traditional other—as an independent person. Un-American in his denial of the primacy of the self so emphatically asserted by his Transcendentalist neighbors, Hawthorne, despite personal and cultural inhibitions, was acutely aware of the personhood of the female other and was able to create female characters who stand out in American literature as women of substance and individuality. His strong woman is not a shadowy figure outside the reality of life, as was the typical woman created by his American contemporaries, a pretty aeolian harp who existed only to be played upon at will by the stronger winds of masculine vanity. She is a person in herself.

CHAPTER 8

CHAPTER 8

THE WOMAN TAKES
CENTER STAGE:
HENRY JAMES

*What was she going to do? . . . Most women
did with themselves nothing at all; they waited
. . . for a man to come their way. . . . Isabel's
originality was that she gave one an impression
of having intentions of her own.*

        Henry James, *The Portrait of a Lady* [1]

What is so revolutionary about Henry James's
The Portrait of a Lady (1880) is his depiction
of the American individualist as a woman—
something that had never been done before
in American literature and has seldom been
done since. Isabel Archer seeks to "suffice to
herself," "planning out her own development, desiring her perfection, observing her
progress" (*Novels*, 3:71–72). Her principal
concern is to realize herself: "I wish to choose
my fate" (*Novels*, 3:229). She rejects her
suitors, Lord Warburton and Caspar Goodwood, not, as critics have insisted, because
of sexual fears, but because they threaten her
individuality. [2] To dismiss Isabel's rejection of
her suitors as simply a puritanical fear of sex
is to miss the connection between this action
and James's portrayal of Isabel as the self-

sufficient individualist. James is very clear about her motivation. She feels that marriage would be analogous to living like an animal in a cage; it is not compatible with her idea of the "free exploration of life" (*Novels*, 3:153, 155). Goodwood and Warburton "deprive her of her sense of freedom," "diminish liberty," and she wants to be free and independent (*Novels*, 3:153, 155–156, 162). Unlike other ladies in American literature, Isabel does not see herself as anyone's satellite but insists that she has "an orbit of her own" (*Novels*, 3:144). She refuses to let either Goodwood or Warburton "take positive possession of her" (*Novels*, 3:162). In other words, at the beginning of the novel Isabel is the embodiment of the American ideal of the self-forming, self-reliant individual.

Not only does Isabel Archer manifest all the traits of the self-assertive American individualist; she also possesses the complacent optimism of the Emersonian idealist, which, in the American myth, supports and sustains the individualist's confidence in himself. James says of Isabel: "She had a fixed determination to regard the world as a place of brightness, of free expansion, of irresistible action; she held it must be detestable to be afraid or ashamed" (*Novels*, 3:68). This attitude toward the world is combined with a similarly Emersonian attitude toward herself: "She had an unquenchable desire to think well of herself. She had a theory that it was only under this provision life was worth living; that one should be one of the best" (*Novels*, 3:68). Like the Transcendentalists in general, she identified herself with the world as a whole: "She carried within herself a great fund of life, and her deepest enjoyment was to feel the continuity between the movements of her own soul and the agitations of the world" (*Novels*, 3:245).[3]

It is not surprising that Isabel Archer has been a favorite character with American feminists, who see in her the self-assertion that has generally been denied women in our literature and in our culture. However, it is important to recognize that James does not countenance this attitude in her. Early in the novel he notes that Isabel is guilty of the "sin of self-esteem," and he criticizes the complacency with which she regards herself (*Novels*, 3:67). Her easy optimism he attributes to her youth and inexperience: "She was too young, too impatient to live, too unacquainted with pain" (*Novels*, 3:72–73). James, then, sees folly in Isabel's confident individualism. Yet, although he does not condone it, neither is he harsh in his criticism of her. He seems to regard her attitude as part of her growing process. At one point he finds it necessary to caution the reader not to be too hasty in judging her: "If there was a great deal of folly in her wisdom those who judge her severely may have the satisfaction of finding that, later, she became consistently wise only at the cost of an amount of folly which will constitute almost a direct appeal to charity" (*Novels*, 3:145).

Readers who have sought a feminist assertion in Isabel Archer have been disappointed with the ending of the novel. Her final act is one of renunciation when she returns to a loveless marriage in which she has been the victim. From James's point of view, however, Isabel's final renunciation allows her to transcend what he portrays in this novel as the evils of self-orientation. Isabel's European experience has taught her that one cannot form one's destiny, that life is *not* a work of art. At the beginning of the novel Isabel had been confident that her own "organization was fine"; she desired to be perfect (*Novels*, 3:68). By the end of the book she realizes that one cannot be fine and live—and she wishes to live (*Novels*, 4:392–393). Since James gives Isabel some of his own sensibilities as an artist,[4] one might say of her approach to life what James in "The Art of Fiction" said of the novelist: the most important quality for a novelist is to be "*sincere.*"[5] Isabel tried to form her life according to an image, but she learned that the world is not always the bright place she thought it was; life involves suffering and renunciation. And finally, she learned that the individual mind is more complex and filled with conflict than her complacency had allowed her to see.[6]

Ultimately, then, *The Portrait of a Lady* denies the validity of the American myth by asserting the necessity for renunciation and suffering, the recognition of inner conflict and self-doubt. But for readers who would regard this novel as one more case of the rug being pulled out from under an independent woman, it is necessary to recognize that James does not apply this philosophy only to women. For James, the self-orientation that is so important a part of American culture is a serious fault in all human beings. The villain in *The Portrait of a Lady* is, after all, a man: Gilbert Osmond. Isabel's husband, the American expatriate, is an exaggeration of all the self-orientation manifested by Isabel.

It is Osmond who insists that life should be a work of art (*Novels*, 4:15). Isabel is originally attracted to him because she feels he is "fine"; he has a fine mind, a fine voice. He is as perfect as a fine drawing (*Novels*, 3:356). James compares him to a "fine gold coin" (*Novels*, 3:329). But his fineness is unreal. As Ralph Touchett observes, it is a pose: Osmond lives only to minister to a mental image. Everything he does is intended to contribute to the formation of the self: "His tastes, his studies, his accomplishments, his collections, were all for a purpose. . . . His solitude, his ennui, his love for his daughter, his good manners, his bad manners, were so many features of a mental image constantly present to him" (*Novels*, 4:145). Osmond is like the American individualist who creates a persona for himself and then seeks only to form that image. Like such an individual, Osmond is constantly preoccupied with self. Living only for the world's opinion, he has become small, narrow, and selfish, says Ralph Touchett (*Novels*, 4:70). In an image reminiscent of Hawthorne, James sums him up thus: "Under all his culture, his cleverness, his amenity, under his good-nature, his facility, his knowledge of life, his egotism lay hidden like a serpent in a bank of flowers" (*Novels*, 4:196).

Of course, the person who lives wholly for the self cannot be moved by the concerns of other people. Mme. Merle says Osmond is heartless (*Novels*, 3:346). And James tells us that Osmond does not feel his relations to other people (*Novels*, 4:71). His daughter is a commodity to him, a beautifully finished product through which he can purchase the world's esteem if he can marry her to a lord (e.g., *Novels*, 4:181–

182). Osmond is interested in other people only for the use they can be to him. When Mme. Merle tells him he should meet Isabel, he asks, "What good will it do me?" (*Novels*, 3:343). And when he marries Isabel, it is for her money and for the way in which he feels she will enhance his image. She has, after all, rejected an English lord, and he is attracted by "the idea of taking to himself a young lady who had qualified herself to figure in his collection of choice objects by declining so noble a hand" (*Novels*, 4:9). She fits his purpose like "handled ivory to the palm," he thinks; to possess such a fine specimen will "publish" his superiority to the world (*Novels*, 4:11–12).

It is obvious that Osmond regards Isabel only as a beautiful object to reflect glory on himself. He wants the "portrait," not the lady. In fact, he becomes irritated when, after their marriage, he finds that there is more to Isabel than an image. Osmond does not want her to have ideas of her own: "He would have liked her to have nothing of her own but her pretty appearance" (*Novels*, 4:194–195). But it is not only her opinions he wishes to efface: "What he had meant had been the whole thing—her character, the way she felt, the way she judged" (*Novels*, 4:195). Her real offense, Isabel realizes, is to have "a mind of her own at all" (*Novels*, 4:200). Like the American individualist discussed in the previous chapters, Osmond sought in a wife not a real person but an image that he could contain within himself. When she questions him, he looks down at her as though she were only "a disagreeable necessity of thought" (*Novels*, 4:263). As Ralph Touchett says, she is expected to be a fine lady who represents only her husband (*Novels*, 4:144–145).[7]

For Isabel, her marriage to Osmond is a mistake. Yet it is not a mistake in the sense that he is in fact her true soul mate. Isabel had desired to be "fine," to be perfect, to be, in fact, a "portrait of a lady." She realizes after her marriage that she had created an image for herself and for Osmond: "She had effaced herself when he first knew her; she had made herself small, pretending there was less of her than there really was" (*Novels*, 4:191). Forced by Osmond to become the exquisite portrait that she thought she wanted to be, Isabel realizes the horror of it. But Osmond will never learn what Isabel has learned. Not only does he want to possess her as an image; but he himself, with all of his posing, is only an image of a man. Reflected in Osmond is the same self-orientation that had guided Isabel. He is an ugly reflection of herself just as truly as Lord Mark's face in the window in *The Wings of the Dove* is a reflection for Merton Densher of the truth about himself—that he is in fact a fortune hunter.[8]

What is significant about *The Portrait of a Lady* as an American novel is that it is told primarily from the point of view of the "lady," not the man who would make her into a portrait. Since James places the center of consciousness in Isabel Archer, we find the point of view of the woman who is being forced to deny her individuality. If that woman is herself an Emersonian individualist, how can she accept the fact that someone wants to efface her personality, her mind, her whole character? How can she consent to be reduced to an image, albeit a pretty one, whose sole function is to represent someone else? For the spirited and independent Isabel, who sees herself as the self-reliant individualist as much as any nineteenth-century American male, it is a horrifying realization. She feels suffocated, locked in the house of Osmond's mind as though in a "house of darkness . . . dumbness" (*Novels*, 4:195–196). She who used to speak freely what she thought now finds she must prepare her answers carefully (*Novels*, 4:178–179). She feels she must defend herself against Osmond, who is contemptuous of anything and anyone that is hers and refuses to grant her any "freedom of mind" (*Novels*, 4:181, 201, 245). Yet he does not want her to be stupid. She knows that. In fact, what he had originally liked about her was her cleverness—but only because he thought it would make her receptive to him: "He had expected his wife to feel with him and for him, and to enter into his opinions, his ambitions, his preferences" (*Novels*, 4:200). Isabel is forced to march to his rigid music, "she who of old had been so free of step" (*Novels*, 4:199). Stunned by the realization that Osmond is "her appointed and inscribed master," she regards this fact "at moments with a sort of incredulous blankness" (*Novels*, 4:245). She finds herself in a dark dead-end alley that seems to lead downward into "realms of restriction and depression" (*Novels*, 4:189). Osmond has made everything wither for her (*Novels*, 4:188).

Just as Margaret Fuller fought against Emerson's attempt to absorb her into his all-encompassing self, so Isabel resists Osmond's voracious appropriation of her. One might ask, what if in Italy Margaret Fuller, instead of meeting an Italian named Ossoli, had met an American named Osmond? She too would have insisted, as Isabel does, that "she was, after all, herself—she couldn't help that" (*Novels*, 4:190).

James's recognition that Isabel is, "after all, herself" is an insight missing from the work of most nineteenth-century American male writers. For James, the woman is not simply an image or reflection of the man; she, too, is a self.[9] However disappointing the ending of *The Portrait of a Lady* may seem to twentieth-century American readers, the fact that the woman is recognized as a self marks it as a milestone in any study of the treatment of women in American literature.

James's disapproval of Isabel Archer's self-assertion does not mean that he did not regard her as a person. In fact, it is because James recognized her as a person that he was able to do what few American novelists have done: create a fully developed female character. She is not a male fantasy figure, on the one hand, or a threatening bitch-goddess, on the other. She is a real person with all of the complexities of an individual.

In his other novels James shows equal sensitivity to the female consciousness. One of James's most interesting women is Christina Light, who appears as a young girl in *Roderick Hudson* (1875) and later reappears as the Princess Casamassima in the novel of that name (1885–1886). Although Christina is not a central character in *Roderick Hudson* and was only intended as one of the determining factors in Hudson's disintegration, James seems unable to treat her simply as the shadowy temptress of a conventional novel. In fact, in his preface to *Roderick Hudson* he comments that he has given Christina more life than the subject required (*Novels*, 1:xx). He shows why she is the way she is, how she was raised by a fortune-hunting mother solely to bring a high price in the marriage market (*Novels*, 1:179–180, 192, 249–254). James sympathetically portrays the tragedy of her life and makes her into a believable, complex character with more self-awareness than Roderick Hudson.

It is not surprising that, having created such an interesting character in Christina, James should take her up again. In *The Princess Casamassima* Christina has left the prince whom she had been forced to marry ten years earlier. The reader, although understanding and sympathizing with Christina's struggle to extricate herself from her stultifying existence, at the same time feels annoyed with her for seeming to amuse herself with other people's lives. If the princess is not a heroine, neither is she a stock female villain. She is an individual, with all of the conflicting motives, strengths, and weaknesses deriving from her circumstances.

Another of James's interesting female characters is Kate Croy in *The Wings of the Dove* (1902). Kate plans an action that in itself is despicable: she persuades Merton Densher to pretend to love and to marry the dying Milly Theale so that when Milly dies, he and Kate will have her money and can marry. But James does not portray Kate as the stereotypical scheming woman. We are inside her consciousness and see her with her selfish father and vulgar sister, who want her to marry well only to benefit themselves. Then we see her with the possessive Mrs. Lowder, who regards her as a beautiful prize to reflect credit on herself. These pressures on Kate are juxtaposed against her own vibrant spirit. We see her from Milly Theale's point of view as a pacing panther, restrained by circumstances from being what she could (*Novels*, 19:282). And we see her from Densher's point of view as a woman with a special "talent for life," whose intelligence and vitality make other women seem like books he has already read (*Novels*, 20:61–62, 176).

It is not necessary to discuss in detail all of James's female characters. Charlotte Stant, Maggie Verver, Milly Theale, Olive Chancellor, Daisy Miller—all are complex human beings. Even James's minor female characters are believable, individual persons: Miss Pynsent, Rosie Muniment, Maria Gostrey, Susan Stringham. James understood and portrayed the reality of woman's "infinite variety"; he was not limited to a few stereotypes.

James's attitude toward the women in his fiction is reflected in his personal life. He regarded women not simply as decorative objects but as people. E. S. Nadal, the second secretary of the United States legation in London and an acquaintance of Henry James, wrote of James's relationship to women: "He seemed to look at women rather as women looked at them. Women look at women as persons; men look at them as women."[10]

James's recognition of the personhood of women is particularly apparent in his comments about his sister Alice. The youngest of the five James children and the only girl, Alice suffered a series of nervous illnesses from the time she was fifteen until she died of cancer at the age of forty-three. During the last six years of her life she lived in England, where from her sofa she commented on social and political affairs with a caustic wit that James recreated in the invalid Rosie Muniment in *The Princess Casamassima*. James was a frequent visitor during Alice's years in England, bringing her news of society and of his activities. According to Alice's comments in her diary, James was a sympathetic and concerned brother, her favorite among the four. It is clear from James's comments that he regarded Alice as a separate individual with a personality of her own. Reading Alice's diary after her death, James commented in a letter to his brother William that he had always been struck by Alice's "extraordinary force of mind and character." The diary reflected her self, "heroic in its individuality, its independence—its face-to-face with the universe for-and-by herself."[11] His ability to see Alice as an individual allowed James to observe her illness with unusual perception. The reason for Alice's illness, he saw, lay somehow in the contrast between "the intensity of her will and personality" and the role available to her in the world. She found no outlet for her marvelous energies and ability. As Alice's diary so clearly shows, there was nothing for her to do as an adult but drink tea and "sit immovable" by the fireside.[12] "How sick one gets of being 'good,'" she wrote at another point in the diary, noting how between the ages of twelve and twenty-four she had been forced to work hard "absorbing into the bone that the better part is to clothe oneself in neutral tints, walk by still waters, and possess one's soul in silence."[13] James understood her dilemma and concluded that "her tragic health was in a manner the only solution of the practical problem of life." (*L*, Lubbock, 1:215–216).

James also recognized that there was more to his mother's character than was visible in her role as wife and mother. In *Notes of a Son and Brother* he marveled at how his mother had lived so exclusively for her husband and children that she seemed to have no identity of her own. The harmony of the family lay primarily in their sense that she had no other life.[14] After his mother's death in 1882, he wrote: "She was our life, she was the house, she was the keystone of the arch. She held us all together."[15] It is significant that James perceived the strength behind the apparent passivity of his mother—which others may have considered simply as a lack of character.[16] It is also notable that he questioned her role and wondered about her as a separate being. Moreover, James realized that the relationship between his parents was a reciprocal one and that the interdependency of his mother and father "showed . . . what, in this world of cleft components, one human being can yet be for another" (*Notes*, p. 178). James's recognition of his mother's separate identity furthered his understanding of the individuality of other people and helped provide him with the insight into human relationships that was so necessary to his writing.

In addition to the relationships with his mother and sister, James enjoyed many long-lasting friendships with women throughout his life. He was interested in strong women of substance: Fanny Kemble, Mrs. Proctor, Mrs. Duncan Stewart, and Edith Wharton were among his many women friends. His relationships with these women were, so far as we know, solely intellectual. He sought their company, as his letters make clear, because they were interesting people to be with. Remarking that he found so many people to be superficial, he noted that it was "a rest and a refreshment" to know someone like Mrs. Kemble, who had such "a deep, rich human nature." Her conversation was "strong meat," and he found her to be "one of the most delightful and interesting of women" (L, Edel, 2:212, 225, 240–241; see also 2:208).

During the last thirteen years of his life, one of James's closest friends was Edith Wharton. Although he mockingly called her his "Angel of Devastation," because of the ruin her tempting invitations to travel brought on his "time and domestic economy," taking him away from his work, he found her company exciting and constantly stimulating. She was "almost too insistently Olympian," a "golden eagle" or "Firebird" whose energy left him exhausted.[17] James regarded her as a brilliant writer and "a very great person."[18] His feeling for her is particularly apparent in his letters to her and to other friends during the period leading up to her divorce. As Millicent Bell points out, James's participation in Wharton's extreme personal troubles was remarkable for a man often thought of as a detached observer of life.[19] He wrote to his friend Gaillard Lapsely in 1911 of the horror of Wharton's situation: "One's pity for her is at the best scarce bearable."[20] The extent of James's relationship with Edith Wharton—and a significant clue to his relationship with people in general—is best expressed in Wharton's own observations in a letter to Charles Eliot Norton in 1907. After James had visited her in France, she wrote of him: "The more one knows of him the more one wonders and admires the mixture of wisdom and tolerance, of sensitiveness and sympathy, that makes his heart even more interesting to contemplate than his mind." [21] Whatever the reason for James's attraction to these women, the important point is that he was able to interact with women as persons; he saw them as people like himself.

Less well known is James's relationship with Constance Fenimore Woolson, the American novelist. James met Woolson in 1880, and they remained close friends until her death in 1894. He wrote of her to William Dean Howells in 1884: "She is a very intelligent woman, and understands when she is spoken to; a peculiarity I prize, as I find it more and more rare." She was, he continued, the only English novelist that he read, with the exception of Howells himself. [22] He wrote a tribute to her work in 1887 and published the revised essay in *Partial Portraits* (1887), his collection of essays on literary masters—an action that is surprising, considering the relative obscurity of Woolson compared with the other writers in the volume. James summed up his feelings about Woolson in a letter to his friend Francis Boott in 1886, when he described her as "an intelligent and sympathetic being." [23]

Following Woolson's death, her sister invited James to retrieve his letters, and apparently he destroyed them. Her letters to him have also disappeared, with the exception of four early letters that were among the papers of James's brother William. These few letters reveal her own admiration for James's work, and they indicate that the relationship was a reciprocal one. Certainly, she never hesitated to criticize James. Particularly significant is her disagreement with James's portrayal of women: "How did you ever dare write a portrait of a lady? Fancy any woman attempting the portrait of a gentleman!" In another letter she urges him to create a really lovable woman:

> Why not give us a woman for whom we can feel a real love? There are surely such in the world. . . . I do not plead that she should be happy; or even fortunate; but let her be distinctly loveable; perhaps, let some one love her very much; but, at any rate, let *her* love very much, and

let us see that she does; let us care for her, and even greatly. If you will only care for her yourself, as you describe her, the thing is done.[24]

Was this comment in James's mind when he created Milly Theale, the most lovable of his female characters, who, like Woolson, died in Venice? It was in the year of Woolson's death that James first set down notes for *The Wings of the Dove*. There are many questions about the relationship between James and Woolson,[25] but one fact is clear: for Henry James, Constance Fenimore Woolson was a significant *person*.

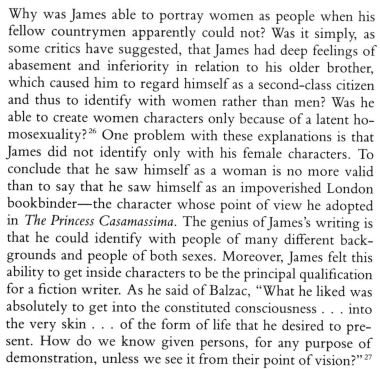

Why was James able to portray women as people when his fellow countrymen apparently could not? Was it simply, as some critics have suggested, that James had deep feelings of abasement and inferiority in relation to his older brother, which caused him to regard himself as a second-class citizen and thus to identify with women rather than men? Was he able to create women characters only because of a latent homosexuality?[26] One problem with these explanations is that James did not identify only with his female characters. To conclude that he saw himself as a woman is no more valid than to say that he saw himself as an impoverished London bookbinder—the character whose point of view he adopted in *The Princess Casamassima*. The genius of James's writing is that he could identify with people of many different backgrounds and people of both sexes. Moreover, James felt this ability to get inside characters to be the principal qualification for a fiction writer. As he said of Balzac, "What he liked was absolutely to get into the constituted consciousness . . . into the very skin . . . of the form of life that he desired to present. How do we know given persons, for any purpose of demonstration, unless we see it from their point of vision?"[27]

To rely on psychological explanations here would lead to the assumption that James's ability to portray strong, independent women is abnormal. In fact, this accomplishment is abnormal only in American literature. That critics have sought to explain James's portrayal of female protagonists in psychosexual terms illustrates how much of an anachronism he was in nineteenth-century American literature. We do not look for hidden feelings of inferiority or homosexuality in the creators of Moll Flanders, Cousine Bette, Anna Karenina, or Becky Sharp. When we read that Flaubert said, "Emma Bovary—*c'est moi*," we don't assume that Flaubert regarded himself as a second-class citizen because he could identify with a woman. Psychological explanations may play a part in James's choice and treatment of his subject matter, as they do with any writer, but they do not help us to understand *why* James was able to portray female characters as people when other American writers could not.

The explanation for James's ability is not primarily psychological but cultural: like Hawthorne, James was not typically American in his attitudes. In the first place, his background obviated an insular view of his country's traditions. He was exposed to many different cultures during his formative years. He traveled back and forth to Europe three times before he was seventeen, living half of the time in various parts of Europe and the other half in Albany, Manhattan, and Newport, Rhode Island. In 1864, when he was twenty-one, his family moved to Boston, and two years later they settled finally in Cambridge, Massachusetts. James spent a year traveling in Europe in 1869–1870, and two years later he returned to France to live. Then in 1875, after an unsuccessful six-month attempt to live in New York, he returned to Europe, declaring, "I take possession of the old world—I inhale it—I appropriate it" (*L*, Edel, 1:484). This time he settled permanently in England, where he lived until his death in 1916.

The reason for James's ability to resist the individualism of his culture, I believe, derived primarily from his feeling of detachment from it. In *Notes of a Son and Brother* James described the attitude of his family upon returning to the United States from Europe at the end of 1860: the family is "tainted . . . with the quality and the effect of detachment. The effect of detachment was the fact of the experience of Europe" (*Notes*, p. 67). Whereas Hawthorne was only isolated from American society, James, during his formative years, was much of the time absent from it. Yet James's attitude of detachment, like Hawthorne's, was a familial one. James recalled feeling that his family did not fit into American culture. His father, for example, was not in business like other American fathers. He remembers pressing his father to tell him something that the boy could offer to the children at school who wanted to know what his father did (*Notes*, pp. 68–69). And in *A Small Boy and Others* he notes how from the time he was a little boy in New York he sensed that his parents were homesick for the ways of English life and became convinced that therein he would find his own direction: "Conviction was the result of the very air of home." [28] As children, he and his brother William were infected by a home atmosphere that extolled the virtues of the Old World (*Small Boy*, pp. 81, 85). But, upon maturity, Henry, unlike his brother, did not take his place in American society. Like Hawthorne during his young manhood, he absented himself from active participation in the American scene. Again the pattern of childhood and family attitudes, coupled with an absence from American culture during the early adult years, made possible the detachment that permitted a lifelong resistance to the individualism of American culture.

James deprecated Americans who were unable to learn from other societies and other cultures. Emerson, he noted, had gone to Europe three times and "was introduced to a more complicated world; but his spirit, his moral taste, as it were, abode always within the undecorated walls of his youth" (*Portraits*, p. 7). In a letter to his mother from Florence in 1869, James complained that the Americans he saw there remained closed to the European experience:

A set of people less framed to provoke national complacency than the latter [Americans] it would be hard to imagine. There is but one word to use in regard to them—

> vulgar; vulgar; vulgar. Their ignorance—their stingy,
> grudging, defiant attitude toward everything European
> —their perpetual reference of all things to some Ameri-
> can standard or precedent which exists only in their own
> unscrupulous wind-bags— . . . these things glare at you
> hideously.   (L, Edel, 1:152)[29]

That America was not the only standard was a lesson that
James had learned early. And throughout his fiction he revealed the complexity of his vision in his portrayal of the
confrontation of Americans and Europeans. He does not
present the one as villain and the other as hero; in James's
work they can learn from each other. The Woollett con-
tingent in *The Ambassadors* and the stiff New Englanders in
The Europeans have much to learn from the Europeans' easy
acceptance of life. Further, American individualists like Christopher Newman have much to learn from European manners
and culture. Yet, at the same time, European customs seem
stiff and inhuman beside the natural dignity and innocent
spontaneity of a Daisy Miller, a Milly Theale, or a Charlotte
Evans and her father. James was interested in humankind, its
foibles and its virtues; he was not limited by national boundaries. He considered himself a novelist of the world, and he
aimed to write a "human comedy" in the tradition of Balzac.[30]

His broader orientation led James to dissent from the
nineteenth-century American's belief in the essential rightness
of the American way. His heresy is particularly evident in his
deviation from the two principal tenets of nineteenth-century
American thought: American expansionism and American
individualism.

In *The American Scene*, which recorded his visit to the
United States in 1904, after a twenty-year absence, James
questioned the whole idea of American growth. At what cost
and to what end did Americans seek to expand, individually
and as a nation? Was mere growth to be an end in itself? Sur-
veying the American scene, James noted, "*The will to grow*
was everywhere written large, and to grow at no matter what
or whose expense."[31] Describing America as a land plun-

dered, he made clear his disapproval of the American faith in progress and of the belief in the positive value of territorial expansion. He wished there were an "unbridgeable abyss" to halt his countrymen's advance across the continent. Americans had despoiled the land, and they had no civilization to put in its place:

> You touch the great lonely land . . . only to plant upon it some ugliness about which, never dreaming of the grace of apology or contrition, you then proceed to brag with a cynicism all your own. You convert the large and noble sanities that I see around me . . . to crudities, to invalidities, hideous and unashamed; and you so leave them to add to the number of the myriad aspects you simply spoil. (*American Scene*, pp. 463–464)

If James did not embrace his countrymen's belief in the grandeur of America's destiny, neither did he subscribe to American individualism. As a writer, he opposed the Transcendentalists, who saw the self as central and who attempted to absorb the outside world into the self. In a review of Whitman's "Drum Taps" in 1865, James criticized Whitman's inability to get outside himself, and he thereby established a credo for his own fiction. Art, he addressed himself to Whitman, "requires, above all things, a suppression of one's self, a subordination of one's self to an idea. This will never do for you, whose plan is to adapt the scheme of the universe to your own limitations."[32]

Not only as an artist, but in his personal life as well, James did not succumb to Whitmanesque self-assertion. Certainly he never portrayed himself as a rugged individualist or confident hero. In his autobiographical *A Small Boy and Others* (1913) and *Notes of a Son and Brother* (1914), James stresses his feelings of inadequacy as a child and young man. Physical and social disabilities reinforced an image of incompetence that James accepted about himself to such an extent that, as he later noted, he offered no resistance when his parents sent him to an engineering school in Switzerland, although he had no interest or ability in mathematics and, despite his diligence, could only meet with daily failure at such a school (*Notes*, pp. 3–4).

One of James's earliest perceptions was that his brother William, who was a year older than he, was always better than he was. William was ahead of him in school; he had more friends; his activities were more interesting; and he seemed more competent in everything. James felt that he himself picked up only the "crumbs and echoes" of his brother's life (*Small Boy*, pp. 8–9, 254; *Notes*, pp. 13, 302, 327). But it was not only his brother who made James feel inadequate. When he was a child, he thought that to change places with *anyone* would be a positive gain. He envied the "otherness" of other people. To him otherness held the same fascination as the sweet concoctions that he looked at "through a confectioner's window" (*Notes*, p. 175)—a phrase echoed in James's description of Hyacinth Robinson, whose position outside society in *The Princess Casamassima* compelled him to look at life "through the glass of the pastry-cook's window" (*Novels*, 6:61). James, who enjoyed the social position unavailable to Hyacinth, nevertheless lacked the confidence and insular self-assurance of the American individualist. Although he was not without personal ambition and possessed his own brand of egotism with respect to his writing, he was too aware of individual limitations and the claims of other people to adopt the self-assertion of the American Narcissus.

James's fictional portraits reflect a philosophy closer to Hawthorne's view of limited man than to the American Transcendentalists' concept of the all-knowing "I." With the exception of Milly Theale in *The Wings of the Dove* and Mr. Longdon in *The Awkward Age*, there are no all-good characters in James's work. And even those two, although they do not exhibit the moral duality of most of James's characters, are far from being the self-confident, all-powerful heroes of American myth. In fact, part of their strength lies in their unassuming natures; they are concerned not with self but with the welfare of others.

If there are no superheroes in James's novels, neither are

there any villains, with the possible exception of Osmond in *The Portrait of a Lady* (and even he can be pitied). This absence of all-bad characters is one reason why his novels seem so ambivalent in tone. James does not judge his characters. As he said of Balzac in a 1905 lecture in the United States, Balzac loved all of his characters. His subject was the "complicated . . . human condition," and he gave his characters all the freedom they needed to act themselves out fully.[33] The same can be said of James. He was not trying to show how exemplary one character was or how evil another. He was fascinated by his characters as people.

Not only are James's characters not morally perfect; they are limited by culture and circumstance. They cannot know everything. Christopher Newman, Merton Densher, Basil Ransom, Lambert Strether, Prince Amerigo, Adam Verver, Olive Chancellor, Christina Light, Kate Croy, Maggie Verver, Charlotte Stant—all are limited in some way. Newman, for example, is held back by cultural limitations; Princess Casamassima is limited by her circumstances; and Strether is restrained by background and custom. No matter how good a Jamesian character's motivations are or how sincere his efforts, he can never be perfect. As Isabel Archer recognizes at the end of *The Portrait of a Lady*, perfection is not part of the human condition.[34]

For the purposes of this study, the important aspect of James's view of the individual is that, like Hawthorne, James does not portray the male figure as the superperson of American myth. His prototypical American, Christopher Newman, finds at the end of *The American* (1877) that he can not do or have everything. His optimistic self-assertion is pulled up short by his European experience, and he realizes that the world outside himself has a reality of its own. When he is confronted with the stone wall of the convent, Newman's "thoroughly contemporaneous optimism" runs into an Old World reality that he cannot overcome (*Novels*, 2:422). When Mrs. Tristram asks him if he tried to scale the wall, he replies: "It's too high—it's beyond me" (*Novels*, 2:536). It is a chastened Newman who decides not to seek revenge on the

Bellegardes. His step is not "the elastic step of a man who has won a victory" but the "quiet measure . . . of a retreat with appearances preserved" (*Novels*, 2:534).

In most of James's work the principal male figure is a self-questioning, complex person. Hyacinth Robinson in *The Princess Casamassima* wavers in Hamlet-like uncertainty before the terrible decision that he cannot make. Ralph Touchett in *The Portrait of a Lady* is an unhappy cynic and invalid, but his introspective questioning contrasts favorably with the cruel self-assertion of Osmond. Lambert Strether in *The Ambassadors* (1903) feels that he has failed in everything. Merton Densher in *The Wings of the Dove* sees himself as a fool and is ultimately ashamed of his own actions. Prince Amerigo in *The Golden Bowl* is bewildered by the white impenetrability of his American wife and father-in-law and believes that "everything is terrible . . . in the heart of man" (*Novels*, 24:349). The Jamesian man, like James himself, is aware of his limitations and does not manifest the confidence and simplistic optimism of the American Dreamer.

Because James did not share his countrymen's belief in individualism and consequently did not draw his male characters in the heroic porportions that dwarf other personalities and points of view, he was aware of and able to portray the other in his fiction. In *The Wings of the Dove*, for example, he conceived of the story of a dying American girl and also created two other totally different consciousnesses—Kate Croy and Merton Densher. In *The Portrait of a Lady* he could be Ralph Touchett, the dying cynic, and at the same time be a spontaneous American girl. *What Maisie Knew* is told from the point of view of a little girl; *The Ambassadors*, from the point of view of a middle-aged man. *The Golden Bowl* gives us the interior minds of the Prince and Maggie, as well as the points of view of the Assinghams, Adam Verver, and Charlotte Stant.

Recognition of James's ability to enter the consciousness of many varied characters is of course not new. What has been consistently overlooked, however, is that this ability de-

rives from James's attitude toward individualism and provides the principal explanation for his portrayal of women. If
American critics have not been able to understand this aspect
of James's writing, it is because they have found it easier
to look for psychosexual explanations for James's ability to
identify with women than to question the narcissistic implications of the American myth.

James's comments outside his fiction reveal a continuing
un-American awareness of and interest in the other. In *Notes
of a Son and Brother*, James explains that George Eliot's first
novel, *Adam Bede*, was rejected by Americans because they
had no interest in people so unlike themselves. James, however, was excited about "such other people" and about the
book that so beautifully "*referred* them . . . to a social order,
making life more interesting and more various." For the
young James, Eliot's novel opened up "the door of the world"
(*Notes*, p. 19). In *The American Scene*, James specifically discusses what he sees as an American failure to be concerned
with other people. James maintains that if the individual is to
develop as a person, he must become aware of other people
and must interact with them:

> Character is developed to visible fineness . . . only by
> friction, . . . only by its having to reckon with a com-
> plexity of forces. . . . No kind of person . . . is a very
> good kind, and still less a very pleasing kind, when its
> education has not been made to some extent by contact
> with other kinds, and, to that degree, by a certain rela-
> tion with them.　　(*American Scene*, pp. 427–428)

In his personal life, too, James was always aware of the other.
His youthful memories of Newport, for example, are of "the
dramatic, the social, the effectively human aspect" (*Notes*,
p. 416). Even in the titles of his autobiographical works, he
portrays himself in his relation to others: "A Small Boy and
Others" and "Notes of a *Son* and *Brother*." What he liked most
about his cousin Minny Temple was the way she enjoyed

seeing other people reveal themselves. She had a "sense for the verity of character and play of life in others" (*Notes*, p. 461).

James's ability to recognize the other as a separate being enabled him to portray the woman as a person. In all of his novels the female characters are just as real, just as complex, and just as interesting—sometimes more interesting—than the male characters. For James, who did not subscribe to the American myth of the individual, the female other was a person in her own right. In *The Portrait of a Lady* he was able to conceive of placing the "centre of the subject in the young woman's own consciousness" (*Novels*, 3:xiv–xvi). Such a novelistic device represented an overt questioning of the pattern of nineteenth-century American literature in which major (male) American writers, except for Hawthorne, depicted the young woman simply as an object in the life of the male individual. As James noted in his preface to *The Portrait of a Lady*, young women in most novels are never allowed to be the "sole ministers" of the novel's theme; other characters carry the action, and the young women do not really "matter" (*Novels*, 3:xiv–xvi). To James, women mattered, both in his life and in his art.

EPILOGUE

In 1833 Emerson wrote in his journal: "Wherever we go[,] whatever we do[,] self is the sole subject we study & learn."[1] Americans have studied this lesson well. The concept of the developing self became the basis for the individualistic march across the continent. The emphasis on self supported the rationale for the drive toward individual achievement embodied in the American success myth. And today the preoccupation with self has become big business, with Americans buying increasing numbers of books on self-development, looking for ever-new therapies to develop self-awareness and self-realization, and responding to a mushrooming number of advertisements that promise to help each of us find the real Me.

Emerson envisioned a world in which the individual would "transfer the world into his own consciousness" and be totally "self-dependent," leaning "entirely on his own character."[2] "The purpose of life," he believed, "seems to be to acquaint a man with himself" (*JMN*, 4:84). In 1837 Emerson predicted that his ideas would lead to the development of a continent wherein "a Nation of men will for the first time exist, because each believes himself inspired by the Divine Soul which also inspires all men" (*Works*, 1:115). Emerson used religious terms to describe what in its consequences is a secular experience: the elevation of the self above the demands of everyday life, and particularly above the claims of the other. And Emersonian philosophy, with all of its implications, is a reflection of the basic principle of American

253

culture: the individual is god, and his energies are best employed in developing his own godhood.

Emerson cannot be blamed for introducing this narcissism into American culture. A belief in the primacy of the individual and an emphasis on the expanding self were apparent in American life before Emerson began to write. However, Emerson, in his role as philosopher and man of letters, *authenticated* this tendency, gave it stature, and made it defensible as a way of life. In Emerson's language a popular tendency not only became acceptable, it became divine. It is no wonder that most of the self-realization books that are published today quote Emerson and Thoreau as authorities.

A necessary consequence of this preoccupation with the self—and one that Emerson recognized and defended—is the solitary life. In defiance of John Donne's admonition that "no man is an island," Emerson asserted in 1841: "In all things I would have the island of a man inviolate" (*Works*, 3:137). And in his journal in 1846 he wrote: "I see not how we can live except alone" (*JMN*, 9:377). In an essay ironically entitled "The Heart," Emerson described the necessary inviolability of the individual in pursuit of self: "Man is insular, and cannot be touched. Every man is an infinitely repellent orb."[3]

A continuing belief in Emersonian self-reliance has perpetuated this image of the solitary individual in America. From the isolated figures of Daniel Boone and Davy Crockett to television's aloof private eye and lonely western gunfighter, America's heroes have been solitary men. The modern single life style may be more consumer-oriented than Thoreau's, but it has wholeheartedly adopted his maxim to "live free and uncommitted."[4]

Just down the shelf from the self-realization books, however, loom the books on "loneliness," which some social commentators have diagnosed as the number one disease in America today. A nation of individuals, each of whom believes himself to be inspired by the "divine Soul," can communicate, as Emerson was aware, only as "a sovereign state to a sovereign state" (*Works*, 1:113) or "as the gods, talking from peak to peak around Mt. Olympus" (*Works*, 3:137). There can be no closeness, no real union in a "lonely crowd" of individuals intent on self-assertion, for, as Emerson complained, other people "untune and dissipate" the individual (*Works*, 7:13). When in 1860 Emerson looked forward to a new religion that would permit the self-development he advocated, he might have been describing the philosophy of present-day Americans:

> It shall send man home to his central solitude, shame these social, supplicating manners, and make him know that much of the time he must have himself to his friend. He shall expect no cooperation, he shall walk with no companion. . . . He needs only his own verdict.
>
> (*Works*, 6:241)

In Emerson's philosophy, then, as in American society, the corollary of the development of the self is the disregard of other selves. The emphasis on the individual leads to a reverence for the solitary life and negates the significance of other people. Other people have no reality except as they reflect the individual and minister to his needs. Emerson wrote in 1841:

> The soul is alone & creates these images of itself which it calls friends. . . . Every one of its thoughts it casts into an incarnation which is a man, a woman, exhausts it of its sweetness & wisdom, & passes on to new. To a strong mind therefore the griefs incident to every earthly marriage are the less, because it has the resource of the all-creating all-obliterating spirit; retreating on its grand essence the nearest persons become pictures merely.
>
> (*JMN*, 8:34)

If other people are only pictures, they can be no threat to the self. The individual immunizes himself to the grief of failures in personal relations by obliterating the intrusive other. He takes what he needs from other people, and when he exhausts one person's "sweetness & wisdom," he moves on to the next. Other people are valuable only insofar as they provide stimulation or motivation for the individual ("Concert fires people to . . . performance" [*Works*, 7:11]) or "confirmation to our own thoughts" (*JMN*, 5:46). The individual enters into associations with other people only on his own terms—that is, to confirm and assert his own ideas and needs. The most incriminating denial of Emerson's philosophy came from his wife, whose satirical critique of Emerson's Transcendentalism, because it was written from the point of view of the other and so clearly represents an agonizing cry for recognition and acknowledgment, offers an important lesson for the individualist who would disregard human relationships in the pursuit of his own perfection:

> Great souls are self-sustained and stand ever erect, saying only to the prostrate sufferer "Get up, and stop your complaining." . . . If you have refused all sympathy to the sorrowful, all pity and aid to the sick, all toleration to the infirm of character, if you have condemned the unintellectual and loathed such sinners as have discovered want of intellect by their sin, then are you a perfect specimen of Humanity.[5]

Emerson's formula for self-preservation and self-fulfillment at the expense of human relationships provides the basis for the individualistic pursuit of the American Dream that has prevented Americans from seeing other people as autonomous beings. In Emerson's philosophy, the individual "must regard all things as having a subjective or relative existence"—relative to himself (*Works*, 1:334). The other person is unreal insofar as he/she is unnecessary or unrelated to the development of the self. Hence those others who are seen as closest to the self will have the greatest reality; those most unlike the self will be outside reality. As Emerson explained in 1836, "Our friends we value as they conform to the ideal type of Man, not as they multiply idiosyncrasies" (*Lectures*, 2:12). To the American individualist, women, minority Americans, and other "others" do not "conform to the ideal type of Man." Of what value, then, are they? They have been placed outside the American Dream. It is not their dream, and to the dreamer they do not count. Intent on the development of the self, the American Narcissus thus denies the value—even the existence—of the other and relegates to abstract otherness the self that is unlike his own. "Mind is the only reality, of which all men and other natures are better or worse reflectors," Emerson affirmed in 1842 (*Works*, 1:333–334). And today the blinders of self still prevent Americans from granting authenticity to others.

If Nathaniel Hawthorne and Henry James were able to create autonomous female characters, it was because theirs was a detachment from *culture* and not, as in the case of Emerson, a detachment from persons. The modern American may not experience the literal or psychological detachment from American culture that was so important a part of James's and Hawthorne's development as writers, but he can learn from their experience. He can examine and question the premises of his culture. If we are to have a literature that portrays all individuals with understanding and depth, we must have writers who can rise above the restrictions of a culture that denies the selfhood of other Americans.

In 1844 Margaret Fuller wrote that there was "no need to clip the wings of any bird that wants to soar and sing."[6] But in the nineteenth century few American writers could perceive women with the unclipped wings of a free American eagle. American literature has been rich and varied, but it has not included a full cast of characters. In nineteenth-century American literature, as in nineteenth-century American life, the male individualist was on center stage and women were cast in weak supporting roles—if they had any role at all. If American writers are to learn anything from the writers of the past, they must begin by looking at American individualism from the "other" side.

NOTES

CHAPTER 1
THE AMERICAN NARCISSUS

1. In the mid-nineteenth century, when Margaret Fuller attempted to apply the Transcendental doctrine of the self to women, she could find no model in American literature or in American life. See Margaret Fuller, *Woman in the Nineteenth Century* (1855). Called the American "Corinne" because she was an anachronism in America, she found her models in such European women as George Sand and Madame de Stael. And it was in Europe that she was able to develop as a person. After her death, her Transcendentalist friends butchered her works when they edited them and did not try to conceal their contempt for her writing. The American public has heard little about her, and until recently her works were so successfully excluded from college syllabi that the average educated person was apt to think Margaret Fuller was a Fuller Brush heiress—if he/she had heard of her at all. It was not until the late 1970s that there was much interest in Fuller scholarship. Recent studies that explore Fuller's life and writings from a feminist perspective include Bell Gale Chevigny, *The Woman and the Myth* (1976); Paula Blanchard, *Margaret Fuller* (1978); and Margaret Vanderhaar Allen, *The Achievement of Margaret Fuller* (1979). Fuller is also the subject of an excellent analysis in Ann Douglas, *The Feminization of American Culture* (1977), pp. 259–288. The most recent addition to Fuller scholarship is the currently appearing *Letters of Margaret Fuller*, edited by Robert N. Hudspeth, two volumes to date (1983).

In 1892 *New England Magazine* published Charlotte Perkins

Gilman's short story "The Yellow Wallpaper," a fascinating study of a woman going insane that speaks forcefully to the twentieth-century woman. Yet Gilman had great difficulty getting the work published, and when it finally appeared, it was either criticized for its morbidity or praised for the wrong reasons. What little attention the story has received since has focused on its atmosphere of mystery; and it is regarded either as a Poesque horror story or as a medical study of insanity. Only very recently has the story been recognized for what it is: a devastating portrait of a woman struggling to free herself from a conventional, personality-destroying marriage based on constricting sex roles. For a good discussion of this story see Elaine R. Hedges's afterword to the Feminist Press reprint of *The Yellow Wallpaper*, pp. 37–63.

In 1899 Kate Chopin's *The Awakening* caused a scandal that ultimately ended Chopin's writing career. The book was banned as immoral and literally dropped out of sight. Until it was discovered in the early 1970s, the only attention it got from American critics was similar to Edmund Wilson's mention of it in *Patriotic Gore* (1962), pp. 590–592. Citing it as an example of the new sensuality in literature, Wilson completely missed the more primary point of the struggle for individuality by a woman. The first recognition of Chopin's theme of female self-fulfillment appeared in Larzer Ziff's 1966 study, *The American 1890s*, pp. 300–305.

A different situation is that of Fanny Fern (Sara Payson Willis Parton), who wrote two very successful novels, *Ruth Hall* (1855) and *Rose Clark* (1856), and was for twenty years a popular (and the first American woman) newspaper columnist. Though immensely popular in her day, she is unknown today. If her work does not deserve its present obscurity (and anyone who reads much of it must agree that it does not; see Hawthorne's comment on *Ruth Hall* in Chapter 7 of this work), why is it still consigned to oblivion? Although some of Fern's earlier collected newspaper pieces were conventionally sentimental, most of her writing was strong, outspoken, and vividly powerful. Her newspaper writing was often delightfully satirical, debunking male vanity and advocating autonomy for women in down-to-earth terms; see *Fern Leaves from Fanny's Portfolio* (1853), *Fresh Leaves* (1857), *Folly As It Flies* (1868), and *Ginger Snaps* (1870). But it was Fern's novel, the autobiographical *Ruth*

Hall, that most disqualified her for lasting recognition in her culture. *Ruth Hall* was the first (and the only nineteenth-century) American novel to portray a female protagonist who succeeds *wholly on her own*. Whereas poor girls in other novels succeed by marrying well, Ruth Hall becomes rich and successful through hard work and her own talents—without the help of and in spite of the cruelty of the men in the novel. And the novel does not even end in marriage. This theme of complete female independence implicitly challenges the exclusiveness of the myth of American male individualism and subverts the traditional role of women—and this helps to account for Fern's fall into oblivion. Although her contemporary readers (primarily female) responded with enthusiasm to her work, such a subversive theme could not sustain popularity in the dominant (male) literary establishment.

2. Richard Chase, *The American Novel and Its Tradition*, p. 64.

3. William Wasserstrom concludes that the majority of heroines in nineteenth-century American fiction are little girls who will never grow up. Wasserstrom, *Heiress of All the Ages*, pp. 25–27, 51, 76–87, 126. Wendy Martin points out that the major tradition in American literature portrays woman as a fallen creature who must be punished. Martin, "Seduced and Abandoned in the New World," pp. 329–346. See also Carolyn Heilbrun, *Toward a Recognition of Androgyny*, p. 63; Heilbrun, review of James Dickey's *Deliverance*; and Judith Fryer, *The Faces of Eve*, p. 23. Ernest Earnest argues that many of the real women in nineteenth-century America were more interesting than the lifeless and sexless heroines of American fiction. Although his explanations help to account for the sexlessness of these characters, they do not explain why American heroines were so lacking in depth and personality or why European writers of the same period were able to create women of character and substance. Earnest, *The American Eve in Fact and Fiction*, pp. 8, 265–267.

4. For perceptive analyses of the problem confronting women readers, see Carolyn Heilbrun, *Reinventing Womanhood*, pp. 74, 94–95, 140, 175; Judith Fetterley, *The Resisting Reader*, pp. xi, xii, xiii; and Nina Baym, "Melodramas of Beset Manhood," pp. 123–139. For a discussion of how this cultural one-sidedness has been reflected in the college curriculum and how it affects women students, see Elaine Showalter, "Women and the Literary Curriculum,"

pp. 855–862. Showalter's *A Literature of Their Own*, although it deals with British literature, is useful in providing a perspective from which to view American fiction. Although, as Showalter points out, the British women novelists wrote from within an experience and culture of their own, apart from the general male culture, it is significant that, in contrast to American experience, a number of nineteenth-century British women were important literary figures in their day and have maintained their prominence in the canon of "classic" British literature.

5. Nina Baym comes closest to an explanation in her recognition of the way American critics have excluded women writers who explore the female experience. Baym, "Melodramas," pp. 123–139.

6. Leslie Fiedler, *Love and Death in the American Novel*, p. 171.

7. See Yehoshua Arieli, *Individualism and Nationalism in American Ideology*, esp. pp. 20, 83, 95–96, 123–124, 174, 183, 193; for a discussion of individualism in American institutions, see pp. 50–51, 62–63, 202–203, 255–271, 277–288, 309–322, 334–335, 341–346.

8. Hector St. Jean de Crèvecoeur, *Letters from an American Farmer*, pp. 56–60, 40, 42.

9. Benjamin Franklin, *Autobiography*, pp. 93, 89; see also pp. 125, 127, 142, 159.

10. Cited in John William Ward, *Andrew Jackson*, p. 210.

11. John Taylor, *An Inquiry into the Principles of the Government of the United States*, pp. 414–415.

12. See Arieli, *Individualism*, p. 184.

13. "The Course of Civilization," pp. 213–214.

14. Alexis de Tocqueville, *Democracy in America*, 2:2, 104–107.

15. Michel Chevalier, *Society, Manners and Politics in the United States*, pp. 116, 368–369, 428–429.

16. James Bryce, *The American Commonwealth*, 2:404–407.

17. David M. Potter, *People of Plenty*.

18. See, e.g., Irwin Wyllie, *The Self-Made Man in America*, pp. 6–7, 170–174; Richard Weiss, *The American Myth of Success*, p. 231; Philip Slater, *The Pursuit of Loneliness*; and Lawrence Chenoweth, *The American Dream of Success*.

19. John William Ward, *Red, White, and Blue*, pp. 10–14, 28–29, 36–37, 53, 151.

20. It is significant that ten years after the appearance of his

study of the American character, David Potter published a followup statement in which he acknowledged that most studies of the American character do not consider women. He attempted to analyze how women have been affected differently by significant events in American history and pointed out that the common generalizations about American character do not apply to women. Potter, "American Women and the American Character," pp. 117–132.

21. Crèvecoeur, *Letters*, pp. 14, 62.

22. Eliza W. Farnham, *Life in Prairie Land*, pp. 36–38. See also Anna Howard Shaw, *The Story of a Pioneer*, pp. 25–28.

23. See John Mack Faragher, *Women and Men on the Overland Trail*, pp. 59–64, 82–86, 99–102, 133–136, 163–168, 187. See also Johnny Faragher and Christine Stansell, "Women and Their Families on the Overland Trail to California and Oregon, 1842–1867," pp. 150–166; Lillian Schlissel, *Women's Diaries of the Westward Journey*; and Christiane Fischer, ed., *Let Them Speak for Themselves*.

24. Alexander Hamilton, "Report on the Subject of Manufactures" (1790), in Hamilton, *Industrial and Commercial Correspondence*, ed. Arthur H. Cole, p. 259. For Washington's attitude, see his letter to Lafayette, in Frank L. McVey, *Modern Industrialism*, pp. 47–48: "Though I would not force the introduction of manufactures . . . yet I conceive much might be done in the way of women, children, and others, without taking one really necessary hand from tilling the earth." Gerda Lerner points out that in Europe the labor in the early factories was performed by displaced farmers, whereas in America men could always make a living by farming and were not willing to enter the factories: "From its beginnings, therefore, American industrialism depended on the labor of women and children." Lerner, *The Woman in American History*, p. 49.

25. Thorstein Veblen, *The Theory of the Leisure Class*, pp. 354–355.

26. See Mary P. Ryan, *Womanhood in America*, pp. 75–117; Barbara Berg, *The Remembered Gate*, pp. 7, 58–59, 73–74.

27. Lerner, *Woman in American History*, pp. 29–30, 45; Lerner, "The Lady and the Mill Girl," pp. 15–60; Lerner, *The Female Experience*, pp. xxix–xxxi.

28. See Barbara Welter, "The Cult of True Womanood," pp. 243–256. Mary Beth Norton, in "The Paradox of Women's

Sphere," points out that historians should not make the mistake of equating prescriptive behavior with real behavior. Norton observes that options for women were opening in the nineteenth century, but she recognizes that they were not available to women as a group.

29. Lerner, "The Lady and the Mill Girl," p. 17.

30. As Mary Beth Norton demonstrates in "The Myth of the Golden Age," and as we have seen with respect to mid–nineteenth-century farm women, it is a fallacy to assume that female participation in production assures equality.

31. Ann Douglas, *Feminization of American Culture*, pp. 8, 11–12, 50–51, 77–78, bases her thesis of women's capitulation to sentimentality on the fact that this and moral influence were all that were left to women by the dominant male culture. Douglas is critical of the way in which women writers made sentimentality central to their writing, but she emphasizes that all other sources of practical power had been removed. Yet for women the results of this separation by sex may not have been wholly negative. Nancy Cott suggests that awareness of gender classification caused by enforced separation gave women the feeling of sisterhood that ultimately made possible the development of feminism. Cott, *The Bonds of Womanhood*, pp. 200–201, 206. Caroll Smith-Rosenberg, in "The Female World of Love and Ritual," reveals the intense ties that bound women together in nineteenth-century America. See also Smith-Rosenberg, "Beauty, the Beast, and the Militant Woman," pp. 197–221.

32. Lerner, *The Female Experience*, p. xxxii.

33. I have not considered the status of black or Native American women in this study because, with only rare exceptions (e.g., Roxy in Twain's *Puddn'head Wilson*), they do not appear as major characters in nineteenth-century American literature.

34. See Anne Firor Scott, *The Southern Lady*, pp. 7, 17. Two nineteenth-century women diarists reveal the powerlessness of the Southern lady with particular acuteness. See Frances Anne Kemble, *Journal of a Residence on a Georgia Plantation in 1838–1839*, pp. 133, 101–102; and Mary Boykin Chesnut, *A Diary from Dixie*, ed. Ben Ames Williams, pp. 21–22, 25–26. For a more complete edition of Chesnut's diary (one that distinguishes between sections written in

the 1860s and the revised diary of the 1880s), see *Mary Chesnut's Civil War*, ed. C. Vann Woodward.

35. Tocqueville, pp. 212–213.

36. Gustave de Beaumont, *Marie*, pp. 19–20.

37. Harriet Martineau, *Society in America*, 2:226.

38. George Savile, Lord Halifax, *Complete Works*, pp. 7–17.

39. Samuel K. Jennings, *The Married Lady's Companion*, pp. 61–68.

40. William A. Alcott, *The Young Wife*, pp. 27–29.

41. Edward A. Clarke, *Sex in Education, or a Fair Chance for Girls*, pp. 31–60; George Austin, *The Perils of American Women*, pp. 292–298.

42. See, for example, Thomas Branagan, *The Excellency of the Female Character Vindicated* (1807), and Charles Brockden Brown, *Alcuin: A Dialogue* (1798). For a comprehensive history of the women's movement in the nineteenth century, see Eleanor Flexner, *Century of Struggle*. For the ideas of the movement in the later nineteenth century, see Aileen S. Kraditor, *The Ideas of the Woman Suffrage Movement, 1890–1920*, and William O'Neill, *Everyone Was Brave*.

43. For examples of the inability of most Americans to achieve unlimited success, see the studies of Stephan Thernstrom, *Poverty and Progress* and *The Other Bostonians*, and Peter R. Decker, *Fortunes and Failures*. Thernstrom and Decker find that, although there was some upward mobility, relatively few men were able to realize the Horatio Alger dream. As Decker says of the men who flocked to San Francisco as to a new El Dorado: "None envisioned failure, only success." Their frustrated expectations most often resulted in a "sense of personal failure, disillusionment, and despair" (pp. 31, 253, 259–260).

44. Kent L. Steckmesser, "The Frontier Hero in History and Legend," pp. 7, 19. This same masculine conqueror has also been the dominant male image in American film. See, e.g., Joan Mellen, *Big Bad Wolves*.

45. W. Eugene Hallon, *Frontier Violence*, pp. 115–117, 197.

46. Constance Rourke, *American Humor*, p. 36.

47. Ibid., pp. 104, 142–144.

48. For an analysis of narcissism from a psychological point of view, see Heinz Kohut, *The Analysis of the Self* and *The Restoration of the Self*. Kohut maintains that narcissism is the result of an early failure of the individual to find confirmation of the self in his environment and his subsequent unwillingness or inability to look to the outside world for self-evaluation.

49. In *The Culture of Narcissism* Christopher Lasch argues that Americans today are motivated by the goal of personal survival. The modern narcissist, he says, denies the validity of the past and is unable to identify with another person "without obliterating the other's identity." Lasch differentiates between the modern narcissist and the nineteenth-century individualist: since the latter had a continent to explore, there was a real situation behind his self-reliance, whereas modern man's narcissism is a defense mechanism. Modern industrialism having made real self-help impossible, modern man is self-questioning and anxious for praise (see pp. 4–5, 8–10, 86). Though perceptive, Lasch's analysis of modern narcissism, I believe, exaggerates the difference between the modern narcissist and the nineteenth-century individualist. The nineteenth-century American was not as confident and all-conquering as he pretended. He too felt anxiety and self-doubt, and in many cases his self-reliant stance was a persona, an image deliberately created in order to live up to the myth of his generation.

50. Richard Slotkin, *Regeneration Through Violence*, pp. 268–300. See John Filson, *The Discovery, Settlement, and Present State of Kentucke*. The solitary image of a Boone without family or friends that exists in our culture and literature is apparent in this reference in *Moby-Dick*: "Almost universally, a lone whale—as a solitary Leviathan is called—proves an ancient one. Like venerable moss-bearded Daniel Boone, he will have no one near him but Nature herself." Herman Melville, *Moby-Dick*, p. 330.

51. For a comprehensive study of this phenomenon in American history, see Albert K. Weinberg, *Manifest Destiny*. Weinberg notes the relationship between American individualism and expansionism (p. 89). In 1825 the *Illinois Gazette* described the United States as a "great country, manifestly called by the Almighty to a destiny which Greece and Rome . . . might have envied." In Louis Hartz, *The Liberal Tradition in America*, p. 89. In 1845 John L.

O'Sullivan coined the now familiar phrase, explaining that it was America's "manifest destiny to overspread the continent." O'Sullivan, "Annexation," p. 5.

52. As Weinberg points out, John Adams had long ago formulated the trend of "continental dominion as the manifest destiny of American Republicanism." But Adams had thought in terms of individual pioneers migrating westward. Weinberg, *Manifest Destiny*, p. 240. Originally, the government's policy was to negotiate for Indian lands, but the frontiersmen refused to wait for treaties. As early as 1796, Washington acknowledged that it would take a "Chinese Wall" to keep American pioneers off Indian land. By the time of Jefferson's presidency, all government efforts to protect Indian land had failed. Bernard W. Sheehan, *Seeds of Extinction*, p. 268. In the first decades of the nineteenth century the government began forcibly removing Southern tribes to make room for whites who wanted their land, and after 1851 the government began to acquire land in the West to which the Indians had been removed. Roy Harvey Pearce, *The Savages of America*, pp. 240–241.

53. Samuel Bowles, *Our New West*, pp. 156–158.

54. By the mid-eighteenth century, Eastern tribes like the Pequods, the Narragansetts, and the Mohicans had disappeared. Hallon, *Frontier Violence*, p. 124, points out that of the 370 treaties made with the Indians since 1789, not one has been kept.

55. William T. Hagan, *American Indians*, p. 29; see also pp. 26, 31–38, 57–64. As Reginald Horsman makes clear, the British Indian agents were often sympathetic to the Indian point of view. Horsman, "British Indian Policy in the Northwest," pp. 55–56, 60–61. One problem that complicated American relations with the Indians was the American mistreatment of Indian women. For a pioneer's view of the difference between the English and Americans in this respect, see U.S. Works Progress Administration, *Told by the Pioneers*, 1:173–174: "The English had gained the confidence of the Indians more than the Americans. Most of the English married Indian women, by both English and Indian laws, and brought up their children in the proper way. Wife desertion was a rare thing among the English."

56. Theodore Roosevelt, *Works*, 10:8 (italics added). Roy Harvey Pearce notes that Americans viewed the Indian as an ab-

stract symbol of "savagism," whose destruction they saw as the inevitable result of the progress of civilization. Pearce, *Savages*, pp. 48–49, 73, 241–242. Bernard W. Sheehan points out that both philanthropists and Indian haters paid little attention to the actualities of Indian experience, treating the Indian "more like a precious abstraction than a living being." Sheehan, *Seeds of Extinction*, pp. 11–12. See also Philip Borden, "Found Cumbering the Soil," pp. 71–97: "Never were substantial numbers of Americans able to accommodate themselves to a view of the Indian as a human being." The resulting tragedy of Indian-white relations is vividly described by Anthony Wallace in *King of the Delawares* and *The Death and Rebirth of the Seneca*.

57. It is important to recognize the difference between this attitude and that of other conquerors on the American continent. In South America the Spanish murdered and tortured Indians, but they did not regard the Indian problem as simply a "hygienic" one. As Frank Tannenbaum points out, the Spanish attempt to bring the Indian inside the Catholic church "gave the Indian identity with the European and a sense that they were both mortal. . . . human beings who had souls." Tannenbaum, *Ten Keys to Latin America*, p. 55. The Canadian attitude also differed from that of the Americans. The North West Mounted Police was formed not to fight the Indians but to protect them. The government's position was that Indians were entitled to the same treatment under the law that white people were, and the Mounties carried out this policy. The difference is vividly spelled out in the body count. In 1876, 300 American soldiers were killed in the Battle of Little Big Horn; the total number of Mounties killed by the Indians in the history of the force is 6. See Ronald Atkin, *Maintain the Right*; Alexander Hill, *From Home to Home*; Alexander Morris, *The Treaties of Canada with the Indians of Manitoba and the North-West Territories*; John Peter Turner, *The North West Mounted Police*.

58. Winthrop D. Jordan, *White Over Black*, pp. 340–341, 540–541.

59. Frank Tannenbaum, in *Slave and Citizen*, and Stanley Elkins, in *Slavery*, compare American slavery and racial attitudes with those in Latin American countries and find that in South America, by the nineteenth century, free Negroes, particularly

mulattoes, were accepted into society more easily than in the United States, intermarrying with whites and occupying positions in the professions. Tannenbaum attributes this difference to the greater power of the Catholic church and the state in South America, which allowed the slave to retain his "human personality" (pp. 48, 53–56, 63–65, 88–91). Elkins, whose book is an extension of Tannenbaum's thesis, claims that unrestrained individualism in America, without the counterbalancing power of external institutions, gave the slaveowner total power over the slave and prevented blacks from developing as individuals (pp. 30–32, 43–44, 61–63, 67, 79–82). Whatever problems there may be in Tannenbaum's and Elkins's analyses (in particular, Elkins's discussions of concentration camps and the American abolitionist movement are problematic), Tannenbaum's essential thesis still stands. As Eugene Genovese, one of Elkins's major critics, notes, religious and legal tradition in South America provided "a setting in which the slave . . . retained a significant degree of manhood in the eyes of society." Genovese, "Rebelliousness and Docility in the Negro Slave," pp. 52, 57, 59. Another of Elkins's critics, Carl N. Degler, offers a detailed comparison of racial attitudes in the United States and Brazil, finding that in Brazil the Negro, and particularly the mulatto, was regarded as more of a person than in the U.S. He cites, for example, the portrayal of Negroes in nineteenth-century Brazilian literature. Degler defines the difference in terms of social distinctions. In Brazil, under slavery, the significant characteristic was legal status, not race. Also significant, he says, was that in Brazil mulattoes were not considered black, whereas in America a person with any amount of black blood was considered black. The Brazilian attitude permitted more social mobility among mixed bloods than in the U.S. See Degler, *Neither Black Nor White*, pp. 9–13, 75–84, 104, 107, 203, 239–240, 255–256.

60. See, e.g., Jordan, *White Over Black*, pp. 401–414; Ronald Takaki, "The Black Child Savage in Ante-Bellum America," pp. 42–43; Richard Weiss, "Racism and Industrialization," p. 143. That this was also true of the Indian is pointed out by Borden, "Found Cumbering the Soil," p. 79.

61. Jordan, *White Over Black*, pp. 130, 134.

62. Degler, *Neither Black Nor White*, pp. 255–256.

63. Franklin, *Autobiography*, pp. 93, 89, 105–106.

64. Ralph Waldo Emerson, *Complete Works*, ed. Edward Emerson, 4:58.

65. Simone de Beauvoir, *The Second Sex*, pp. xvi, xxv.

66. Moreover, as Nina Baym points out, although most of these women writers were able to portray realistic detail and description, they were often too bound by stereotype to create authentically human, fully developed female characters. Baym, *Woman's Fiction*, p. 299.

CHAPTER 2
TRANSCENDENTALISM AND THE SELF

1. Ralph Waldo Emerson, *The Journals and Miscellaneous Notebooks*, ed. William H. Gilman et al., 16 vols. (Cambridge, Mass.: Harvard Univ. Press, 1960–1982), 9:85 (hereafter cited as *JMN* in the text).

2. Quentin Anderson, *The Imperial Self*, pp. 207, 217.

3. Harold Bloom maintains that Emerson and Whitman are very American because their creation was built on the assumption that "our new experience perpetually forgets the old"—the belief that one can disavow all prior events, influences, and other people. Emerson's statement in 1866 that "for every seeing soul, there are two absorbing facts,—'I and the Abyss,'" Bloom interprets thus: "For 'the Abyss,' we can read: tradition, history, the other, while for 'I' we can read 'any American.' The final price paid for the extreme discontinuities of Emersonian vision is that we are left with a simple, chilling formula: the American Sublime equals *I and the Abyss*." And Whitman, who wholly absorbs the external world, is, says Bloom, "alas, even more American." Bloom, *Poetry and Repression*, pp. 236–266.

4. Ralph Waldo Emerson, *Complete Works*, ed. Edward W. Emerson, Centenary Edition, 12 vols. (Boston: Houghton Mifflin, 1903–1904), 1:187–188, 32, 43 (hereafter cited in this chapter as *Works*).

In a recent analysis of "Nature," Eric Cheyfitz (*The Trans-Parent*) attempts to show by psychological interpretation of language and metaphor that Emerson was more concerned with the "Not me" than his writing indicates and that the call to masculine self-assertion was in conflict with a subversive feminine quality within him. Although this thesis is valuable as a means of forcing us to examine Emerson's overconfident masculinity and optimistic self-assertion, Cheyfitz's conclusions are weakened by frequent misreadings of Emerson's prose. For example, he concludes from a passage on Idealism at the end of the section entitled "Spirit" (*Works*, 1:62–63) that there was a conflict in Emerson's mind between the assertion of the unity of Mind and Matter (which Cheyfitz calls the masculine and the feminine) and the separateness of Nature (Matter) expressed in this passage on Idealism (pp. 146–148). However, if the passage is looked at in context, it becomes clear that Emerson is only posing it as a possible answer to his rhetorical question. He goes on to show why Idealism's answer is incomplete, the reason being precisely *because* it does not recognize this unity (*Works*, 1:63). In a further misreading, Cheyfitz assumes that when Emerson says "in actual life the marriage is not celebrated" (*Works*, 1:74), he means that there is no actual union of Spirit and Matter (pp. 70, 167). But Emerson is clearly referring to something else: two faculties of man—his empirical understanding and his faith—which man must use together if he is to see the essential unity (*Works*, 1:72–74).

Cheyfitz's argument is further weakened by overreadings. At one point, he asserts that when Emerson says that the unity of all things can be found "under the undermost garment of Nature" (*Works*, 1:44), he is directing us to look at the female organ of (Mother) Nature (p. 165). Aside from the fact that in the nineteenth-century the "undermost garment" would conceal much more than the female organ, Emerson would have had to have been very confused to be thinking of simply the female organ when what he is talking about is the unity of a multitude of objects and thoughts. Cheyfitz backs up this questionable assumption by a further overreading—that when Emerson urges man not to rely only on empirical science for his knowledge of the world because this prevents "the manly contemplation of the whole" (*Works*, 1:66), Emerson means not only the "whole," in the sense of "all," but the "hole"—again the sexual organ of woman (pp. 165–166). To give any credence to this meaning, even an unconscious one, a reader would have to know whether the term "hole" had this association for Emerson, and, if so, whether he would regard the mere "contemplation" of it as "manly."

5. The *Letters of Ralph Waldo Emerson*, ed. Ralph L. Rusk, 6 vols. (New York: Columbia Univ. Press, 1939), 1:388 (hereafter cited in this chapter as *Letters*). One of the few things that Emerson did enjoy in Europe was his visit on July 13, 1833, to the Cabinet of Natural History in Paris, particularly the collection of stuffed birds—significantly a solitary entertainment (*JMN*, 4:198–200).

6. Emerson's subsequent trips to Europe were much more satisfying. But on those visits he was the "great man" whom others came to see and listen to and pay homage to. Those were "ego trips" during which he was the center.

7. Particularly significant is his portrayal of Napoleon, whom he admired for his strong will and absolute self-reliance: "Horrible anecdotes may no doubt be collected, from his history, of the price at which he bought his successes; but he must not therefore be set down as cruel, but only as one who knew no impediment to his will" (*Works*, 4:233–234). And in an 1863 journal entry, in which he insists on the need for egotism, he included Napoleon in his list of the benefactors of mankind: "Take egotism out and you would castrate the benefactors." *Journals of Ralph Waldo Emerson*, ed. Edward W. Emerson and Waldo Emerson Forbes, 10 vols. (Boston and New York: Houghton Mifflin, 1909–1914), 9:519 (hereafter cited as *Journals*, in the text). For an analysis of Emerson's fascination with Napoleon, see Perry Miller, "Emersonian Genius and the American Democracy," pp. 27–44.

8. For example, when he visited West Point in 1863, he wrote in his journal: "I think it excellent that such tender youths should be made so manly and masterly in rough exercises of horse and guns" (*Journals*, 9:512).

9. In Ralph Rusk, *Life of Ralph Waldo Emerson*, p. 423.

10. Emerson was also impressed with American technology. See his praise of sawmills, the operation of which he called a "noble sight" (*JMN*, 4:389). Also significant is his attitude toward the railroad. Always emphasizing the benefits that have come from the development of the railroad, he said in *The Conduct of Life* (1860)

that no lover of mankind has benefited the country as much as the men who built the railroads (*Works*, 6:256).

11. Emerson's attitude toward other minorities was just as callous. In 1862 he wrote to Abel Adams of how glad he was to see settlers driving back the "spiteful Mormons," and he was always contemptuous of the immigrant (*Letters*, 5:287; *Journals*, 8:226; *Works*, 11:422). By 1844 Emerson's attitude toward the black race had softened somewhat, and he noted that abolition in the West Indies had had the effect of humanizing the Negro (*Works*, 2:268).

12. Emerson's stance during the Civil War is thoroughly documented in Daniel Aaron, *The Unwritten War*, pp. 34–38.

13. Phillips Russell, *Emerson, The Wisest American*, pp. 31, 69.

14. Rusk, *Life of Emerson*, p. 88.

15. Gay Wilson Allen, *Waldo Emerson*, pp. 226–227.

16. See also "Margaret Fuller's 1842 Journal," ed. Joel Myerson, pp. 331–332, 338.

17. Ibid., p. 338.

18. Stephen Whicher, "Emerson's Tragic Sense," pp. 221–228, concludes that Emerson's serenity was an act of faith that his horror at reality forced him to adopt to save himself.

19. Rusk, *Life of Emerson*, p. 231.

20. As Gay Wilson Allen points out, however, he was not able to write the final compensating stanzas until some time after Waldo's death. Allen, *Waldo Emerson*, p. 397.

21. In "Margaret Fuller's 1842 Journal," p. 326.

22. In James Eliot Cabot, *A Memoir of Ralph Waldo Emerson*, 1:353–354, 357–358, 366.

23. Ibid, p. 371.

24. Ellen Tucker Emerson, *The Life of Lidian Jackson Emerson*, ed. Delores Bird Carpenter, pp. 82–83. The validity of Lidian's satiric portrayal is apparent in such statements as this one from Emerson's 1840 essay, "Circles," which portrays how the individual's constant quest to develop the self impels him to disregard other people:

> The continued effort to raise himself above himself, to work a pitch above his last height, betrays itself in a man's relations. . . . A man's growth is seen in the successive choirs of his friends. For every friend whom he loses for a

truth, he gains a better. . . . O blessed Spirit, whom I forsake for these [friends], they are not thou! Every personal consideration that we allow costs us heavenly state. We sell the thrones of angels for a short and turbulent pleasure. How often must we learn this lesson? Men cease to interest us when we find their limitations.
See Emerson, *Essays, First Series*, pp. 307–308.

25. From "Margaret Fuller's 1840 Journal," pp. 331–332.

26. Russell, *Emerson*, pp. 79–80.

27. Allen, *Waldo Emerson*, pp. 147, 240.

28. Rusk, *Life of Emerson*, p. 215.

29. Early in her marriage Lidian wrote to her sister that she could not get over the fact that she was privileged to live with two such remarkable men as Emerson and his brother Charles: "Sometimes it comes over me as *so* strange that I should be housed with these two wonderful beings—turning out coffee for them and helping them to pie." See Rusk, *Life of Emerson*, p. 225.

30. Ibid, p. 266.

31. Cabot, *A Memoir of Emerson*, 1:229; Rusk, *Life of Emerson*, p. 213.

32. See Rusk, *Life of Emerson*, p. 226.

33. See also *The Correspondence of Emerson and Carlyle*, ed. Joseph Slater, p. 184. In Shelley's play, Asia is married to Prometheus, which also makes Emerson's name for Lidian a comment on his view of himself.

34. *The Early Lectures of Ralph Waldo Emerson*, ed. Stephen E. Whicher, Robert E. Spiller, and Wallace E. Williams, 3 vols. (Cambridge, Mass.: Harvard Univ. Press, 1959–1972), 2:102–103 (hereafter cited as *Lectures* in the text).

35. For an excellent discussion of how the physical illnesses induced by cultural factors were intensified by the lack of knowledge or understanding and by the outright hostility of doctors, see Ann Douglas Wood, "The Fashionable Diseases," pp. 25–52. Barbara Welter, *Dimity Convictions*, pp. 57–70, shows how women's diseases and doctors' attitudes toward women were in large part determined by the definition of women in society.

36. Ellen Tucker Emerson, *Life of Lidian Emerson*, p. 73.

37. For a description of Emerson's statement, see the *Boston Daily Advertiser*, May 27, 1869, p. 4.

38. Printed in the *New York Times*, July 30, 1869.

CHAPTER 3
THE GENDER OF AMERICAN INDIVIDUALISM

1. In *The Letters of Ralph Waldo Emerson*, ed. Ralph L. Rusk, 6 vols. (New York: Columbia Univ. Press, 1939), 3:253 (hereafter cited in this chapter as *LRWE*).

2. Ralph Waldo Emerson, *The Journals and Miscellaneous Notebooks*, ed. William H. Gilman et al., 4:81.

3. Henry David Thoreau, *Walden*, vol. 2 of *The Writings of Henry David Thoreau*, Walden Edition, 20 vols. (1906: rpr. New York: AMS Press, 1968), pp. 353–354 (hereafter cited as *Walden* in the text).

4. Leon Edel, *Henry David Thoreau*, p. 6. As Perry Miller points out, the Journal was not simply a spontaneous record of events. Polished and revised with all the care an artist gives a favorite work, it became an end in itself—"a mode for expressing the self." Miller maintains that Thoreau was even more self-oriented than Emerson was, and he cites the greater arrogance of Thoreau's requests for permission to use the Harvard Library: "He spoke as though the cultivation of his own consciousness were the ultimate profession." Thoreau, *Consciousness in Concord: Thoreau's Hitherto "Lost Journal," 1840–1841*, ed. Perry Miller (Boston: Houghton Mifflin, 1958), pp. 30, 34–36 (hereafter cited as *Consciousness* in the text).

5. *The Journal of Henry David Thoreau*, vols. 7–20 of *The Writings of Henry David Thoreau*, Walden Edition (volume references are to the Journal numbers), 2:101 (hereafter cited as *Journal* in the text).

6. *Consciousness*, p. 101. In 1880 Robert Louis Stevenson noted that in his relations with other people, "Thoreau is dry, priggish, selfish. It is profit he is after in these intimacies . . . profit to himself." Robert Louis Stevenson, "Henry David Thoreau," p. 82.

7. See Quentin Anderson, review of *The Best of Thoreau's Journals*, ed. Carl Bode, *New York Times Book Review*, July 4, 1971, pp. 1, 16–18.

8. See Ellery Channing, *Thoreau, the Poet Naturalist*, ed. F. B. Sanborn, p. 24; Walter Harding, *The Days of Henry Thoreau*, p. 184.

9. F. B. Sanborn, *The Life of Henry David Thoreau*, p. 353.

10. Quoted in Horace Traubel, *With Walt Whitman in Camden*, 1:212–213.

11. *The Journals of Ralph Waldo Emerson*, ed. Edward W. Emerson and Waldo Emerson Forbes, 9:34.

12. Henry David Thoreau, *Familiar Letters and Index*, vol. 6 of *The Writings of Henry David Thoreau*, Walden Edition, pp. 185–186 (hereafter cited in this chapter as *Letters*).

13. *Consciousness*, p. 45.

14. For Thoreau's comments on the Indians, see *A Week on the Concord and Merrimack Rivers*, vol. 1 of *The Writings of Henry David Thoreau*, Walden Edition, pp. 51–56, 82–84, 124.

15. Richard Lebeaux has theorized that Thoreau's love for his brother was complicated by the hostility of oedipal guilt (his brother being a father figure to him) and by guilt he felt because of his rivalry with his brother for the affections of Ellen Sewall (which was in turn complicated by oedipal guilt). Lebeaux, *Young Man Thoreau*, pp. 120–121, 131, 140, 151, 155–156, 166, 175–177. Although Lebeaux's attempts to fit Thoreau to the theories of Erikson and Freud are not conclusive (there is hardly sufficient data for all the conclusions he draws, particularly with respect to Thoreau's relationship with his mother, pp. 33, 46–48, 51–52), he is certainly correct in his conclusion that the *Walden* identity that Thoreau created was more independent than the real man (p. 215). Or, as Richard Bridgman says in *Dark Thoreau*, p. 284: "For all his independence and abrasive outspokenness, Thoreau was an emotionally vulnerable man."

16. In the chapter "Where I Lived and What I Lived For," Thoreau mentions that he had originally agreed to buy the Hollowell place but that the farmer told him his wife had changed her mind. He comments parenthetically, "Every man has such a wife" (*Walden*, p. 91). Although this comment could be interpreted as a stereotyped judgment of women (and most critics tend to take the comment

literally; see, e.g., Lebeaux, *Young Man Thoreau*, p. 156), it can be interpreted as indicating that Thoreau believed that the farmer was using his wife as an excuse for going back on his bargain. The comment can mean simply that when a man reneges on a deal, it is common practice to use his wife as an excuse: "Every man has such a wife."

17. Cited in Henry Seidel Canby, *Thoreau*, pp. 160–163. From an unpublished manuscript in the Huntington Library, San Marino, Calif.

18. Canby theorizes that this fragment was a tribute to Lidian Emerson, whom Thoreau had described as like a sister to him, but it seems much more likely that it refers to his own sister. Canby, *Thoreau*, pp. 160–163. See also the Journal passage (1850) that refers to his sister (*Journal*, 2:78).

19. See, e.g., Lebeaux, *Young Man Thoreau*, passim; Jonathan Katz, *Gay American History*, pp. 481–494; and Clayton Hoagland, "The Diary of Thoreau's 'Gentle Boy,'" pp. 473–489. In contrast, Edward Wagenknecht, in *Henry David Thoreau*, pp. 79–94, discusses Thoreau's sexuality, pointing out his acceptance of natural functions, and examines in a wider context the question of latent homosexuality.

20. Even *A Week on the Concord and Merrimack Rivers*, which is the story of an expedition with his brother John and was written as a memorial to his brother, is strangely silent on Thoreau's feeling for his brother. It records what they saw and heard and contains an abstract essay on friendship, but it offers nothing of the "otherness" of John.

21. Ralph Waldo Emerson, *Complete Works*, ed. Edward W. Emerson, 4:313.

22. *Memoirs of Margaret Fuller Ossoli*, ed. Ralph Waldo Emerson, W. H. Channing, and J. F. Clarke, 2 vols. (1884; rpr. New York: Burt Franklin, 1972), 1:98–100 (hereafter cited as *Memoirs* in the text).

23. Margaret Fuller, *Woman in the Nineteenth Century, and Kindred Essays*, ed. Arthur B. Fuller (New York: Jewett, 1855), pp. 36–38, 177 (hereafter cited as *Woman* in the text).

24. Thomas Wentworth Higginson, *Margaret Fuller Ossoli*, p. 29. Margaret Fuller had also taken opium for her severe head-

aches and back pains. See Madeleine B. Stern, *The Life of Margaret Fuller*, pp. 141, 165.

25. Whitman writes in *Leaves of Grass* (p. 48) that "there is nothing greater than the mother of men." And in *Democratic Vistas* he describes the ideal woman as "the perfect human mother." *Collected Writings of Walt Whitman*, ed. Floyd Stovall, 2:389, 393. When Whitman writes that women are important, he means as breeders of men and even suggests the necessity of selective breeding to ensure the development of men with native power and intelligence. *Collected Writings*, 2:397.

26. Margaret Fuller, *Life Without and Life Within*, ed. A. B. Fuller (1860; rpr. Upper Saddle River, N.J.: Literature House, 1970) p. 276 (hereafter cited in this chapter as *Life*).

27. Paula Blanchard, *Margaret Fuller*, pp. 182, 184–185, independently arrives at this conclusion and points to the journal Fuller kept while visiting Emerson in 1842. This journal confirms my contention that Fuller was not complaining about a rejected love but was asserting the need to establish her own identity.

28. Mason Wade, *Margaret Fuller*, p. 95.

29. Margaret Fuller, *Papers on Literature and Art*, 2:132.

30. Emerson, *Journals and Miscellaneous Notebooks*, 11:258.

31. Emerson did not think that Fuller's work warranted any real research (*Journals and Miscellaneous Notebooks*, 11:431–432). But when he was approached by Horace Greeley and William Henry Channing, he agreed to edit the *Memoirs*. If Americans in general were not willing to take seriously the work of a woman who insisted that she was an individual, Emerson's attitude in the *Memoirs* only confirmed this opinion. Writing as a presumed friend, he undercut Fuller wherever he could. His criticism ranged from petty comments like the claim that her writings about nature were no good because she was too nearsighted to see nature properly (*Memoirs*, 1:263–264) to more damning general remarks like his assertion that her writing was all style and no content, that, like all women, she allowed herself to be influenced too much by personal feelings (*Memoirs*, 1:279). Moreover, his condescending tone constantly poked fun at her pretensions to individuality, as when he referred to her "mountainous Me" (*Memoirs*, 1:236) and when he

reported her comment that she could not find in America an intellect comparable to her own and criticized Emerson's reverence for a certain youth. Emerson comments, "Meantime, we knew that she neither had seen, nor would see, his subtle superiorities" (*Memoirs*, 1:234).

32. Caroline W. Healey, *Margaret and Her Friends*, pp. 43–46. That Emerson's presence at the Conversation also served to illustrate the difference in their philosophies is evident from the comment of another woman who was present: "Mr. Emerson only served to display her powers. With his study reiteration of his uncompromising idealism, his absolute denial of the fact of human nature, he gave her opportunity and excitement to unfold and illustrate her realism and acceptance of conditions. . . . She proceeds in her search after the unity of things, the divine harmony, not by exclusion as he does, but by comprehension" (*Memoirs*, 1:349–350).

33. Nancy Milford, *Zelda*. Elizabeth Hardwick, *Seduction and Betrayal*, p. 89, recognizes the significance of Milford's focusing on the wife, thus giving us the "other side of the question." For a discussion of Emerson's use of these letters in his essay "Friendship," see Ralph Rusk's footnotes in *The Letters of Ralph Waldo Emerson*, 2:250, 254, 324, 333, 336; J. Bard McNulty, "Emerson's Friends and the Essay on Friendship," pp. 390–394. For his use of the letters in his poetry, see Carl E. Strauch, "Hatred's Swift Repulsions," pp. 65–103.

34. Emerson, *Journals and Miscellaneous Notebooks*, 7:509.

35. Letter and poem printed partly in Rusk, *Letters*, 3:252–254, and partly in Higginson, *Margaret Fuller Ossoli*, pp. 70–71.

36. *Margaret Fuller*, ed. Perry Miller, p. 132.

37. See Ann Douglas, *The Feminization of American Culture*, pp. 273–277, for a discussion of other factors that may have been involved in the Fuller-Emerson relationship. Douglas speculates about the unconscious need each had for the other—Emerson finding in Fuller's criticism of him a representation of the guilt he felt at his metaphorical existence, and Fuller finding in Emerson the rejection she perhaps required for self-fulfillment.

38. Margaret Fuller, *At Home and Abroad*, ed. Arthur B. Fuller (1856; Boston: Roberts Brothers, 1874), pp. 46–48 (hereafter cited

as *At Home* in the text). An excellent fictional portrayal of this phenomenon and its consequences is found in O. E. Rolvaag, *Giants in the Earth* (1924; translated and published in the United States in 1927).

39. In her perceptive analysis of Margaret Fuller's role in American culture, Ann Douglas recognizes that Fuller was able to perceive the subtle, psychological oppression of minority groups and other disadvantaged peoples because she had felt status oppression as a woman. Douglas, *Feminization*, pp. 282, 284.

40. Emerson, *Complete Works*, 1:161; 4:4.

41. Emerson, *Complete Works*, 11:403.

42. Joseph Jay Deiss, *The Roman Years of Margaret Fuller*, p. 148.

43. Fuller met Mazzini at the home of Thomas Carlyle. It was not the arrogant Carlyle, Emerson's friend, who attracted Margaret Fuller, but Mazzini, whose concern for the Italian people was ridiculed by Carlyle as "rose-water imbecilities." Jane Carlyle, who, Fuller commented, could not speak when Carlyle was there (he shouted down everyone else), remarked sadly to Fuller later: "These are but opinions to Carlyle; but to Mazzini, who has given his all . . . it is a matter of life and death." See Wade, *Margaret Fuller*, p. 189.

44. Deiss, *Roman Years*, pp. 23, 88–89, 135. As Deiss says, Fuller even saw the problem with Mazzini—that he was all politics and no economics (*At Home*, p. 320). Just how in tune she was with events is suggested by the fact that at the time she wrote this, Marx and Engels were publishing the *Communist Manifesto* in England.

45. American men tended to agree with Emerson, who was amazed that Margaret Fuller had been courted by men in Europe and that she had received offers of marriage (*Memoirs*, 1:281).

46. The only evidence as to the date of the marriage is contained in a letter from Ossoli's sister Angela to Fuller's sister Ellen, saying that Ossoli had written to her from Florence in late 1849 or 1850 that they had been married there. Deiss speculates that any other evidence was destroyed by the Fuller family because of the scandal feared from a belated marriage and that this letter was probably overlooked because it was written in Italian (Deiss, *Roman Years*, pp. 291–292). Bell Gale Chevigny, *The Woman and the Myth*, p. 400, concludes that the evidence is insufficient to tell when, or even if, the marriage took place. But Paula Blanchard,

Margaret Fuller, p. 328, points out that in the spring of 1850 Fuller suddenly began using the title Marchesa, which seems to support Deiss's thesis.

47. Cited in Deiss, *Roman Years*, p. 107.

48. See also a letter to her sister, Ellen Channing, December 11, 1849, in Chevigny, *The Woman and the Myth*, pp. 487–489 (from a manuscript in the Houghton Library, Harvard University).

49. Margaret Fuller, *Woman in the Nineteenth Century*, ed. A. B. Fuller, rev. ed. (Boston: Roberts Brothers, 1874), pp. 298–300.

CHAPTER 4
SOLITARY MAN
AND SUPERFLUOUS WOMAN

1. James Fenimore Cooper, *Complete Works*, Leatherstocking Edition, 32 vols. (New York: Putnam, 1893?), 24:312 (hereafter cited in this chapter as *Works*).

2. James Russell Lowell, *Poetical Works*, p. 137.

3. William Dean Howells, *Heroines of Fiction*, 1:111.

4. Leslie Fiedler, *Love and Death in the American Novel*, p. 175.

5. Richard Chase, *The American Novel and Its Tradition*, p. 64.

6. Kay Seymour House, *Cooper's Americans*, p. 14.

7. D. H. Lawrence, *Studies in Classic American Literature*, pp. 58, 61.

8. James Fenimore Cooper, *Letters and Journals*, ed. James Franklin Beard, 6 vols. (Cambridge, Mass.: Harvard Univ. Press, 1968), 4:345 (hereafter cited in this chapter as *Letters*).

9. Herman Melville, review of *The Sea Lions*, p. 370.

10. Chase, *American Novel*, p. 64.

11. Donald Davie, *The Heyday of Sir Walter Scott*, p. 127.

12. Earlier in the same novel Anna Updyke pleads for Mary with childlike simplicity, throwing herself on the mercy of the court in an impulsive outburst of heartfelt emotion (*Works*, 24:406). In *The Spy*, where Frances Wharton pleads in a similar way at her brother's trial, Cooper emphasizes her beauty, innocence, and deep emotion (*Works*, 6:320–323). After the strain of such a public display of feeling, Frances falls senseless to the floor, and Anna has to

be led from the room by ladies. "She is too delicate for the touch of a constable," writes Cooper (*Works*, 24:407). Mary Monson, however, remains calm and rational throughout her own trial; she neither weeps nor faints, but conducts herself with dignity and intelligence. Some of the facts behind Cooper's animosity toward Mary Monson are pointed out by Barbara Ann Bardes and Suzanne Gossett in "Cooper and the Cup and Saucer Law," pp. 499–518.

13. In *Notions of the Americans Picked Up by a Traveling Bachelor*, 2 vols. (London: Henry Colburn, 1828), 1:255–256 (hereafter cited as *Notions* in the text), Cooper specifically states that the beautiful creatures he admires are very young. There is nothing more beautiful, he says, than an "American beauty between the ages of 15 and 18." After marriage, he says, American women "decay prematurely" and become uninteresting to anyone but their husbands.

14. See the introduction to *The Correspondence of James Fenimore Cooper*, 1:3, by his grandson, James Fenimore Cooper.

15. James Fenimore Cooper, *The American Democrat* (New York: Funk and Wagnalls, 1969), pp. 38–39 (hereafter cited as *Democrat* in the text).

16. W. C. Brownell, *American Prose Masters*, pp. 31–35.

17. W. H. Gardiner, review of *The Spy* in *North American Review*, July, 1822 and review of *The Last of the Mohicans*, in ibid., July 1826.

18. Fiedler, *Love and Death*, pp. 175, 190–203.

19. In the preface to *The Pilot* (1824), Cooper states somewhat impatiently that the book was not written for "females." His aim "was to illustrate vessels and the ocean rather than to draw any pictures of sentiment and love," though he hoped there would be enough of the latter to satisfy (*Works*, 7:vii). In the original preface to *The Two Admirals* (1842) he wrote: "The reader will do us the justice to regard *The Two Admirals* as a sea story and not as a love story. Our admirals are our heroes; as there are two of them, those who are particularly fastidious on such subjects are quite welcome to term one the heroine, if they see fit." William Charvat points out in his preface to *The Last of the Mohicans* (Riverside Edition [Boston: Houghton Mifflin, 1958], p. vii) that the insipid love story of the genteel hero and heroine was simply a pandering to public taste. It is significant that *Lionel Lincoln* (1825), which did not include such

a love story, was a financial failure. As Kay Seymour House notes in *Cooper's Americans*, p. 182, Cooper could not afford to ignore public taste; he was not only supporting his own family but had assumed responsibility for the debts and families of his five dead brothers. See also, James Grossman, *James Fenimore Cooper*, p. 17.

20. Francis Parkman, review, pp. 147, 151.

21. Allan Nevins, ed., *The Leatherstocking Saga*, p. 5.

22. Gardiner, *North American Review* (July 1822), pp. 250–282; Lewis Leary, introduction to *Home as Found* (New York: Capricorn Books, 1961), pp. viii–ix.

23. Since the appearance of the first Leatherstocking novel, readers have compared Nathaniel Bumppo to Daniel Boone. The *Niles Weekly Register* of Dec. 3, 1825, explored at length the similarities between the two (p. 217). In 1939 John E. Bakeless pointed out specific similarities between Boone's exploits and parts of *The Last of the Mohicans*, in *Daniel Boone*, pp. 133–139. And Henry Nash Smith noted in *Virgin Land* that both Bumppo and Boone were said to be driven westward by the advance of civilization (pp. 59–60, 67–68).

24. See, e.g., Mark Twain's classic criticism of Cooper in 1895. Among other things, Twain ridicules Leatherstocking's miraculous feats and comments, "Nothing is impossible to a Cooper person." *North American Review*, 161 (July 1895), 1–12, in *The Writings of Mark Twain* (New York: Harpers, 1899), 12:71.

25. Lawrence, *Studies*, p. 51.

26. Ibid., pp. 59, 62–63.

27. House, *Cooper's Americans*, p. 327.

28. Leary, introduction to *Home as Found*, p. vi.

29. James Fenimore Cooper, *Towns of Manhattan*, unpublished manuscript, the introduction to which appears in *New York*, p. 37.

30. James Grossman, in his analysis of Cooper's attitude toward his country, points out that, after his return from Europe, Cooper lost faith in the American masses and, as for example in the anti-rent strikes, put his faith in the wealthy few. What was originally a defense of high breeding and the democratic "gentleman" became ultimately a defense of wealth (Grossman, *Cooper*, pp. 7–9, 253–254). Cooper's disillusionment with the masses derived from his fear that the masses, through their vulnerability to the persua-

sion of demagogues and other forces, would infringe on the rights of the individual.

31. As Ludwig Lewisohn commented in *Expression in America*, p. 56, "Bumppo's long career of murder is based upon prejudices as vulgar and cruel as those of his foes." Cooper's attitude toward other Americans is particularly apparent in his definition of female beauty. In *Afloat and Ashore* Miles Wallingford observes that in New York only the native American females were noteworthy for their beauty, "the true, native portion of the population, and not the throng from Ireland and Germany who now crowd the streets, and who certainly, as a body, are not in the least remarkable for personal charms." The real charm of woman, Cooper felt, belonged "almost exclusively to the Anglo-Saxon race: that expression of the countenance which so eminently betokens feminine purity and feminine tenderness united" (*Works*, 16:294, 347).

32. For a discussion of Cooper's attitude toward Indians, see New York Historical Association, *James Fenimore Cooper*, pp. 56–59. The chapter on Cooper's Indians points out that Cooper completely misunderstood the Iroquois, whose Six Nation confederacy gave Benjamin Franklin the idea for the Union and who had long been allies of the English colonies. Cooper portrays the Iroquois as inherently evil tools of the French. He apparently took his idea of the Six Nations from John Heckewelder's 1819 history of the Indian tribes around Pennsylvania and New York. Cooper's lament for a vanishing people in *The Last of the Mohicans* does not mean that he intended to write an epic of the American Indian. As Lucy Lockwood Hazard points out in *The Frontier in American Literature*, p. 99, the same lament appears in Sabin's *Kit Carson Days*, but the hero of the book is Carson, not the Indian. With the exception of Chingachgook's family and Hard-Heart in *The Prairie*, Cooper's portrayal of Indians in his Leatherstocking novels is negative. They are "varmints," devils, demons, reptiles, knaves, or rascals. And, although Natty insists that whites and Indians have their own gifts, as Joel Porte points out in *The Romance in America*, pp. 11–20, it is clear that white gifts are better.

33. See George Dekker, *James Fenimore Cooper, the Novelist*, pp. 64–75. (The American title is *James Fenimore Cooper, the American Scott*.)

34. As James R. Lowell said in "A Fable for Critics" (*Poetical Works*, p. 137):

His Indians, with proper respect be it said,
Are just Natty Bumppo, daubed over with red,
And his very Long Toms are the same useful Nat,
Rigged up in duck pants and a sou'wester hat.

CHAPTER 5
THE MASCULINE SEA

1. Herman Melville, *The Writings of Herman Melville*, vols. 1–5, 7, 8 (Evanston and Chicago: Northwestern Univ. Press and Newberry Library, 1968–   ), 5:46 (hereafter cited in this chapter as *Writings*).

2. In his 1929 biography of Melville, Lewis Mumford pointed out that Melville had left women out of his fiction and concluded that there must have been "something in Herman Melville's life that caused him to dissociate women from his account of man's deepest experience." See Mumford, *Herman Melville*, p. 201. Newton Arvin, *Herman Melville*, pp. 86, 129, also notes the lack of women in Melville's work. More recently, Charles J. Haberstroh, Jr., in *Melville and Male Identity*, p. 22, asserts that Melville's "powerful uncertainties about his ability, or even desire" to play the responsible masculine role caused him to shy away from the fictional treatment of women, whom he saw as entrappers.

3. *The Melville Log*, ed. Jay Leyda, 2 vols. (1951; rpr. New York: Gordian Press, 1969), 1:83 (hereafter cited as *Log* in the text).

4. There is conflicting evidence concerning the reality of Fayaway. Lewis Mumford cites an American traveler, Henry Augustus Wise, who said that he had met a girl named Fayaway from Typee working in a French commissary in Nukuheva. Mumford, *Herman Melville*, p. 52. But a traveler, Alfred G. Jones, on board a ship in harbor in the Marquesas recorded in his journal in 1855 that he met a native chief who knew some of the people mentioned in Melville's book but that there was no one named Fayaway, that the name was not a part of the language (*Log*, 2:505–506).

5. Herman Melville, *Moby-Dick*, ed. Harrison Hayford and Hershel Parker (New York: Norton, 1967), p. 442 (hereafter cited as *Moby-Dick* in the text).

6. Isabel is specifically related to the "ungraspable phantom" image associated with the white whale. In *Moby-Dick* Ishmael says of the whale, "there floated into my inmost soul, endless processions of the whale, and, mid most of them all, one grand hooded phantom" (*Moby-Dick*, p. 16). This passage is strikingly similar to Melville's description of the change that Isabel wrought in Pierre: "He felt that what he had always before considered the solid land of veritable reality, was now being audaciously encroached upon by bannered armies of hooded phantoms, disembarking in his soul" (*Writings*, 7:49). When Pierre thinks of how he has turned from Lucy, he sees himself "in pursuit of some vague, white shape, and lo! two unfathomable dark eyes met his, and Isabel stood mutely . . . before him" (*Writings*, 7:312). Like Ahab, who determines to "strike through the mask" (*Moby-Dick*, p. 144), Pierre declares to the vision of the Black Knight of Truth that his concern with Isabel has conjured up, "lo! I strike through thy helm" (*Writings*, 7:66).

7. Some Melville critics have made the mistake of associating Lucy, the "good" maiden, with what is good in the novel: the heaven-aspiring search for truth. See, e.g., F. O. Matthiessen, *American Renaissance*, pp. 481, 484; Lawrance Thompson, *Melville's Quarrel with God*, pp. 247, 250. The "heavenly" associations of Lucy, however, do not represent the heaven assaulted by Titans but rather the heavenly bliss that might have followed a life spent in unassuming mortal preoccupations. Pierre recognizes that, had he spurned Isabel for Lucy, he would have "been happy through a long life on earth, and perchance through a long eternity in heaven."

8. Although Melville reveals his admiration of the concept represented by landlessness in both *Pierre* and *Moby-Dick*, there is an unmistakable difference in the tone of the two novels. In *Moby-Dick* the passage on landlessness concludes: "Terrors of the terrible! is all this agony so vain? Take heart, take heart, O Bulkington! Bear thee grimly, demigod! Up from the spray of thy ocean-perishing— straight up, leaps thy apotheosis!" *Pierre* contains all of this agony, but the exultant inspiration of this statement does not properly fit in the novel. In *Pierre* Melville seems to have surrendered to all of

Pierre's woe. There is no Ishmael to maintain a balance in the narration of the novel, and the "little Lucy," as a representative of "all that's kind to our mortalities," fails to command the sympathy and respect that Starbuck does. Nor does Pierre himself have the stature of an Ahab. Further, the wild writing indicates that Melville is not wholly in control of his material, which in fact often become warmly personal, particularly the discussions of Pierre as an unappreciated author (*Writings*, 7:244–264, 283–285, 302, 306, 338–339).

9. I can find no evidence that Pierre's and Isabel's love was physically consummated, although each admitted a physical attraction to the other that went beyond the relationship of brother and sister. See *Writings*, 7:192, 272–273, 276, 312–313, 334.

10. Herman Melville, *The Apple-Tree Table and Other Sketches*, pp. 181, 209.

11. Herman Melville, *Selected Writings*, (New York: Modern Library, 1952), p. 453 (hereafter cited as *Selected Writings* in the text).

12. See *Log*, 2:648–649, 714, for Melville's marking of Emerson's *Essays*, 1862 and 1870. See also *Pierre* (*Writings*, 7:262, 280, 290–300) and *The Confidence Man: His Masquerade*, ed. Hershel Parker (New York: Norton, 1971), pp. 161–170 (hereafter cited as *Confidence Man* in the text).

13. *The Letters of Herman Melville*, ed. Merrell R. Davis and William H. Gilman (1960; rpr. New Haven: Yale Univ. Press, 1965), pp. 76, 78–79 (hereafter cited in this chapter as *Letters*).

14. "Hawthorne and His Mosses" (1851), reprinted in the Norton edition of *Moby-Dick*, p. 545.

15. The work in which Melville came closest to creating separately defined characters is *Billy Budd*, which I have not discussed here because of its total lack of female characters. Yet even in this work Billy and Claggart do not attain the complexity necessary for fully drawn characters. Billy, like the women in Melville's works, is the other—to such an extent that his death seems only an abstraction. (However indignant one may be at the injustice of the situation, one is not moved by Billy's death the way one would be by the death of a realized character.) Claggart, though interesting as a study in "innate depravity," is only a vehicle for the problem that faces Captain Vere. It is, after all, Vere's story. Vere is confronted

with the same problem that challenges Melville's other protagonists: whether to act according to earth's time or heaven's. Like Ahab and Pierre, "Starry" Vere is aware of heavenly time, but his decision is contrary to theirs. They are destroyed because they insist on acting according to what Melville calls a "heavenly chronometer," whereas Vere forces himself to overrule his heavenly awareness of Billy's innocence, and he acts instead according to the earthly rules of military law and duty.

16. Raymond Weaver, *The Shorter Novels of Herman Melville*, p. xi.

17. Nathaniel Hawthorne, *English Notebooks*, ed. Randall Stewart, p. 437.

18. Eleanor Melville Metcalf, *Herman Melville*, pp. 206, 133–134, 215–217, 76–77; Mumford, *Herman Melville*, p. 288.

19. Metcalf, *Herman Melville*, pp. 258–259. Some of these books are noted in Melville's *Log*; see for example, 2:716, where is noted the book Melville gave to his wife in 1870, *Walks About the City and Environs of Jerusalem*.

20. Richard Chase, *Herman Melville*, pp. 100–101, calls *Moby-Dick* an American epic and points out Melville's use of the American folk hero and other aspects of folk culture. He also emphasizes Melville's devotion to the American theme of power and expansion (pp. 65–77, 94–100).

21. Haberstroh, *Melville and Male Identity*, p. 17.

22. Herman Melville, *Journal Up the Straits, October 11, 1856–May 5, 1857*, ed. Raymond Weaver (New York: Cooper Square, 1971), p. 179 (hereafter cited as *JUS* in the text).

23. Melville, "Hawthorne and His Mosses," pp. 545–546.

24. Metcalf, *Herman Melville*, pp. 37–38.

25. See, e.g., Raymond Weaver, *Herman Melville*, p. 340; Mumford, *Herman Melville*, p. 219; Richard Brodhead, *Hawthorne, Melville, and the Novel*, p. 174; Arvin, *Herman Melville*, p. 128; and Edwin Haviland Miller, *Melville*, pp. 78–81, 116–117.

26. See Herman Melville, *Collected Poems*, ed. Howard Vincent, p. 219.

27. Weaver, *Herman Melville*, p. 54.

28. The correspondence between Maria Melville and her

brothers indicates that she received financial help from them, but not without constant prodding. See *Log*, 1:98–99.

29. Metcalf, *Herman Melville*, pp. 204–205.

30. Ibid., p. 42.

31. Ibid., p. 55.

32. Ibid., p. 259.

33. Mumford, *Herman Melville*, p. 136.

34. Metcalf, *Herman Melville*, p. 250.

35. Ibid., p. 259.

36. Ibid., pp. 51–52; *Log*, 1:266–267.

37. Metcalf, *Herman Melville*, p. 113.

38. Ibid., pp. 218, 225.

39. Mumford, *Herman Melville*, p. 86.

40. Ibid., pp. 86–87; Weaver, *Herman Melville*, pp. 340, 379–380.

41. Metcalf, *Herman Melville*, p. 42.

42. Walter D. Kring and Jonathan S. Carey, "Two Discoveries Concerning Herman Melville," p. 140.

43. Although Melville was at sea during some of her visits, he would have had ample time before he went to sea and after he returned in 1844 to become thoroughly acquainted with Elizabeth.

44. Mumford, *Herman Melville*, pp. 86, 219.

45. In 1834 the British Shakespearean actress Fanny Kemble was married to Pierce Butler, a wealthy American, after completing a two-year triumphant tour of the United States. In 1835 she published a journal of her tour, against the violent objections of her husband, who, when his exhortations failed, offered the publishers a sum of money to stop publication. Although he did not prevent this journal from appearing, Butler, who was heir to a Georgia plantation and owner of 700 slaves, successfully opposed the publication of Fanny's antislavery writing for the duration of their marriage. It was not until 1863 that Kemble published her *Journal of a Residence on a Georgia Plantation, 1838–1839*, which recorded her hatred of slavery.

The problems of the Kemble-Butler marriage were many and complex, but the central one can be said to have been the question of a wife's subordination to her husband. Butler wrote to Fanny in

1843 that their marriage could succeed only "if you can consent to submit your will to mine." She replied that, although she loved him, she could not promise unquestioning obedience: "I consider it my duty not to submit my conduct to another human being." Butler found it incredible that his wife would insist on her independence: "Her declarations on this matter of equal rights were so perversely frequent, and so emphatic, that there appeared to be no hope of reconciling our differences." See Constance Wright, *Fanny Kemble and the Lovely Land*, pp. 43, 100–101; John Anthony Scott, *Fanny Kemble's America*, pp. 98, 108–109. See also Margaret Armstrong, *Fanny Kemble*, pp. 314–316.

46. Metcalf, *Herman Melville*, p. 125.

47. Herman Melville, *Journal of a Visit to London and the Continent, 1849–50*, ed. Eleanor Melville Metcalf (Cambridge, Mass.: Harvard Univ. Press, 1948), pp. 72–73 (hereafter cited as *JLC* in the text).

48. Quoted in Mumford, *Herman Melville*, p. 131.

49. Metcalf, *Herman Melville*, p. 115; *Log*, 1:420.

50. Metcalf, *Herman Melville*, p. 234; *Log*, 2:747.

51. Metcalf, *Herman Melville*, pp. 93–94.

52. Other critics who have commented on the extreme difficulties of Melville's handwriting include Weaver, ed., *JUS*, pp. xxviii–xxix, and Howard C. Horsford, ed., *Journal of a Visit to Europe and the Levant, October 11, 1856–May 6, 1857*, pp. 43–46.

53. Horsford points out in his introduction to the *Journal of a Visit to Europe* that the journal reveals a preoccupation with death (pp. 21–22).

54. Leon Howard, *Herman Melville*, p. 198, notes Melville's dependence on English sales.

55. Metcalf, *Herman Melville*, pp. 91–93, 106.

56. Hawthorne, *English Notebooks*, pp. 432, 437.

57. Arvin, *Herman Melville*, p. 204.

58. That Melville was able to hold his own with Holmes is suggested by this description of a conversation that took place between them in late 1855: it "was conducted with the most amazing skill and brilliancy on both sides" (*Log*, 2:506).

CHAPTER 6
OLD LADIES
AND LITTLE GIRLS

1. Albert Bigelow Paine, *Mark Twain*, 4:1613.

2. Ernest Hemingway, *The Green Hills of Africa*, p. 16.

3. Leslie Fiedler, *Love and Death in the American Novel*, p. 7.

4. William Dean Howells, *My Mark Twain*, p. 175.

5. Mary M. Fairbanks, who was seven years older than he and married to Abel W. Fairbanks, the publisher of the Cleveland *Herald*.

6. See, e.g., Mark Twain, *The Complete Works*, American Artists Edition, 24 vols. (New York: Harper, 1935), 1:148, 183, 198; 2:202, 266–267, 281 (hereafter cited in this chapter as *Works*). See also, *Mark Twain's Notebooks and Journals*, ed. Frederick Anderson et al., 3 vols. (Berkeley and Los Angeles: Univ. of California Press, 1975–1979), 1:344 (hereafter cited in this chapter as *Notebooks*).

7. Twain identified his contributions to *The Gilded Age* in letters to Mrs. Fairbanks and Dr. John Brown. For a listing of them, see the introduction to *The Adventures of Colonel Sellers*, ed. Charles Neider, pp. xii, xiii.

8. Perhaps one reason for the charming picture of the child Laura is Twain's memory of the real Laura Hawkins, a young girl he knew when he was a thirteen-year-old publisher's apprentice in Hannibal. Paine, *Mark Twain*, 1:80.

9. *Mark Twain to Mrs. Fairbanks*, ed. Dixon Wecter (San Marino, Calif.: Huntington Library, 1949), pp. 170–171 (hereafter cited as *Fairbanks* in the text).

10. Mark Twain, "Huck Finn and Tom Sawyer Among the Indians," pp. 34–51.

11. See Mary Ellen Goad, *The Image and the Woman in the Life and Writings of Mark Twain*, p. 65.

12. As James M. Cox notes in *Mark Twain*, p. 246, "The bitter plot of *Pudd'nhead Wilson* overrides the character of Roxana, reducing her vernacular to dialect and severing her humor from the sources of her instinctive power."

13. *Complete Essays of Mark Twain*, ed. Charles Neider (Gar-

den City, N.Y.: Doubleday, 1963), p. 323 (hereafter cited as *Essays* in the text).

14. Paine, *Mark Twain*, 3:998.

15. Clara Clemens, *My Father, Mark Twain*, p. 127.

16. Maxwell Geismar, *Mark Twain*, p. 152.

17. Cox, *Mark Twain*, pp. 256–260, 263.

18. Quoted in Bernard DeVoto, *Mark Twain's America*, p. 280.

19. Paine, *Mark Twain*, 3:1030.

20. Ibid., 1:75.

21. Van Wyck Brooks, *The Ordeal of Mark Twain*, pp. 52–59.

22. See, e.g., DeVoto, *Mark Twain's America*, pp. 80–86; Gladys Carmen Bellamy, *Mark Twain as a Literary Artist*, p. 32; Goad, *Image and the Woman*, pp. 10–11.

23. Brooks, *Ordeal*, p. 52.

24. Paine, *Mark Twain*, 1:93.

25. See, e.g., "History Repeats Itself," in *Works*, 19:330.

26. Paine, *Mark Twain*, 1:3.

27. Rachel M. Varble, *Jane Clemens*, pp. 57–58.

28. In Dixon Wecter, *Sam Clemens of Hannibal*, pp. 83, 86.

29. Varble, *Jane Clemens*, pp. 67, 142.

30. Paine, *Mark Twain*, 1:3.

31. Varble, *Jane Clemens*, pp. 222–223.

32. Ibid., pp. 53–54, 80, 160, 94–95, 123–124, 215–216, 180–181, 298, 153–154, 226. See also *The Love Letters of Mark Twain*, ed. Dixon Wecter (New York: Harper, 1949), pp. 134–137 (hereafter cited in this chapter as *Love Letters*); Philip S. Foner, *Mark Twain*, p. 127.

33. Varble, *Jane Clemens*, pp. 281–282.

34. See Leon T. Dickinson, "Mark Twain's Revisions in Writing *The Innocents Abroad*," pp. 139–157.

35. For Twain's exhortations to Mrs. Fairbanks to reform him, see, e.g., *Fairbanks*, pp. 106–108, 16, 50.

36. As Mary Ellen Goad has observed, it was really just a game he was playing. Goad, *Image and the Woman*, pp. 18–19.

37. See Paine, *Mark Twain*, 1:354, 367.

38. See Cox, *Mark Twain*, p. 64.

39. Paine, *Mark Twain*, 1:339.

40. Ibid., 1:352–353, 367–369.

41. Mary Ellen Goad makes this point in *Image and the Woman*, p. 27.

42. As Dixon Wecter says, he was in love with "ideal womanhood." *Love Letters*, p. 3.

43. Ibid., pp. 34, 92–97. See also, Ralph Waldo Emerson, *Complete Works*, ed. Edward W. Emerson, 11:403.

44. Paine, *Mark Twain*, 2:411.

45. Mary Lawton, *A Lifetime with Mark Twain*, p. 240.

46. See Arthur L. Scott, "The *Century Magazine* Edits *Huckleberry Finn*," pp. 356–362.

47. Paul J. Carter, Jr., "Olivia Clemens Edits *Following the Equator*," pp. 194–209.

48. See Bellamy, *Twain as Artist*, p. 33.

49. Paine, *Mark Twain*, 2:650–651.

50. That Eve was a portrait of Livy is suggested by Paine in his biography of Twain, (4:1225–1226), and by Joseph Ridgely in his introduction to *The Diaries of Adam and Eve* (New York: American Heritage Press, 1971), p. 1 (hereafter cited as *Diaries* in the text). In one of his letters to Mary Benjamin Rogers after his wife's death, Twain answers her guess that he used her (Mary) for his portrait of Eve by saying that he had, and then he compares her to his wife and mother. Of course, this admission may have been only a polite reply to her query. See *Mark Twain's Letters to Mary*, ed. Lewis Leary, p. 42.

51. Paine, *Mark Twain*, 3:987.

52. Ibid., pp. 990–994.

53. Clara Clemens, *My Father, Mark Twain*, pp. 179–180. On May 8, 1869, Twain wrote that if he lost Livy he would lose memory and reason also: she was necessary to his sanity. Cited in Cox, *Mark Twain*, p. 75; from the Mark Twain Papers, University of California, Berkeley.

54. Justin Kaplan, *Mr. Clemens and Mark Twain*, p. 340.

55. Geismar, *Mark Twain*, p. 245.

56. Clara Clemens, *My Father, Mark Twain*, p. 251.

57. Howells, *My Mark Twain*, p. 76.

58. Paine, *Mark Twain*, 2:524 (interview with Paine).

59. Lawton, *Lifetime*, pp. 31, 38, 234.

60. Paine, *Mark Twain*, 2:730.

61. Cox, *Mark Twain*, pp. 76–81. Mary Ellen Goad is the only critic I have found who discusses Livy as a person separate from Mark Twain.

62. Lawton, *Lifetime*, p. 227.

63. See also, *Mark Twain's Autobiography*, ed. Albert Bigelow Paine, 2 vols. (New York: Harper, 1924), 2:26 (hereafter cited as *Autob.*, Paine, in the text).

64. *Mark Twain's Letter to Will Bowen*, ed. Theodore Hornberger, pp. 18–20; my italics.

65. Paine, *Mark Twain*, 4:1613.

66. *Mark Twain and the Three R's*, ed. Maxwell Geismar, p. 196.

67. Mark Twain, *Life as I Find It*, ed. Charles Neider (Garden City, N.Y.: Hanover House, 1961), pp. 352–364 (hereafter cited as *Life* in the text).

68. See Bernard DeVoto, *Mark Twain at Work*, p. 15; Bellamy, *Twain as Artist*, p. 31.

69. See Alexander Jones, "Mark Twain and Sexuality," pp. 596–616.

70. Delancey Ferguson, *Mark Twain*, pp. 219 ff.

71. *Love Letters*, pp. 3–4. During his courtship of Livy, for example, Twain is said to have commented to his friend George Wiley, "You know I never had wish or time to bother with women, and I can give that girl the purest best love any man can give her." In *1601*, the Elizabethan fantasy that Twain had privately printed in 1882, Sir Walter Raleigh speaks of men in North America who "copulate not until they be five and thirty years of age"—Twain's approximate age at marriage (*1601*, p. 36). See also Samuel Webster, *Mark Twain, Business Man*, p. 102.

72. Jones, "Mark Twain and Sexuality," pp. 598–599.

73. Lawton, *Lifetime*, pp. 211–212; Clara Clemens, *My Father, Mark Twain*, pp. 201–202. For a good discussion of Twain as a strict father, see Edward Wagenknecht, *Mark Twain*, pp. 163–164.

74. Clara Clemens, *My Father, Mark Twain*, pp. 912–913.

75. Wagenknecht, *Mark Twain*, p. 164.

76. Quoted in Caroline Thomas Harnsberger, *Mark Twain*, pp. 140–142 (from an unpublished letter).

77. Mark Twain, *The Mammoth Cod and Address to the Stomach Club*, ed. G. Legman, pp. 18–21, 11.

78. Despite Twain's concern with female purity, he cannot be said actually to have believed that even proper women were the sexless creatures that his fiction implies. His *Letters from the Earth*, written around 1906 but not published until 1962, fifty-two years after his death, reveals a man who not only prized the pleasures of sex for men but also recognized the full extent of the sex drive in women. He calls sexual intercourse the "first delight," the "Supreme Art." Man has created a heaven, says Twain, and left out of it "the one ecstasy that stands first and foremost in the heart of every individual of his race." Humanity may have lost a lot when Adam and Eve were thrown out of the Garden, but it gained one pleasure worth all the rest: sexual intercourse. Twain even characterizes woman as ultimately more sexual than man; man's ability wanes as he grows older, and he is always limited in his performance, whereas woman is competent every day of her life. It is women who should have harems, says Twain, not men. Mark Twain, *Letters from the Earth*, ed. Bernard DeVoto (New York: Harper, 1968), pp. 15, 25, 42–44 (hereafter cited as *Earth* in the text).

79. Leslie Fiedler, *Love and Death in the American Novel*, pp. 265–266.

80. Harnsberger, *Mark Twain*, 139–140.

81. Cited in Kenneth Andrews, *Nook Farm*, p. 39 (from a letter of Molly Clemens to Jane Clemens, Nov. 26, 1872, Samuel C. Webster Collection).

82. In Wagenknecht, *Mark Twain*, p. 165.

83. *Mark Twain in Eruption*, ed. Bernard DeVoto (New York: Harper, 1940), pp. 316, 319 (hereafter cited as *Eruption* in the text).

84. Clara Clemens, *My Father, Mark Twain*, p. 57.

85. Lawton, *Lifetime*, p. 305.

86. James B. Pond, "Across the Continent with Mark Twain," p. 7.

87. Twain wrote home appreciatively of the "thundering outburst of spontaneous applause" that greeted his name at dinners and told his mother: "I have had a jolly time, and I do hate to go away from these English folks; they make a stranger feel entirely at home." See *Love Letters*, pp. 177–179; Paine, *Mark Twain*, 2:465–470.

88. See Justin Kaplan, *Mr. Clemens and Mark Twain*, p. 229.

89. Clara Clemens, *My Father, Mark Twain*, pp. 202–203.

90. Ibid., p. 261; Paine, *Mark Twain*, 3:972, 1111, 1113–1114.

91. Cited in Kaplan, *Mr. Clemens and Mark Twain*, p. 381.

92. Paine, *Mark Twain*, 4:1341; Howells, *My Mark Twain*, p. 96.

93. Kaplan, *Mr. Clemens and Mark Twain*, p. 380.

94. Paine quotes Twain as having told him he was tired of wearing drab colors as for a funeral and wanted to wear something that reflected a happier spirit. Paine, *Mark Twain*, 4:1341–1342.

95. How closely Twain identified himself with Tom is apparent in Katy Leary's description of how Twain laughed out loud when reading *Tom Sawyer* to his daughter Jean and told her it was as real then as the day he did those things. Lawton, *Lifetime*, p. 347.

96. Twain's attitude toward his children was the same. In 1891, when he was to lecture at Bryn Mawr College, where his favorite daughter, Susy, was a student, she met him at the station and begged him not to tell the ghost story about the golden arm. He promised he would not. But when he got up on stage and found himself searching for something to say, he thought of the ghost story and told it. Susy ran out of the hall weeping, and he later apologized to her. It is clear that having an effective story to tell and the success of his lecture were more important to him than Susy's feelings. See Kaplan, *Mr. Clemens and Mark Twain*, pp. 309–310; Edith Colgate Salsbury, ed., *Susy and Mark Twain*, pp. 287–288. Their account is taken from a letter from Susy's classmate at Bryn Mawr, Mrs. Charles M. Andrews, to Dixon Wecter, Feb. 26, 1949, Mark Twain Papers, University of California, Berkeley.

97. Paine, *Mark Twain*, 3:1235–1236.

98. Ibid., 2:511–512.

99. Twain compared Grant to Napoleon. See Mark Twain, *Letters*, ed. Albert Bigelow Paine, 2 vols. (New York: Harper, 1917), 1:364–365 (hereafter cited in this chapter as *Letters*). Perhaps one of the greatest moments in Twain's life came when he was able to shatter Grant's famous reserve. After a speech celebrating Grant's birthday in 1879, he wrote to Livy: "I fetched him! I broke him up,

utterly! . . . The audience *saw* that for once in his life he had been knocked out of his iron serenity" (*Letters*, 1:370–372). Twain admired power, and he liked the feeling of power himself. He wrote to Livy in 1870, just before they were married, of how he enjoyed the feeling of power over a lecture audience, for example. Explaining his technique of using pauses, he described how "an audience captured in that way *belongs* to the speaker, body and soul, for the rest of the evening." Cited in Kaplan, *Mr. Clemens and Mark Twain*, pp. 86–87. Lionel Trilling maintains that all of Twain's ventures into business are evidence not so much of a desire for prestige and money but of a search for power. Lionel Trilling, review of Samuel Webster, *Mark Twain, Business Man*, in *New York Times Book Review*, Feb. 3, 1946, pp. 1, 14, in Lewis Leary, ed., *Mark Twain's Wound*, p. 181.

100. Cited in Kaplan, *Mr. Clemens and Mark Twain*, p. 158 (from the Mark Twain Papers, University of California, Berkeley).

101. Brooks, *Ordeal*, pp. 122–123.

102. Howells, *My Mark Twain*, pp. 7–8, 66, 80.

103. Paine, *Mark Twain*, 2:480.

104. Ibid., 2:519.

105. In *Roughing It*, Twain says that he went crazy along with the rest of the population (*Works*, 6:251).

106. See Livy's letter to her sister in Paine, *Mark Twain*, 2:978, and Howell's comment in *My Mark Twain*, p. 80.

107. Horace L. Traubel, ed., *Camden's Compliment to Walt Whitman*, pp. 64–65.

108. For a description of Twain's relationship with his "Angel Fish," see Hamlin Hill, *Mark Twain*, pp. xxvii, 127–128, 195, 203–204.

CHAPTER 7
THE CLAIMS OF THE OTHER

1. Nathaniel Hawthorne, *The Centenary Edition of the Works of Nathaniel Hawthorne*, 14 vols. (Columbus: Ohio State Univ. Press, 1962–   ), 3:123 (hereafter cited in this chapter as *Works*).

2. *Love Letters of Nathaniel Hawthorne*, ed. C. E. Frazer Clark, Jr. (1907; rpr. Washington, D.C.: NCR Microcard Editions, 1972), p. 73 (hereafter cited in this chapter as *Love Letters*).

3. See Nathaniel Hawthorne, *English Notebooks*, ed. Randall Stewart (1941; New York: Russell and Russell, 1962), pp. 619–620, 654 (hereafter cited as *English Notebooks* in the text). See also Julian Hawthorne, *Nathaniel Hawthorne and His Wife*, 2 vols. (Boston and New York: Houghton Mifflin, 1884), 1:256–257; 2:151, vols. 14–15 of *The Works of Nathaniel Hawthorne*, ed. George Parsons Lathrop, (hereafter cited as *NHW* in the text).

4. *The Complete Writings of Nathaniel Hawthorne*, Old Manse Edition, 22 vols. (Boston: Houghton Mifflin, 1900), 17:3 (hereafter cited in this chapter as *Writings*).

5. Quoted in Michael Bell, *Hawthorne and the Historical Romance of New England*, p. 175.

6. Nathaniel Hawthorne, *The Letters of Hawthorne to William Ticknor 1851–1869*, ed. C. E. Frazer Clark, Jr., 2 vols. (1910; rpr. Newark, N.J.: Carteret Book Club, 1972), p. 78 (hereafter cited in this chapter as *Letters*).

7. See, e.g., Bell, *Hawthorne*, pp. 175–180, who says that Hawthorne has Hester return to Boston and prevents her from taking any positive action as a kind of punishment for her bold thoughts. However, given Hawthorne's attitude toward reformers, the ending of *The Scarlet Letter* is not a punishment. Hester's choice, which brings her into the community and strengthens her ties with humanity instead of insulating her further as the role of reformer would do, is, for Hawthorne, the best choice that anyone could make under the circumstances.

8. Hawthorne's relationship with Fanny Kemble is suggested by Julian, who tells of how she "often rode up to the door on her strong black horse, and conversed in heroic phrases, with the inmates of the red house" in Lenox (*NHW*, 1:362–363). She later wrote to Hawthorne from England, telling him of the success of *The Scarlet Letter* there and advising him to take out English copyrights (*NHW*, 1:409). See also, Horatio Bridge, *Personal Recollections of Nathanial Hawthorne*, p. 127.

9. Elizabeth, as an elder sister, had managed Sophia's affairs until Sophia was over thirty years old, and apparently she felt that

she could continue to do so after Sophia was married—and manage Hawthorne's affairs as well. Hawthorne resented her interference and told her so. His real annoyance with her came when she tried to convert the Hawthornes to her own ardent abolitionism. See Rose Hawthorne Lathrop, *Memories of Hawthorne*, pp. 334–337; Louise Hall Tharp, *The Peabody Sisters of Salem*, pp. 207–208, 224–225, 286–288; *Letters*, 2:24–25; *Writings*, 17:434–435.

10. See, e.g., Rose Lathrop, *Memories*, pp. 69, 72.

11. See Hubert H. Hoeltje, *Inward Sky*, p. 201. For Hawthorne's comments on Margaret Fuller, see, e.g., *The American Notebooks* (*Works*, 8:342–343, 374). The editors of the Centenary Edition, following Randall Stewart's notes to his early edition of *The American Notebooks*, briefly trace Hawthorne's relationship with Fuller. See *Works*, 8:641, and Randall Stewart, ed., *American Notebooks*, pp. 315–316. When Sophia told Margaret Fuller that she planned to marry Hawthorne, Fuller wrote in May 1842: "If ever I saw a man who combined delicate tendencies to understand the heart of woman, with quiet depth and manliness enough to satisfy her, it is Mr. Hawthorne." *Memoirs of Margaret Fuller Ossoli*, ed. Ralph Waldo Emerson et al., 1:187–189.

12. The manuscript of Vol. 3, from which this quotation is taken, can be found in the Berg Collection at the New York Public Library, whereas the other volumes of the French and Italian Notebooks are in the Morgan Library.

13. See Joseph Jay Deiss, *The Roman Years of Margaret Fuller*, pp. 178, 288, 291–292. Mozier's authority for Ossoli's background and Fuller's literary powers is not convincing, however. He was not in Rome at all and could not have known of Ossoli's family. Moreover, the six months that he knew Margaret in Florence were not a good time to judge her literary powers. She was frantically trying to earn enough money to live and to secure passage to America by doing such odd jobs as tutoring Mozier's daughter. Her paltry finances, in fact, were partly responsible for her death; she could not afford to pay for passage on the safer and faster steamships and came over on a sailing vessel. In any case, Hawthorne's comments on Mozier do not make him seem to be a very reliable source for information on Margaret Fuller. Hawthorne observed that Mozier had been living in Italy for seventeen years but was still wholly Ameri-

canized, which indicates that Mozier would be judging Fuller's conduct by the more restrictive American standards of female behavior. Hawthorne also notes that Miss Lander told him that Mozier stole the idea for one of his works from a student at the French Academy. And on October 21 Hawthorne wrote, with respect to a dispute in which Mozier was involved, that he tended to believe the other party because he did not have faith in Mozier's veracity.

14. Malcolm Cowley, *The Portable Hawthorne*, pp. 19–20; Edward Wagenknecht, *Nathaniel Hawthorne, Man and Writer*, pp. 145–146. Wagenknecht notes that Hawthorne's attitude toward George Eliot was ambiguous. Although he did not wish to meet her because of the irregularity of her union with Lewes, he showed great interest in her. Mrs. Charles Bray reports that when she met him at dinner, "he spent the whole time asking her questions about the novelist."

15. Bell, *Hawthorne*, pp. 173–178.

16. Nina Baym argues convincingly that Hawthorne's mother was the inspiration for Hester Prynne. See Baym, "Hawthorne and His Mother," pp. 1–25.

17. Tharp, *Peabody Sisters*, p. 157.

18. *Nathaniel Hawthorne Journal, 1974*, ed. C. E. Frazer Clark, Jr., p. 3.

19. Tharp, *Peabody Sisters*, p. 190.

20. Stewart, ed., *American Notebooks*, pp. xv–xvii; Frederick Crews, *The Sins of the Fathers*, pp. 12–14.

21. Cited in *The American Notebooks* (*Works*, 8:686), from a manuscript in the Boston Public Library. Fields's letters to Sophia are in the Berg Collection, New York Public Library. According to the editors of the Centenary Edition: "Her letters to Fields show that she relied heavily on his judgment. In effect, he taught her how to edit according to contemporary standards and his decisions must have often determined what was included, what excluded. Given her dependency on Fields, the general reticence of contemporary taste, and a natural respect for privacy, Sophia could scarcely be expected to produce a text which would satisfy modern standards."

22. Holograph Journal, Dec. 11, 28, 1843, Berg Collection, New York Public Library.

23. James R. Mellow, *Nathaniel Hawthorne in His Times*, p. 196 (from a manuscript in the Huntington Library, San Marino, Calif.).

24. Two surviving letters have been published, both of which tell of her love for Hawthorne but contain no improprieties. (*NHW*, 1:208–209; Rose Lathrop, *Memories*, p. 46).

25. Ralph Waldo Emerson, *The Journals and Miscellaneous Notebooks*, ed. William H. Gilman, 7:21.

26. See *NHW*, 1:464; 2:304. Also see James T. Fields, *Yesterdays with Authors*, pp. 107–108. Fields says that many friends urged him to try to persuade Hawthorne not to dedicate the book to Pierce, and he quotes Hawthorne's answer to his letter. See also Randall Stewart, *Nathaniel Hawthorne*, p. 233.

27. In Rose Lathrop, *Memories*, p. 136.

28. By "mud" Hawthorne did not mean the distasteful, unpleasant things of life that Stendhal saw reflected in the mirror on the roadway. He was concerned with the realities of human nature.

29. In a note to her edition of Hawthorne's *French and Italian Notebooks*, Sophia Hawthorne described how Hawthorne once took up a rose and, smiling, remarked: "This is perfect. On earth a flower only can be perfect." Nathaniel Hawthorne, *Passages from the French and Italian Notebooks*, p. 120.

30. One wonders just how complimentary this remark is even to Emerson's poetry. Certainly "austere" is a strange adjective to use with tenderness, and elsewhere Hawthorne expresses his distaste for poetry in general (*Letters*, 1:202).

31. Hyatt Waggoner points out the importance of the past in Hawthorne's work, particularly in "Alice Doane's Appeal." In comparing Hawthorne with the Transcendentalists, he comments on Hawthorne's superior wisdom in recognizing that the past can be transcended only if it is faced and dealt with. Waggoner, *Hawthorne, A Critical Study*, pp. 44–45, 261.

32. Jac Tharpe, *Nathaniel Hawthorne*, p. 137, points out that Hilda's and Kenyon's refusal to act causes evil. Hilda's rejection of Miriam leads to Miriam's final loss of feminine restraint, and Kenyon's reserve leaves Miriam without a confidant, which leads to her complicity in the murder. Critics have tended to associate Hilda

with Hawthorne's wife, Sophia. She is a copyist, as Sophia was, and she is associated with doves. However, she only possesses one-half of Sophia's characteristics and lacks all of the qualities that made Sophia human. I think a more important influence on Hawthorne's conception of Hilda was not his wife but his daughter Una. Hilda is a grown-up Pearl, and Hawthorne's American Notebooks reveal how closely Una is portrayed in the impish Pearl. Hawthorne's English friend Henry Bright assumed that Hilda was Una (*NHW*, 2:240). Particularly significant is the fact that Kenyon's feelings about Rome when Hilda is missing and he is afraid that he will never see her again reflect Hawthorne's state of mind when Una was dangerously ill in Rome and he thought she might die.

33. Kenyon says Donatello "had glimpses of . . . those dark caverns, into which all men must descend, if they would know anything beneath the surface and illusive pleasures of existence" (*Works*, 4:262; see also 4:172, 272–274, 282, 380–381, 434–435, 460).

34. Sophia Hawthorne quotes the same phrase to describe Hawthorne himself in a letter to her mother in 1850. In Rose Lathrop, *Memories*, p. 136.

35. See, e.g., Bell, *Hawthorne*, pp. 112–117.

36. In "Main Street" and *The Scarlet Letter* Hawthorne writes that English women like Hester Prynne are morally and materially stronger and have a warmer beauty than the pale, thin American women. *Works*, 1:50–52; 11:56–57.

37. Quoted in Mellow, *Hawthorne in His Times*, p. 34. See also Bridge, *Recollections of Hawthorne*, pp. 125–126, 149, 151.

38. Crews, for example, sees in Hawthorne's work evidence of an unresolved oedipal complex and incest feelings and concludes that Hawthorne's concept of the artist is in "flight from unacceptable truth." Crews, *Sins of the Fathers*, pp. 241, 211; see also pp. 38, 57, 59, 240–257.

39. See, e.g., his letter to his mother, March 13, 1821, in which he discusses and dismisses the various professions, concluding: "Oh that I was rich enough to live without a profession! What do you think of my becoming an author?" Quoted in Mellow, *Hawthorne in His Times*, pp. 25–26.

40. See, e.g., Charles J. Haberstroh's discussion of the conflicts in Melville caused by his family's pressures "for male ag-

gressiveness and worldly success." Haberstroh, *Melville and Male Identity*, p. 17.

41. George Parsons Lathrop, *A Study of Hawthorne*, p. 335.

42. Mellow, *Hawthorne in His Times*, p. 46.

CHAPTER 8
THE WOMAN TAKES
CENTER STAGE

1. Henry James, *The Novels and Tales*, New York Edition, 24 vols. (New York: Scribner's, 1907–1909), 3:87 (hereafter cited as *Novels* in the text).

2. If sexual fear does enter into Isabel's decision, it is not a question of frigidity but a part of the general fear that a woman with Isabel's aspirations would have of anything that threatened to engulf her. First to recognize this aspect of her character was Dorothea Krook, *The Ordeal of Consciousness in Henry James*, p. 366. See also Linda Ray Pratt, "The Abuse of Eve by the New World Adam," pp. 166–167; Rachel M. Brownstein, *Becoming a Heroine*, p. 251.

3. Richard Chase, *The American Novel and Its Tradition*, p. 131, notes that Isabel "subscribes to the American romance of the self." Richard Poirier, *The Comic Sense of Henry James*, p. 257, associates Isabel with American Transcendentalism. Edward Wagenknecht, *Eve and Henry James*, pp. 37–38, describes her as Emersonian. And Diana Trilling, "The Liberated Heroine," pp. 1163–1167, sees a link between Isabel Archer and twentieth-century female liberation novels, which, she says, have adopted the self-culture of traditional male American thought. Describing what she calls a "relatively new presence" in literature—"a fictional creation whose first concern is the exploration and realization of female selfhood"—Trilling cites James's *The Portrait of a Lady* as one of the forerunners of this phenomenon and notes that Isabel's search for self-fulfillment is "particularly American" in its intense idealism and expansiveness.

4. Quentin Anderson, *The American Henry James*, pp. 195–196, points out that Isabel becomes James's artist striving to create form.

5. Henry James, *Partial Portraits*, ed. Leon Edel (Ann Arbor: Univ. of Michigan Press, 1969), p. 407 (hereafter cited as *Portraits* in the text).

6. F. W. Dupee, *Henry James*, pp. 123–124, notes that Isabel escapes from the American innocence of imagining that one can do what one likes to learn of evil and suffering in Europe. And F. O. Matthiessen, *Henry James*, p. 186, points out that James shows the value of renunciation in portraying Isabel's mistaken belief that one can do what one likes: "The American life of his day, in its reckless plunge to outer expansiveness and inner defeat, had taught him that as his leading spiritual theme."

7. As Quentin Anderson says in *The American Henry James*, pp. 44–45, 186–188, Osmond wants to appropriate Isabel to represent himself. And it is her self-absorption that causes her to be trapped by him.

8. Tony Tanner recognizes that Isabel sees in Osmond what she seeks to become, but he notes that at the end of the novel, when she says "brother" to the dying Ralph, she recognizes in Ralph her true soul mate. Tanner, "The Fearful Self," pp. 147, 157.

9. When James wrote to his brother William after Minny Temple's death that she was a beautiful image in his mind, he was careful to point out that when she was alive, she could not be an image; it is only *because* she is dead that she can exist as an unchanging image. Henry James, *Letters*, ed. Leon Edel (Cambridge, Mass.: Harvard Univ. Press, 1974–   ), 1:225–229 (hereafter cited as *L*, Edel, in the text).

10. In Edel, *Henry James*, 2:359.

11. Henry James, *The Letters of Henry James*, ed. Percy Lubbock, 2 vols. (New York: Scribner's, 1920), 1:215–216 (hereafter cited as *L*, Lubbock, in the text).

12. *The Diary of Alice James*, ed. Leon Edel, p. 149.

13. Ibid., pp. 64, 95.

14. Henry James, *Notes of a Son and Brother* (New York: Scribner's, 1914), pp. 176–179 (hereafter cited as *Notes* in the text).

15. Henry James, *The Notebooks of Henry James*, ed. F. O. Matthiessen and Kenneth B. Murdock (New York: Oxford Univ. Press, 1947), pp. 40–41 (hereafter cited in this chapter as *Notebooks*).

16. See, e.g., the comment of Lilla Cabot Perry, who called

Mrs. James banal and "stupid-seeming." Cited in the introduction to *The Diary of Alice James*, pp. 5–6.

17. Edel, *Henry James*, 5:207, 340, 352; Millicent Bell, *Edith Wharton and Henry James*, pp. 157, 161, 147.

18. Edel, *Henry James*, 5:202, 352.

19. Bell, *Wharton and James*, p. 189.

20. Ibid., pp. 170–173.

21. Ibid., p. 137.

22. Edel, *Henry James*, 3:94–95.

23. Ibid., p. 195.

24. Edel, *Henry James*, 3:88–89.

25. James was very discreet in his relationship with Woolson, and only a select few of his friends knew of it. For two months in 1887 they shared a villa in Florence with no other friends present (Edel, *Henry James*, 3:198–207), and the following year they met in Geneva, where they spent three weeks in neighboring hotels—a rendezvous that James deliberately omitted from letters that he wrote from Geneva to his brother and friends, except Francis Boott, one of the few friends who knew of James's friendship with Woolson (Edel, *Henry James*, 3:251–253). From 1883 to 1886 Woolson lived in England, and in 1890 she settled there, Leon Edel surmises, to be close to James, even though she disliked and suffered from the English climate. Edel, *Henry James*, 3:284. Edel further speculates that the relationship was platonic but that there was some kind of agreement between James and Woolson, and that she left England at the end of 1893 because of the failure of that agreement or of her expectations. Edel, *Henry James*, 3:315–320. It is also possible that it was James who suffered a failure of expectations. In any case, they remained friends. James was so strongly affected by Woolson's apparent suicide in Venice in 1894 that he found it impossible to attend the funeral. He wrote to a friend: "A close and valued friend of mine—a close friend for many years with whom I was extremely intimate and to whom I was greatly attached (Miss Fenimore Woolson, the American novelist, a singularly charming and distinguished woman) died last Wednesday. . . . It is too horrible to me to write about." Quoted in Edel, *Henry James*, 3:360.

26. See Edel, *Henry James*, 2:386, 492–493, and Richard Hall, "The Sexuality of Henry James," pp. 25–31, who make much of

the point that after William's marriage in July 1878, James's major protagonists tended to be female. Of course, *Daisy Miller* was written before the marriage, and Christina Light was created four years earlier. Furthermore, some of his best male protagonists—Lambert Strether, Hyacinth Robinson—came long afterward. To draw such conclusions on the basis of the tenuous evidence available (most of which relies upon a personal interpretation of the fiction, e.g., the novel *Confidence*) overlooks other forces active in James's life at the time, including his reading and his European experience.

27. James, "The Lesson of Balzac," pp. 175–176.

28. Henry James, *A Small Boy and Others* (New York: Scribner's, 1913), p. 84 (hereafter cited as *Small Boy* in the text).

29. In an 1895 notebook entry, James described Americans as the barbarians of the Roman Empire. *Notebooks*, p. 207.

30. James was a long-time admirer of Balzac, whose comprehensive view of humanity was a model for him. He even wanted to have twenty-three volumes in his collected works, as Balzac did in the *Comédie humaine*. See Edel, *Henry James*, 2:195–197; 5:280–284, 322–324.

31. Henry James, *The American Scene*, ed. Leon Edel (Bloomington: Indiana Univ. Press, 1969), p. 54 (hereafter cited as *American Scene* in the text).

32. Henry James, *Views and Reviews* (Boston: Ball, 1908), p. 108 (hereafter cited as *Views* in the text). Although later comments on Whitman indicate that James could take pleasure in his poetry, there is no indication that he changed his opinion of Whitman's self-absorption. See "Review of Calamus," in *The Poetry and Prose of Walt Whitman*, ed. Louis Untermeyer, pp. 1038–1039; Edith Wharton, *A Backward Glance*, p. 186.

33. James, "The Lesson of Balzac," pp. 175–176.

34. James's opinion of the individual who always thinks he knows all the answers is apparent in his treatment of reformers. Paul Muniment in *The Princess Casamassima* is so sure he is right that he will sacrifice his good friend to the cause; Miss Birdseye in *The Bostonians* is lovable but ineffective; and Olive Chancellor in the latter novel is a sympathetic character and a marvelous creation, but her doctrinaire ideas not only contract her own life but also encourage her to seek to possess another individual—though Ran-

som's ultimate possession of Verena is not portrayed as being any better. For an interesting discussion of this novel that convincingly answers the critics who, reading their own prejudices into it, have interpreted Ransom's possession of Verena as a positive ending, see Judith Fetterly, *The Resisting Reader*, pp. 113–115, 118, 144–151. In both novels, it is the human concerns that interest James. In a letter to Charles Eliot Norton in March 1873, James wrote: "There is such a flood of precepts and so few examples—so much preaching, advising, rebuking and reviling, and so little *doing*. . . . I regard the march of history very much as a man placed astride of a locomotive, without knowledge or help, would regard the progress of that vehicle. To stick on, somehow, and even to enjoy the scenery as we pass, is the sum of my aspirations" (*L*, Edel, 1:362–363). James did not portray any one character as a master engineer. He warned against the dangers of "megalomania" and maintained that he would content himself "with living in the realities of things." Quoted in Edel, *Henry James*, 5:472–474.

EPILOGUE

1. Ralph Waldo Emerson, *The Journals and Miscellaneous Notebooks*, ed. William H. Gilman et al. 16 vols. (Cambridge, Mass.: Harvard Univ. Press, 1960–1982), 4:67–68 (hereafter cited as *JMN* in the text).

2. Ralph Waldo Emerson, *Complete Works*, Centenary Edition, ed. Edward W. Emerson, 12 vols. (Boston: Houghton Mifflin, 1903), 1:334, 338 (hereafter cited in this chapter as *Works*).

3. Ralph Waldo Emerson, *The Early Lectures*, ed. Stephen E. Whicher et al., 3 vols. (Cambridge, Mass.: Harvard Univ. Press, 1959–1972), 2:279 (hereafter cited as *Lectures* in the text).

4. Henry David Thoreau, *The Complete Writings*, 2:93.

5. Ellen Tucker Emerson, *The Life of Lidian Jackson Emerson*, ed. Delores Bird Carpenter, pp. 82–83.

6. Margaret Fuller, *Woman in the Nineteenth Century*, p. 175.

BIBLIOGRAPHY

Aaron, Daniel. *The Unwritten War.* New York: Knopf, 1973.

Adams, Abigail. *Letters of Mrs. John Adams.* Boston: Wilkins, Carter, 1848.

Alcott, William A. *The Young Wife.* Boston: George W. Light, 1839.

Allen, Gay Wilson. *Waldo Emerson.* New York: Viking, 1981.

Allen, Margaret Vanderhaar. *The Achievement of Margaret Fuller.* University Park: Pennsylvania State Univ. Press, 1979.

Anderson, Quentin. *The American Henry James.* New Brunswick, N.J.: Rutgers Univ. Press, 1957.

————. *The Imperial Self.* New York: Knopf, 1971.

————. Review of *The Best of Thoreau's Journals,* ed. Carl Bode. *New York Times Book Review,* July 4, 1971, pp. 16–18.

Andrews, Kenneth. *Nook Farm: Mark Twain's Hartford Circle.* Seattle: Univ. of Washington Press, 1950.

Anthony, Katherine. *First Lady of the Revolution.* New York: Doubleday, 1958.

Arieli, Yehoshua. *Individualism and Nationalism in American Ideology.* Cambridge, Mass.: Harvard Univ. Press, 1964.

Armstrong, Margaret. *Fanny Kemble: A Passionate Victorian.* New York: Macmillan, 1938.

Arvin, Newton. *Herman Melville.* New York: Viking, 1966.

Atkin, Ronald. *Maintain the Right: The Early History of The North West Mounted Police.* New York: John Day, 1973.

Austin, George. *The Perils of American Women.* In Nancy Cott, ed., *Root of Bitterness: Documents of the Social History of American Women.* New York: Dutton, 1972.

BIBLIOGRAPHY

Austin, James C. *Fields of the "Atlantic Monthly."* San Marino, Calif.: Huntington Library, 1953.

Bakeless, John E. *Daniel Boone: Master of the Wilderness.* New York: Morrow, 1939.

Bardes, Barbara Ann, and Suzanne Gossett. "Cooper and the Cup and Saucer Law: A New Reading of *The Ways of the Hour.*" *American Quarterly*, 32 (Winter 1980), 499–518.

Baym, Nina. "Hawthorne and His Mother: A Biographical Speculation." *American Literature*, 54 (March 1982), 1–25.

———. "Melodramas of Beset Manhood: How Theories of American Fiction Exclude Women Authors." *American Quarterly*, 33 (Summer 1981), 123–139.

———. *Woman's Fiction: A Guide to Novels by and About Women in America, 1820–1870.* Ithaca, N.Y.: Cornell Univ. Press, 1978.

Beard, Mary R. *America Through Women's Eyes.* New York: Macmillan, 1933.

Beaumont, Gustave de. *Marie.* Stanford, Calif.: Stanford Univ. Press, 1958.

Beauvoir, Simone de. *The Second Sex.* 1949. Translated by H. M. Parshley. New York: Knopf, 1953.

Bell, Michael. *Hawthorne and the Historical Romance of New England.* Princeton: Princeton Univ. Press, 1971.

Bell, Millicent. *Edith Wharton and Henry James.* New York: Braziller, 1965.

Bellamy, Gladys Carmen. *Mark Twain as a Literary Artist.* Norman: Univ. of Oklahoma Press, 1950.

Berg, Barbara. *The Remembered Gate: Origins of American Feminism. The Woman and the City, 1800–1860.* New York: Oxford Univ. Press, 1978.

Blanchard, Paula. *Margaret Fuller: From Transcendentalism to Revolution.* New York: Delacorte/Seymour Lawrence, 1978.

Bloom, Harold. *Poetry and Repression.* New Haven: Yale Univ. Press, 1976.

Borden, Philip. "Found Cumbering the Soil: Manifest Destiny and the Indian in the Nineteenth Century." In Gary B. Nash and Richard Weiss, eds., *The Great Fear: Race in the Mind of America*, pp. 71–97. New York: Holt, Rinehart, and Winston, 1970.

Bowles, Samuel. *Our New West*. Hartford, Conn.: Hartford Publishing Co., 1869.

Branagan, Thomas. *The Excellency of the Female Character Vindicated*. 1807. Rpr. New York: Arno Press, 1972.

Bridge, Horatio. *Personal Recollections of Nathaniel Hawthorne*. New York: Haskell House Publishers, 1968.

Bridgman, Richard. *Dark Thoreau*. Lincoln: Univ. of Nebraska Press, 1982.

Brodhead, Richard. *Hawthorne, Melville, and the Novel*. Chicago: Univ. of Chicago Press, 1976.

Brooks, Van Wyck. *The Ordeal of Mark Twain*. New York: Dutton, 1970.

Brown, Alice. *Mercy Warren*. New York: Scribner's, 1896.

Brown, Charles Brockden. *Alcuin: A Dialogue*. 1798. Rpr. New York: Grossman Publishing, 1971.

Brownell, W. C. *American Prose Masters*. Cambridge, Mass.: Harvard Univ. Press, 1963.

Brownstein, Rachel M. *Becoming a Heroine: Reading About Women in Novels*. New York: Viking, 1982.

Bryant, William Cullen. "Discourse on the Life, Character, and Genius of James Fenimore Cooper." In *Memorial of James Fenimore Cooper*. New York: Putnam's, 1852.

Bryce, James. *The American Commonwealth*. 2 vols. London: Macmillan, 1888.

Bucke, Richard. *Walt Whitman*. Philadelphia: David McKay, 1883.

Cabot, James Eliot. *A Memoir of Ralph Waldo Emerson*. 2 vols. Boston: Houghton Mifflin, 1887.

Canby, Henry Seidel. *Thoreau*. Boston: Houghton Mifflin, 1939.

———. *Walt Whitman: An American*. Boston: Houghton Mifflin, 1943.

Carter, Paul J., Jr., "Olivia Clemens Edits *Following the Equator*." *American Literature*, 30 (1958–1959), 194–209.

Channing, Ellery. *Thoreau: The Poet Naturalist*. Edited by F. B. Sanborn. Boston: Charles F. Goodspeed, 1902.

Chase, Richard. *The American Novel and Its Tradition*. New York: Anchor Books, 1957.

———. *Herman Melville: A Critical Study*. New York: Hafner, 1971.

Chenoweth, Lawrence. *The American Dream of Success: The Search for Self in the Twentieth Century*. North Scituate, Mass.: Duxbury Press, 1974.

Chesnut, Mary Boykin. *A Diary from Dixie*. Edited by Ben Ames Williams. Boston: Houghton Mifflin, 1949.

————. *Mary Chesnut's Civil War*. Edited by C. Vann Woodward. New Haven: Yale Univ. Press, 1981.

Chevalier, Michel. *Society, Manners and Politics in the United States: Being a Series of Letters on North America*. New York: Augustus M. Kelley, 1966.

Chevigny, Bell Gale. *The Woman and the Myth: Margaret Fuller's Life and Writings*. Old Westbury, N.Y.: Feminist Press, 1976.

Cheyfitz, Eric. *The Trans-Parent: Sexual Politics in the Language of Emerson*. Balitmore: Johns Hopkins Univ. Press, 1981.

Clarke, Edward A. *Sex in Education, or a Fair Chance for Girls*. Boston: Houghton Mifflin, 1892.

Clemens, Clara. *My Father, Mark Twain*. New York: Harper Bros., 1931.

Clemens, Samuel Langhorne. *See* Twain, Mark.

Cooper, James Fenimore. *The American Democrat*. New York: Funk and Wagnalls, 1969.

————. *Complete Works*. Leatherstocking Edition. 32 vols. New York: Putnam, 1893?

————. *The Correspondence of James Fenimore Cooper*. 2 vols. New Haven: Yale Univ. Press, 1922.

————. *A Letter to His Countrymen*. New York: Wiley, 1834.

————. *Letters and Journals*. Edited by James Franklin Beard. 6 vols. Cambridge, Mass.: Harvard Univ. Press, 1968.

————. *New York*. New York: Samuel Aiwax Jacobs for William Farquar Payson, 1930.

————. *Notions of the Americans Picked up by a Traveling Bachelor*. 2 vols. London: Henry Colburn, 1828.

Corbin, Hannah Lee. Correspondence with her brother, Richard Lee. *Historical Magazine*, 1 (Boston, 1859), 360–361.

Cott, Nancy. *The Bonds of Womanhood*. New Haven: Yale Univ. Press, 1977.

————, ed. *Root of Bitterness: Documents of the Social History of American Women*. New York: Dutton, 1972.

"The Course of Civilization." *United States Democratic Review*, 6

(1839), 208–217.

Cowley, Malcolm. *The Portable Hawthorne*. New York: Viking, 1967.

Cox, James M. *Mark Twain: The Fate of Humor*. Princeton: Princeton Univ. Press, 1966.

Crèvecoeur, Hector St. Jean de. *Letters from an American Farmer*. 1782. Rpr. London: J. M. Dent, 1962.

Crews, Frederick. *The Sins of the Fathers*. New York: Oxford Univ. Press, 1966.

Davie, Donald. *The Heyday of Sir Walter Scott*. New York: Barnes and Noble, 1961.

Decker, Peter R. *Fortunes and Failures: White Collar Mobility in Nineteenth-Century San Francisco*. Cambridge, Mass.: Harvard Univ. Press, 1978.

Degler, Carl N. *Neither Black Nor White: Slavery and Race Relations in Brazil and the United States*. New York: Macmillan, 1971.

Deiss, Joseph Jay. *The Roman Years of Margaret Fuller*. New York: Crowell, 1969.

Dekker, George. *James Fenimore Cooper, The Novelist*. London: Routledge and Kegan Paul, 1967. American title: *James Fenimore Cooper, The American Scott*.

DeVoto, Bernard. *Mark Twain at Work*. Cambridge, Mass.: Harvard Univ. press, 1942.

DeVoto, Bernard. *Mark Twain's America*. Chautauqua, N. Y.: Chautauqua Institution, 1933.

Dickinson, Leon T. "Mark Twain's Revisions in Writing *The Innocents Abroad*." *American Literature*, 19 (May 1947), 139–157.

Douglas, Ann. *The Feminization of American Culture*. New York: Knopf, 1977.

Drake, Samuel. *Annals of Witchcraft*. 1869. Rpr. New York: R. Blom, 1967.

Dupee, F. W. *Henry James*. New York: William Sloane Associates, 1951.

Earnest, Ernest. *The American Eve in Fact and Fiction, 1775–1914*. Urbana: Univ. of Illinois Press, 1974.

Edel, Leon. *Henry David Thoreau*. Minneapolis: Univ. of Minnesota Press, 1970.

———. *Henry James*. 5 vols. Philadelphia: Lippincott, 1953–1977.

Elkins, Stanley. *Slavery: A Problem in American Institutional and Intellectual Life*. New York: Grosset and Dunlap, 1963.

Emerson, Ellen Tucker. *The Life of Lidian Jackson Emerson*. Edited by Delores Bird Carpenter. Boston: Twayne, 1980.

Emerson, Ralph Waldo. *Complete Works*. Centenary Edition. Edited by Edward W. Emerson. 12 vols. Boston: Houghton Mifflin, 1903–1904.

———. *The Correspondence of Emerson and Carlyle*. Edited by Joseph Slater. New York: Columbia Univ. Press, 1964.

———. *The Early Lectures of Ralph Waldo Emerson*. Edited by Stephen E. Whicher et al. 3 vols. Cambridge, Mass.: Harvard Univ. Press, 1959–1972.

———. *Essays, First Series*. Boston: Houghton Mifflin, 1904.

———. *The Journals and Miscellaneous Notebooks of Ralph Waldo Emerson*. Edited by William H. Gilman et al. 16 vols. Cambridge, Mass.: Harvard Univ. Press, 1960–1982.

———. *The Journals of Ralph Waldo Emerson*. Edited by Edward W. Emerson and Waldo Emerson Forbes. 10 vols. Boston: Houghton Mifflin, 1909–1914.

———. *The Letters of Ralph Waldo Emerson*. Edited by Ralph L. Rusk. 6 vols. New York: Columbia Univ. Press, 1939.

———. Letter to the Essex County Woman's Suffrage Association. *New York Times*, July 30, 1869.

———. Speech to the New England Woman's Suffrage Association. *Boston Daily Advertiser*, May 27, 1869.

Faragher, John Mack. *Women and Men on the Overland Trail*. New Haven: Yale Univ. Press, 1979.

Faragher, Johnny, and Stansell, Christine. "Women and Their Families on the Overland Trail to California and Oregon, 1842–1867." *Feminist Studies*, 2 (1975), 150–166.

Farnham, Eliza W. *Life in Prairie Land*. New York: Harper, 1846.

"The Fate of Mexico." *Democratic Review*, 41 (1858), 343.

Ferguson, Delancey. *Mark Twain: Man and Legend*. New York: Bobbs-Merrill, 1943.

Fern, Fanny [Sara Payson Willis Parton]. *Fern Leaves from Fanny's Portfolio*. Auburn: Derby and Miller, 1853.

———. *Folly As It Flies*. New York: Carleton, 1868.

———. *Fresh Leaves*. New York: Mason Bros., 1857.

————. *Ginger-Snaps*. New York: Carleton, 1870.

————. *Ruth Hall*. New York: Mason Bros., 1855.

Fetterley, Judith. *The Resisting Reader: A Feminist Approach to American Fiction*. Bloomington: Indiana Univ. Press, 1978.

Fiedler, Leslie. *Love and Death in the American Novel*. New York: Dell, 1969.

Fields, Annie Adams. *Nathaniel Hawthorne*. 1899. Rpr. Boston: Folcroft Library Editions, 1971.

Fields, James T. *Yesterdays with Authors*. Boston: Houghton Mifflin, 1925.

Filson, John. *The Discovery, Settlement and Present State of Kentucke*. 1784. Introduction by William H. Masterson. Rpr. New York: Corinth, 1962.

Fischer, Christiane, ed. *Let Them Speak for Themselves: Women in the American West, 1849–1900*. Hamden, Conn.: Shoe String Press, 1977.

Flexner, Eleanor. *Century of Struggle*. Cambridge, Mass.: Harvard Univ. Press, 1959.

Foner, Philip S. *Mark Twain: Social Critic*. 1958. Rpr. New York: International Publishers, 1966.

Franklin, Benjamin. *Autobiography*. New York: W. J. Black, 1941.

Fredrickson, George M. *White Supremacy: A Comparative Study in American and South African History*. New York: Oxford Univ. Press, 1981.

Fryer, Judith. *The Faces of Eve*. New York: Oxford Univ. Press, 1976.

Fuller, Margaret [Margaret Fuller Ossoli]. *At Home and Abroad*. 1856. Edited by Arthur B. Fuller. Boston: Roberts Brothers, 1874.

Fuller, Margaret. *The Letters of Margaret Fuller*. Edited by Robert N. Hudspeth. 2 vols. to date. Ithaca, N.Y.: Cornell Univ. Press, 1983.

————. *Life Without and Life Within*. 1860. Edited by A. B. Fuller. Rpr. Upper Saddle River, N.J.: Literature House, 1970.

————. *Margaret Fuller: American Romantic*. Edited by Perry Miller. New York: Doubleday, 1963.

————. "Margaret Fuller's 1842 Journal." Edited by Joel Myerson. *Harvard Library Bulletin*, 21 (1973), 320–340.

————. *Memoirs of Margaret Fuller Ossoli*. 1884. Edited by R. W. Emerson, W. H. Channing, and J. F. Clarke. 2 vols. Rpr. New York: Burt Franklin, 1972.

————. *Papers on Literature and Art*. 1846. Rpr. New York: AMS Press, 1972.

————. *Woman in the Nineteenth Century, and Kindred Essays*. Edited by Arthur B. Fuller. New York: Jewett, 1855. Expanded from "The Great Lawsuit: Man Versus Men, Woman Versus Women," *The Dial*, 4 (July 1843), 1–47.

Gardiner, W. H. Review. *North American Review*, 15 (July 1822), 250–282.

————. Review. *North American Review*, 23 (July 1826), 150–197.

Geismar, Maxwell. *Mark Twain: An American Prophet*. Boston: Houghton Mifflin, 1970.

Genovese, Eugene. "Rebelliousness and Docility in the Negro Slave: A Critique of the Elkins Thesis." In Ann J. Lane, ed., *The Great Debate Over Slavery: Stanley Elkins and His Critics*, pp. 43–74. Urbana: Univ. of Illinois Press, 1971.

Gilman, Charlotte Perkins. *The Yellow Wallpaper*. Old Westbury, N.Y.: Feminist Press, 1973.

Goad, Mary Ellen. *The Image and the Woman in the Life and Writings of Mark Twain*. Emporia: Kansas State Teachers College, 1971.

Godkin, E[dwin]. L[awrence]. *Problems of Modern Democracy*. New York: Scribner's, 1896.

Grossman, James. *James Fenimore Cooper*. New York: William Sloane Associates, 1949.

Haberstroh, Charles J., Jr. *Melville and Male Identity*. Rutherford: Associated Univ. Presses, 1980.

Hagan, William T. *American Indians*. Chicago: Univ. of Chicago Press, 1961.

Hall, Richard. "The Sexuality of Henry James." *New Republic*, April 28, 1979, pp. 25–31.

Hallon, W. Eugene. *Frontier Violence: Another Look*. New York: Oxford Univ. Press, 1974.

Hamilton, Alexander. *Industrial and Commercial Correspondence*. Edited by Arthur H. Cole. New York: Augustus M. Kelley, 1968.

Hansen, Chadwick. *Witchcraft at Salem*. New York: Braziller, 1969.

Harding, Walter. *The Days of Henry Thoreau*. New York: Knopf, 1965.

Hardwick, Elizabeth. *Seduction and Betrayal: Women and Literature*. New York: Random House, 1974.

Harnsberger, Caroline Thomas. *Mark Twain: Family Man*. New York: Citadel Press, 1960.

Hartz, Louis. *The Liberal Tradition in America*. New York: Harcourt Brace, 1955.

Hawthorne, Julian. *Memoirs of Julian Hawthorne*. Edited by Edith Hawthorne. New York: Macmillan, 1938.

———. *Nathaniel Hawthorne and His Wife*. 2 vols. Boston and New York: Houghton Mifflin, 1884. Vols. 14–15 of *The Works of Nathaniel Hawthorne*. Edited by George Parsons Lathrop.

Hawthorne, Nathaniel. *American Notebooks*. Edited by Randall Stewart. New Haven: Yale Univ. Press, 1932.

———. *The Centenary Edition of the Works of Nathaniel Hawthorne*. 14 vols. to date. Columbus: Ohio State Univ. Press, 1962–

———. *Complete Writings of Nathaniel Hawthorne*. Old Manse Edition. 22 vols. Boston: Houghton Mifflin, 1900.

———. *English Notebooks*. Edited by Randall Stewart. New York: Russell and Russell, 1941.

———. French and Italian Notebooks. Manuscript. 5 vols. J. Pierpont Morgan Library, New York. Vol. 3 is in the Berg Collection of the New York Public Library.

———. "The French and Italian Notebooks of Nathaniel Hawthorne." Edited by Norman Holmes Pearson. 3 vols. Ph.D. diss., Yale Univ., 1941.

———. Journal, April 3, 1858. Berg Collection, New York Public Library.

———. Journal, October 21, 1858. Morgan Library, New York.

———. *The Letters of Hawthorne to William Ticknor, 1851–1869*. 1910. Edited by C. E. Frazer Clark, Jr. 2 vols. Rpr. Newark, N.J.: Carteret Book Club, 1972.

———. *Love Letters of Nathaniel Hawthorne*. 1907. Edited by C. E. Frazer Clark, Jr. Rpr. Washington, D.C.: NCR Microcard Editions, 1972.

———. *Nathaniel Hawthorne Journal, 1974*. Edited by C. E. Frazer Clark, Jr. Englewood, Colo. Microcard Editions, 1975.

———. *Passages from the French and Italian Notebooks.* 1870–1871. Boston: Houghton Mifflin, 1883. Vol. 10 of *The Works of Nathaniel Hawthorne.* Edited by George Parsons Lathrop.

Hawthorne, Sophia. Holograph Journal, December 11, 1843. Berg Collection, New York Public Library.

———. Manuscript letter, May 30, 1841. Berg Collection, New York Public Library.

———. *Notes in England and Italy.* 8th ed. New York: Putnam Sons, 1882.

Hazard, Lucy Lockwood. *The Frontier in American Literature.* New York: Crowell, 1927.

Healey, Caroline W. *Margaret and Her Friends.* New York: Arno, 1972.

Heilbrun, Carolyn. *Reinventing Womanhood.* New York: Norton, 1979.

———. Review of James Dickey, *Deliverance. Saturday Review,* January 29, 1972, pp. 41–44.

———. *Toward a Recognition of Androgyny.* New York: Knopf, 1973.

Hemingway, Ernest. *The Green Hills of Africa.* New York: Scribner's, 1956.

Higginson, Thomas Wentworth. *Margaret Fuller Ossoli.* Boston: Houghton Mifflin, 1884.

Hill, Alexander. *From Home to Home.* 1885. Rpr. New York: Argonaut Press, 1966.

Hill, Hamlin. *Mark Twain: God's Fool.* New York: Harper, 1973.

Hoagland, Clayton. "The Diary of Thoreau's 'Gentle Boy.'" *New England Quarterly,* 28 (1955), 473–489.

Hoeltje, Hubert H. *Inward Sky: The Mind and Heart of Nathaniel Hawthorne.* Durham, N.C.: Duke Univ. Press, 1962.

Holliday, Carl. *Woman's Life in Colonial Days.* 1922. Rpr. New York: Ungar, 1960.

Holloway, Emory, and V. Schwartz, eds. *I Sit and Look Out.* New York: Columbia Univ. Press, 1932.

Horsman, Reginald. "British Indian Policy in the Northwest." *Mississippi Valley Historical Review,* 45 (June 1958–1959), 51–66.

House, Kay Seymour. *Cooper's Americans.* Columbus: Ohio State Univ. Press, 1965.

Howard, Leon. *Herman Melville*. Berkeley: Univ. of California Press, 1951.

Howells, William Dean. *Heroines of Fiction*. 2 vols. New York: Harper and Bros., 1901.

———. *Life in Letters*. Edited by Mildred Howells. Garden City, N.Y.: Doubleday, 1928.

———. *My Mark Twain*. New York: Harper and Bros., 1910.

James, Alice. *The Diary of Alice James*. Edited by Leon Edel. New York: Dodd Mead, 1964.

James, Henry. *The American Scene*. Edited by Leon Edel. Bloomington: Indiana Univ. Press, 1969.

———. "The Lesson of Balzac." *Atlantic Monthly*, 96 (July 1905), 175–176.

———. *Letters*. Edited by Leon Edel. 2 vols to date. Cambridge, Mass.: Harvard Univ. Press, 1974– .

———. *The Letters of Henry James*. Edited by Percy Lubbock. 2 vols. New York: Scribner's, 1920.

———. *The Notebooks of Henry James*. Edited by F. O. Matthiessen and Kenneth B. Murdock. New York: Oxford Univ. Press, 1947.

———. *Notes of a Son and Brother*. New York: Scribner's, 1914.

———. *The Novels and Tales of Henry James*. New York Edition. 24 vols. New York: Scribner's, 1907–1909.

———. *Partial Portraits*. Edited by Leon Edel. Ann Arbor: Univ. of Michigan Press, 1969.

———. "Review of Calamus." In Walt Whitman, *The Poetry and Prose*, ed. Louis Untermeyer, pp. 1038–1039. New York: Simon and Schuster, 1949.

———. *A Small Boy and Others*. New York: Scribner's, 1913.

———. *Views and Reviews*. Boston: Ball, 1908.

Jennings, Samuel K. *The Married Lady's Companion*. New York: Lorenzo Dow, 1808.

Jones, Alexander. "Mark Twain and Sexuality." *PMLA*, 71 (September 1956), 596–616.

Jordan, Winthrop D. *White Over Black: American Attitudes Toward the Negro, 1550–1812*. Chapel Hill: Univ. of North Carolina Press, 1968.

Kaplan, Justin. *Mr. Clemens and Mark Twain: A Biography*. New York: Simon and Schuster, 1966.

Katz, Jonathan. *Gay American History*. New York: Crowell, 1976.

Kelley, Cornelia. *Early Development of Henry James*. Urbana: Univ. of Illinois Press, 1930.

Kemble, Frances Ann. *Journal of a Residence on a Georgia Plantation in 1838–1839*. Edited by John A. Scott. New York: Knopf, 1961.

Kohut, Heinz. *The Analysis of the Self*. New York: International Universities Press, 1971.

———. *The Restoration of the Self*. New York: International Universities Press, 1977.

Kraditor, Aileen S. *The Ideas of the Woman's Suffrage Movement, 1890–1920*. New York: Columbia Univ. Press, 1965.

Kring, Walter D., and Jonathan S. Carey. "Two Discoveries Concerning Herman Melville." *Proceedings of the Massachusetts Historical Society*, 87 (1975), 137–141.

Krook, Dorothea. *The Ordeal of Consciousness in Henry James*. London: Cambridge Univ. Press, 1963.

Lasch, Christopher. *The Culture of Narcissism: American Life in an Age of Diminishing Expectations*. New York: Norton, 1978.

Lathrop, George Parsons. *A Study of Hawthorne*. 1876. Rpr. New York: AMS Press, 1969.

Lathrop, Rose Hawthorne. *Memories of Hawthorne*. New York: AMS Press, 1969.

Lawrence, D. H. *Studies in Classic American Literature*. 1923. Rpr. New York: Viking, 1971.

Lawton, Mary. *A Lifetime with Mark Twain: The Memories of Katy Leary. . . .* New York: Haskell House, 1972.

Leary, Lewis, ed. *Mark Twain's Wound*. New York: Crowell, 1962.

Leavis, F. R. *The Great Tradition*. London: Chatto and Windus, 1950.

Lebeaux, Richard. *Young Man Thoreau*. Amherst: Univ. of Massachusetts Press, 1977.

Leonard, Eugenie, et al. *The American Woman in Colonial and Revolutionary Times, 1565–1800*. Philadelphia: Univ. of Pennsylvania Press, 1962.

————. *The Dear Bought Heritage.* Philadelphia: Univ. of Pennsylvania Press, 1965.

Lerner, Gerda. *The Female Experience: An American Documentary.* Indianapolis: Bobbs-Merrill, 1977.

————. *The Majority Finds Its Past: Placing Women in History.* New York: Oxford Univ. Press, 1979.

————. *The Woman in American History.* Menlo Park, Calif.: Addison-Wesley, 1971.

Levine, George. "Isabel, Gwendolyn, and Dorothea." *Journal of English Literary History,* 30 (September 1963), 244–257.

Lewisohn, Ludwig. *Expression in America.* New York: Harper, 1932.

Lowell, James Russell. *Poetical Works.* Boston: Houghton Mifflin, 1882.

McNulty, J. Bard. "Emerson's Friends and the Essay on Friendship." *New England Quarterly,* 19 (1946), 390–394.

MacPike, Loralee. "Environment as Psychological Symbolism in 'The Yellow Wallpaper.'" *American Literary Realism,* 8 (Summer 1975), 286–288.

McVey, Frank L. *Modern Industrialism.* New York: D. Appleton and Co., 1923.

Martin, Wendy. "Seduced and Abandoned in the New World." In Vivian Gornick and B. K. Moran, eds., *Woman in Sexist Society,* pp. 329–346. New York: Signet, 1971.

Martineau, Harriet. *Society in America.* 1837. 3 vols. Rpr. New York: AMS Press, 1966.

Matthiessen, F. O. *American Renaissance.* New York: Oxford Univ. Press, 1941.

————. *Henry James: The Major Phase.* New York: Oxford Univ. Press, 1944.

Mellen, Joan. *Big Bad Wolves: Masculinity in the American Film.* New York: Pantheon, 1980.

Mellow, James R. *Nathanial Hawthorne in His Times.* Boston: Houghton Mifflin, 1980.

Melville, Herman. *The Apple-Tree Table and Other Sketches.* Princeton: Princeton Univ. Press, 1922.

————. *The Battle-Pieces.* Edited by Hennig Cohen. New York: Thomas Yoseloff, 1963.

————. *Clarel: A Poem and Pilgrimage in the Holy Land*. Edited by Walter Bezanson. New York: Hendricks House, 1960.

————. *Collected Poems*. Edited by Howard Vincent. Chicago: Packard and Co., 1947.

————. *The Confidence Man: His Masquerade*. Norton Critical Edition. Edited by Hershel Parker. New York: Norton, 1971.

————. *Journal of a Visit to Europe and the Levant, October 11, 1856–May 6, 1857,* Edited by Howard C. Horsford. Princeton: Princeton Univ. Press, 1955.

————. *Journal of a Visit to London and the Continent, 1849–50*. Edited by Eleanor Melville Metcalf. Cambridge, Mass.: Harvard Univ. Press, 1948.

————. *Journal up the Straits, October 11, 1856–May 5, 1857*. Edited by Raymond Weaver. New York: Cooper Square, 1971.

————. *The Letters of Herman Melville*. Edited by Merrell R. Davis and William H. Gilman. New Haven: Yale Univ. Press, 1965.

————. *The Melville Log*. Edited by Jay Leyda. 2 vols. New York: Gordian Press, 1969.

————. *Moby-Dick*. Norton Critical Edition. Edited by Harrison Hayford and Hershel Parker. New York: Norton, 1967.

————. Review of James Fenimore Cooper, *The Sea Lions. The Literary World*. 4 (April 28, 1849), 370.

————. *Selected Writings*. New York: Modern Library, Random House, 1952.

————. *The Writings of Herman Melville*. Vols. 1–5, 7, 8. Evanston: Northwestern Univ. Press and Newberry Library, 1968– .

Metcalf, Eleanor Melville. *Herman Melville: Cycle and Epicycle*. Westport, Conn.: Greenwood Press, 1970.

Milford, Nancy. *Zelda: A Biography*. New York: Harper, 1970.

Miller, Edwin Haviland. *Melville: A Biography*. New York: Braziller, 1975.

Miller, Perry, "Emersonian Genius and the American Democracy." *New England Quarterly*, 26 (March 1953), 27–44.

————, and Thomas A. Johnson, eds. *The Puritans*. 2 vols. New York: Harper, 1963.

Morris, Alexander. *The Treaties of Canada with the Indians of Manitoba and the North-West Territories*. Toronto: Belfords, Clarke, and Co., 1880.

Mumford, Lewis. *Herman Melville.* New York: Literary Guild, 1929.

Nevin, John. "Human Freedom." *American Whig Review,* 7 (1848), 406–418.

Nevins, Allan, ed. *The Leatherstocking Saga.* New York: Pantheon Books, 1954.

New York Historical Association. *James Fenimore Cooper: A Reappraisal.* Cooperstown, N.Y., 1954.

Niles Weekly Register, 29 (December 3, 1825), 217.

Norton, Mary Beth. "The Myth of the Golden Age." In Ruth Berkin and Mary Beth Norton, eds., *Women of America: A History,* pp. 37–47. Boston: Houghton Mifflin, 1979.

———. "The Paradox of Women's Sphere." In Ruth Berkin and Mary Beth Norton, eds., *Women of America: A History,* pp. 139–149. Boston: Houghton Mifflin, 1979.

O'Neill, William. *Everyone Was Brave: A History of Feminism in America.* Chicago: Quadrangle, 1969.

Ossoli, Margaret Fuller. *See* Fuller, Margaret.

O'Sullivan, John L. "Annexation." *Democratic Review,* 17 (1845), 5.

Outland, Ethel R. *The "Effingham" Libels on Cooper. . . .* Madison: Univ. of Wisconsin Studies in Language and Literature, no. 28, 1929.

Paine, Albert Bigelow. *Mark Twain: A Biography.* 4 vols. in 2. New York: Harper Bros., 1912.

Parkman, Francis. Review. *North American Review,* 74 (January 1852), 147, 151.

Parton, Sara Payson Willis. *See* Fern, Fanny.

Patmore, Coventry. *The Angel in the House.* London: Dutton, 1905.

Pearce, Roy Harvey. *The Savages of America: A Study of the Indians and the Idea of Civilization.* Baltimore: Johns Hopkins University Press, 1960.

Poirier, Richard. *The Comic Sense of Henry James.* New York: Oxford Univ. Press, 1960.

Pond, James B. "Across the Continent with Mark Twain." *Saturday Evening Post,* September 29, 1900, pp. 6–7.

Porte, Joel. *The Romance in America.* Middletown, Conn.: Wesleyan Univ. Press, 1969.

Potter, David M. "American Women and the American Character."

In Barbara Welter, ed., *The Woman Question in American History*, pp. 117–132. Hinsdale, Ill.: Dryden Press, 1973.

———. *People of Plenty: Economic Abundance and the American Character*. Chicago: Univ. of Chicago Press, 1954.

Pratt, Linda Ray. "The Abuse of Eve by the New World Adam." In Susan Koppelman Cornillon, ed., *Images of Women in Fiction*, pp. 155–174. Bowling Green, Ohio: Bowling Green Univ. Press, 1972.

Railton, Stephen. "Thoreau's Resurrection of Virtue." *American Quarterly*, 24 (May 1972), 210–227.

Roosevelt, Theodore. *Works*. Vol. 10. New York: Scribner's, 1924.

Ross, Nancy Wilson. *Westward the Women*. New York: Knopf, 1944.

Rourke, Constance. *American Humor: A Study of the National Character*. New York: Harcourt Brace, 1931.

Rusk, Ralph. *Life of Ralph Waldo Emerson*. New York: Columbia, Univ. Press, 1967.

Russell, Phillips. *Emerson, The Wisest American*. New York: Blue Ribbon Books, 1929.

Ryan, Mary P. *Womanhood in America: From Colonial Times to the Present*. New York: Franklin Watts, 1979.

Salsbury, Edith Colgate, ed. *Susy and Mark Twain*. New York: Harper, 1965.

Sanborn, F[ranklin]. B[enjamin]. *The Life of Henry David Thoreau*. Boston: Houghton Mifflin, 1917.

Sandoz, Mari. *Crazy Horse*. New York: Hastings House, 1942.

Savile, George, Lord Halifax. *Complete Works*. Oxford: Clarendon Press, 1912.

Schainess, Natalie. "A Psychiatrist's View: Images of Women—Past and Present, Overt and Obscured." *American Journal of Psychotherapy*, June 1969, pp. 77–97.

Schlissel, Lillian. *Women's Diaries of the Westward Journey*. New York: Schocken Books, 1982.

Schopp-Schilling, Beate. "'The Yellow Wallpaper': A Rediscovered 'Realistic' Story." *American Literary Realism*, 8 (Summer 1975), 284–286.

Scott, Anne Firor. *The Southern Lady: From Pedestal to Politics*. Chicago: Univ. of Chicago Press, 1970.

Scott, Arthur L. "The *Century Magazine* Edits *Huckleberry Finn*."

American Literature, 27 (1955–1956), 356–362.

Scott, John Anthony. *Fanny Kemble's America.* New York: Crowell, 1973.

Shaw, Anna Howard. *The Story of a Pioneer.* New York: Harper, 1915.

Sheehan, Bernard W. *Seeds of Extinction: Jeffersonian Philanthropy and the American Indian.* Chapel Hill: Univ. of North Carolina Press, 1973.

Showalter, Elaine. *A Literature of Their Own: British Women Novelists from Brontë to Lessing.* Princeton: Princeton Univ. Press, 1977.

————. "Women and the Literary Curriculum." *College English*, 32 (March 1971), 855–862.

Slater, Philip. *The Pursuit of Loneliness: American Culture at the Breaking Point.* Boston: Beacon Press, 1971.

Slotkin, Richard. *Regeneration Through Violence: The Mythology of the American Frontier, 1680–1860.* Middletown, Conn.: Wesleyan Univ. Press, 1973.

Smith, Henry Nash. "Emerson's Problem of Vocation: A Note on the American Scholar." *New England Quarterly*, 12 (March 1939), 52–67.

————. *Mark Twain's Fable of Progress: Political and Economic Ideas in "A Connecticut Yankee."* New Brunswick, N.J.: Rutgers Univ. Press, 1964.

————. *Mark Twain: The Development of a Writer.* Cambridge, Mass.: Belknap Press of Harvard Univ. Press, 1962.

————. *Virgin Land.* Cambridge, Mass.: Harvard Univ. Press, 1950.

Smith, Janet, ed. *Mark Twain on the Damned Human Race.* New York: Hill and Wang, 1962.

Smith, Page. *Daughters of the Promised Land: Women in American History.* Boston: Little, Brown, 1970.

Smith-Rosenberg, Caroll. "Beauty, the Beast, and the Militant Woman." In Nancy F. Cott and Elizabeth H. Pleck, eds., *A Heritage of Her Own: Toward a New Social History of American Women*, pp. 197–221. New York: Simon and Schuster, 1979.

————. "The Female World of Love and Ritual: Relations Between Women in Nineteenth-Century America." In Nancy F. Cott and Elizabeth H. Pleck, eds., *A Heritage of Her Own: Toward a New Social History of American Women*, pp. 311–342. New York: Simon and Schuster, 1979.

Starkey, Marion. *The Devil in Massachusetts*. 1949. Rpr. New York: Doubleday, 1961.

Steckmesser, Kent L. "The Frontier Hero in History and Legend." In Leonard Dinnerstein and Kenneth T. Jackson, eds., *American Vistas: 1877 to the Present*, pp. 3–19. New York: Oxford Univ. Press, 1971.

Stein, Gertrude. *The Making of Americans*. New York: Harcourt, Brace and World, 1962.

Stern, Madeleine B. *The Life of Margaret Fuller*. New York: Dutton, 1942.

Stevenson, Robert Louis. "Henry David Thoreau: His Character and Opinions." From *Cornhill Magazine*, 41 (June 1880), 665–682. In Wendell Glick, ed., *The Recognition of Henry David Thoreau*, pp. 65–88. Ann Arbor: Univ. of Mich. Press, 1969.

Stewart, Randall. *Nathaniel Hawthorne: A Biography*. New Haven: Yale Univ. Press, 1948.

Stratton, Joanna L. *Pioneer Women: Voices from the Kansas Frontier*. New York: Simon and Schuster, 1981.

Strauch, Carl E. "Hatred's Swift Repulsions." *Studies in Romanticism*, 7 (Winter 1968), 65–103.

Takaki, Ronald. "The Black Child Savage in Ante-Bellum America." In Gary Nash and Richard Weiss, eds., *The Great Fear: Race in the Mind of America*, pp. 27–44. New York: Holt, Rinehart and Winston, 1970.

Tannenbaum, Frank. *Slave and Citizen: The Negro in the Americas*. New York: Vintage, 1946.

——. *Ten Keys to Latin America*. New York: Knopf, 1963.

Tanner, Tony. "The Fearful Self: Henry James' *The Portrait of a Lady*." In Tanner, ed., *Henry James*, pp. 143–159. London: Macmillan, 1968.

Taylor, John. *An Inquiry into the Principles of the Government of the United States*. Fredericksburg: Green and Kady, 1814.

Tharp, Louise Hall. *The Peabody Sisters of Salem*. Boston: Little, Brown, 1950.

Tharpe, Jac. *Nathaniel Hawthorne: Identity and Knowledge*. Carbondale: Southern Illinois Univ. Press, 1967.

Thernstrom, Stephan. *The Other Bostonians: Poverty and Progress in the American Metropolis*. Cambridge, Mass.: Harvard Univ. Press, 1973.

—————. *Poverty and Progress: Social Mobility in a Nineteenth-Century City*. Cambridge, Mass.: Harvard Univ. Press, 1964.

Thompson, Lawrance. *Melville's Quarrel with God*. Princeton: Princeton Univ. Press, 1952.

Thoreau, Henry David. *Consciousness in Concord: Thoreau's Hitherto "Lost Journal," 1840–1841*. Edited by Perry Miller. Boston: Houghton Mifflin, 1958.

—————. *The Writings of Henry David Thoreau*. 1906. Walden Edition. 20 vols. Rpr. New York: AMS Press, 1968.

Tocqueville, Alexis de. *Democracy in America*. 2 vols. New York: Knopf, 1954.

Traubel, Horace L. *Camden's Compliment to Walt Whitman*. Philadelphia: McKay, 1889.

—————. *With Walt Whitman in Camden*. 1905. 5 vols. Rpr. New York: Rowman and Littlefield, 1961.

Trilling, Diana. "The Liberated Heroine." (London) *Times Literary Supplement*, October 13, 1978, pp. 1163–1167.

Turner, Frederick Jackson. *The Significance of the Frontier in American History*. New York: Henry Holt, 1920.

Turner, John Peter. *The North West Mounted Police*. 2 vols. Ottawa: Kings Printer, 1950.

Twain, Mark [Samuel Langhorne Clemens]. *The Adventures of Colonel Sellers*. Edited by Charles Neider. New York: Doubleday, 1965.

—————. *The Autobiography of Mark Twain*. Edited by Charles Neider. New York: Harper Bros., 1959.

—————. *Complete Essays*. Edited by Charles Neider. Garden City, N.Y.: Doubleday, 1963.

—————. *The Complete Works*. American Artists Edition. 24 vols. New York: Harper and Bros., 1935.

—————. "Dear Master Wattie: The Mark Twain–David Watt Bowser Letters." *Southwestern Review*, 45 (Spring 1960), 105–121.

———. *The Diaries of Adam and Eve*. Edited by Joseph Ridgely. New York: American Heritage Press, 1971.

———. "Huck Finn and Tom Sawyer Among the Indians." *Life Magazine*, 65 (December 20, 1968), 34–51.

———. *Letters*. Edited by Albert Bigelow Paine. 2 vols. New York: Harper Bros., 1917.

———. *Letters from the Earth*. Edited by Bernard DeVoto. New York: Harper, 1968.

———. *Life as I Find It*. Edited by Charles Neider. Garden City, N.Y.: Hanover House, 1961.

———. *The Love Letters of Mark Twain*. Edited by Dixon Wecter. New York: Harper Bros., 1949.

———. *The Mammoth Cod and Address to the Stomach Club*. Edited by G. Legman. Milwaukee: Maledicta Inc., 1976.

———. *Mark Twain and the Three R's: Race, Religion, Revolution— and Related Matters*. Edited by Maxwell Geismar. Indianapolis: Bobbs Merrill, 1973.

———. *Mark Twain–Howells Letters*. Edited by Henry Nash Smith, William M. Gibson, and Frederick Anderson. 2 vols. Cambridge, Mass.: Harvard Univ. Press, 1960.

———. *Mark Twain in Eruption*. Edited by Bernard DeVoto. New York: Harper, 1940.

———. *Mark Twain's Autobiography*. Edited by Albert Bigelow Paine. 2 vols. New York: Harper, 1924.

———. *Mark Twain's Letters to Mary*. Edited by Lewis Leary. New York: Columbia Univ. Press, 1961.

———. *Mark Twain's Letter to Will Bowen*. Edited by Theodore Hornberger. Austin: Univ. of Texas Press, 1941.

———. *Mark Twain's Notebooks and Journals*. Edited by Frederick Anderson et al. 3 vols. Berkeley: Univ. of California Press, 1975–1979.

———. *Mark Twain to Mrs. Fairbanks*. Edited by Dixon Wecter. San Marino, Calif.: Huntington Library, 1949.

———. *1601: Conversation as It Was by the Social Fireside in the Time of the Tudors*. Edited by Franklin J. Meine. New York: Lyle Stuart, 1962.

———. *The War Prayer*. New York: Harper, 1968.

———. *The Writings of Mark Twain.* 22 vols. New York: Harper's, 1899–1900.

United States Works Progress Administration. *Told by the Pioneers: Tales of Pioneer Life.* 3 vols. in 1. WPA Project no. 5841. Olympia, Wash., 1937–1938.

Upham, Charles W. *Salem Witchcraft.* 1867. 2 vols. New York: Ungar, 1959.

Van Doren, Mark. *Nathaniel Hawthorne.* New York: William Sloane Associates, 1949.

Varble, Rachel M. *Jane Clemens: The Story of Mark Twain's Mother.* Garden City, N.Y.: Doubleday, 1964.

Vaughan, Alden T. *New England Frontier: Puritans and Indians: 1620–1675.* Boston: Little, Brown, 1965.

Veblen, Thorstein. *The Theory of the Leisure Class.* New York: Modern Library, 1934.

Wade, Mason. *Margaret Fuller: Whetstone of Genius.* New York: Viking, 1940.

Wagenknecht, Edward. *Eve and Henry James.* Norman: Univ. of Oklahoma Press, 1978.

———. *Henry David Thoreau: What Manner of Man?* Amherst: Univ. of Massachusetts Press, 1981.

———. *Mark Twain: The Man and His Work.* Norman: Univ. of Oklahoma Press, 1961.

———. *Nathaniel Hawthorne, Man and Writer.* New York: Oxford Univ. Press, 1961.

Waggoner, Hyatt. *Hawthorne, A Critical Study.* Cambridge, Mass.: Harvard Univ. Press, 1955.

Wallace, Anthony. *The Death and Rebirth of the Seneca.* New York: Knopf, 1970.

———. *King of the Delawares: Teedyuscung.* Philadelphia: Univ. of Pennsylvania Press, 1949.

Ward, John William. *Andrew Jackson: Symbol for an Age.* New York: Oxford Univ. Press, 1962.

———. *Red, White, and Blue.* New York: Oxford Univ. Press, 1969.

Wasserstrom, William. *Heiress of All the Ages.* Minneapolis: University of Minnesota Press, 1959.

Weaver, Raymond. *Herman Melville: Mariner and Mystic.* 1921. Rpr. New York: Cooper Square Publishers, 1968.

————. *The Shorter Novels of Herman Melville.* New York: Horace Liveright, 1932.

Webster, Samuel. *Mark Twain, Business Man.* Boston: Little, Brown, 1946.

Wecter, Dixon. *Sam Clemens of Hannibal.* Boston: Houghton Mifflin, 1961.

Weinberg, Albert K. *Manifest Destiny: A Study of Nationalist Expansionism in American History.* Gloucester, Mass.: Peter Smith, 1958.

Weiss, Richard. *The American Myth of Success.* New York: Basic Books, 1969.

————. "Racism and Industrialization." In Gary B. Nash and Richard Weiss, eds., *The Great Fear: Race in the Mind of America,* pp. 121–143. New York: Holt, Rinehart and Winston, 1970.

Welter, Barbara. "The Cult of True Womanhood: 1820–1860." In Wendy Martin, ed. *American Sisterhood,* pp. 243–256. New York: Harper and Row, 1972.

————. *Dimity Convictions: The American Woman in the Nineteenth Century.* Athens: Ohio Univ. Press, 1976.

Wharton, Edith. *A Backward Glance.* New York: D. Appleton Century, 1934.

Whicher, Stephen. "Emerson's Tragic Sense." In Wilson Smith, ed., *Essays in American History,* pp. 221–228. Hinsdale, Ill.: Dryden Press, 1975.

White, Elizabeth Wade. "The Tenth Muse—A Tercentenary Appraisal of Anne Bradstreet." *William and Mary Quarterly,* 8 (1957), 355–377.

Whitman, Walt. *Collected Writings of Walt Whitman: Prose Works, 1892.* Edited by Floyd Stovall. 2 vols. New York: New York Univ. Press, 1963–1964.

————. *Leaves of Grass.* Norton Critical Edition. Edited by Sculley Bradley and Harold W. Blodgett. New York: Norton, 1973.

Wilson, Edmund. *Patriotic Gore.* New York: Oxford Univ. Press, 1962.

Winsor, Justin. *Memorial History of Boston.* Edited by William F. Poole. 4 vols. Boston: Osgood and Co., 1880–1881.

Winthrop, John. *Winthrop's Journal*. Edited by James K. Hosmer. 2 vols. New York: Scribner's, 1908.

Wood, Ann Douglas. "The Fashionable Diseases." *Journal of Interdisciplinary History*, 4 (Summer 1973), 25–52.

Woodward, W. Elliot, ed. *Records of Salem Witchcraft*. 2 vols. in 1. New York: DeCapa Press, 1969.

Wright, Constance. *Fanny Kemble and the Lovely Land*. New York: Dodd Mead, 1972.

Wyllie, Irwin. *The Self-Made Man in America*. New Brunswick, N.J.: Rutgers Univ. Press, 1954.

Ziff, Larzer. *The American 1890s: Life and Times of a Lost Generation*. New York: Viking, 1966.

INDEX

Abstraction: in Emerson, 29–30, 38, 74–75; in Fuller, 85–87; in Thoreau, 57, 61, 68–69; women as, in Melville, 116–117, 119–120, 121, 123, 124; women as, in Twain, 151, 156
Adams, Abel, 37
Adams, John, 267n. 52
Alcott, Bronson, 39, 41, 56, 57
Alcott, William A.: *The Young Wife*, 11
Allen, Gay Wilson, 36, 44, 273n. 20
American society: compared to European, 3, 4, 10, 85, 105, 133, 203, 224, 246; and Cooper, 110–112; and Emerson, 31–35; and Fuller, 86; and individualism, 4–6, 14–16, 55–56, 69–71, 253–257; and Melville, 132–133; and the role of women, 6–11; and Thoreau, 62–65; and Twain, 180–181, 184
Anderson, Quentin, 303n. 4, 304n. 7; *The Imperial Self*, 23

Anthony, Susan B., 11
Arieli, Yehoshua, 262n. 12
Arvin, Newton, 146, 285n. 2
Austin, George: *The Perils of American Women*, 11

Bakeless, John E., 283n. 23
Balzac, Honoré de, 243, 246, 249
Baym, Nina, 261n. 4, 270n. 66, 300n. 16
Beaumont, Gustave de: *Marie*, 10
Beauvoir, Simone de: *The Second Sex*, 17
Beecher, Henry Ward, 173–174
Beecher, Isabella, 173–174
Bell, Michael, 198
Bell, Millicent, 241
Bennoch, Francis, 197
Blacks, 15–16, 35, 153–54
Blake, Harrison, 60
Blanchard, Paula, 259n. 1, 278n. 27, 280n. 46
Bloom, Harold, 270n. 3
Bonaparte, Napoleon, 180, 272n. 7
Boone, Daniel, 11–12, 13–14, 283n. 23